D1542648

MAKING WAY FOR GENIUS

MAKING WAY FOR GENIUS

The Aspiring Self in
France from the Old
Regime to the New

Kathleen Kete

Yale UNIVERSITY PRESS
New Haven & London

Published with assistance from the Annie Burr Lewis Fund and from the foundation established in memory of Calvin Chapin of the Class of 1788, Yale College.

Yale University Press books may be purchased in quantity for educational, business, or promotional use. For information, please e-mail sales.press@yale.edu (U.S. office) or sales@yaleup.co.uk (U.K. office).

Set in Galliard type by IDS Infotech Ltd., Chandigarh, India.
Printed in the United States of America.

Library of Congress Cataloging-in-Publication Data

Kete, Kathleen.
    Making way for genius : the aspiring self in France from the old regime to the new / Kathleen Kete.
        p. cm.
    Includes bibliographical references and index.
    ISBN 978-0-300-17482-3 (cloth : alk. paper) 1. France—Intellectual life—18th century. 2. France—Intellectual life—19th century. 3. Ambition—Social aspects—France—History—18th century. 4. Ambition—Social aspects—France—History—19th century. 5. Self—France—History—18th century. 6. Self—France—History—19th century. 7. Individuality—France—History—18th century. 8. Individuality—France—History—19th century. I. Title.
    DC33.4.K47 2012
    944--dc23

                                                              2011046015

A catalogue record for this book is available from the British Library.

This paper meets the requirements of ANSI/NISO Z39.481–992 (Permanence of Paper).

10 9 8 7 6 5 4 3 2 1

TO DAN AND JULIA

CONTENTS

ACKNOWLEDGMENTS

It was a pleasure to write this book, and it is with pleasure that I acknowledge the help I received along the way. Trinity College provided funds for summer travel and research, and I am grateful to the Dean of Faculty, Rena Fraden, and members of the Faculty Research Committee for their support. The Department of History is a congenial place to work, and I thank my colleagues for their collegiality, especially Susan Pennybacker (now at the University of North Carolina) and Gary Reger. Zayde Antrim, Sean Cocco, Jeff Bayliss, and I completed manuscripts at almost exactly the same time, and our race across the finish line was a team effort. Zayde was kind enough to read bits of the manuscript that I worried over. I hope my help to her has been as welcome. Barbara Benedict in the Department of English invited me into the Connecticut Eighteenth-Century Scholars Seminar and advised on the manuscript as well.

Sections of this book were presented at the Nineteenth-Century French Studies Colloquium, the American Society for Eighteenth-Century Studies, the Hall Center for the Humanities at the University of Kansas (at the invitation of Lisa Bitel, now at the University of Southern California), the Interdisciplinary Nineteenth-Century Studies Conference, the International Germaine de Staël Symposium, the Western Society for French History, several meetings of French Historical Studies, and Harvard University's Center for European Studies. I thank members of these audiences for their generous comments, especially Madelyn Gutwirth and the late Frank Paul Bowman. Jo Margadant offered to read the manuscript after my presentation on Cuvier at French Historical Studies, and this gesture buoyed me, as did her later comments on the draft. Darrin M. McMahon, with whom I presented at a panel on genius in Québec City, generously let me read sections of his forthcoming *Genius: A History*. A version of chapter 3 appeared as "Stendhal and the Trials of Ambition in Postrevolutionary France" in *French Historical Studies* 28, no. 3, a special issue, "Interdisciplinary Perspectives on French Literature and History," ed. Robert A. Schneider and Whitney Walton (2005). I thank Duke University Press for permission to republish this material. I am also very grateful to Whitney Walton and the anonymous readers for suggestions for revision, which considerably strengthened my argument.

Old friends stayed the course. Harriet Ritvo read a draft of the manuscript. My heartfelt thanks to Patrice Higonnet for reading everything over several times. His generosity toward former students can be repaid only by emulating his professionalism and kindness. My own aspiring self was enabled in graduate school at Harvard and I want to thank Simon Schama for bringing an outlier into the fold. Steve Pincus, a colleague then, helped bring my book to Yale. At Yale University Press, Laura Davulis and her assistant, Christina Tucker, have been the perfect editors. Ann Twombly's excellent copyediting did much to improve the book. All remaining errors are my own. And I am very grateful to the two anonymous readers of the manuscript for Yale, whose comments were exactly what I needed to bring the project to completion.

Research trips to Paris—as life itself—were enlivened by the company of the funny and talented Julia E. Kete and made comfortable by the hospitality of the Corfee-Morlots and Margaret Higonnet. Mary Lou Kete at the University of Vermont extended professional advice and sororal support; Nancy Kete and John Beale offered enthusiasm and their house in North Truro. The best parts of this book were written in the light of Highland Lighthouse and within its circle of family love. As always, Dan McGrath's loving support and our happiness together sustained this project, and the book is dedicated to him and Julia.

1

THE ASPIRING SELF IN FRANCE FROM THE OLD REGIME TO THE NEW

From the Old Regime to the New

"Great, unregulated, furious, horrible, execrable, pernicious." This was how the Académie française, responsible for control over the French language, modified its definition of *ambition* in 1694. The connotation remained negative into the next century, the "excessive desire for honor and greatness" becoming an "uncontrolled passion for glory and fortune" in the 1760s and into the new regime.[1] This book about the aspiring self in France begins broadly with an abstract of old regime efforts aimed at regulating this passion, at least on the part of elites, so that we might see how modern views of competition—highly ambivalent, and drenched in anxiety as well—took root in their collapse. My focus in this section is on efforts to control ambition more than the measuring of success in so doing. That concerns about ambition were laced through the political culture of the old regime and that they spilled over into the Revolution is the theme of these prefatory remarks.

The first effort was the court society, famously created in the seventeenth century to deflect the attention of the nobility from the pursuit of sovereignty to a formalized competition for the king's favor at Versailles. In this system, as the duc de Saint-Simon reminded himself, "He who has ambitions must be well informed."[2] All (though always imperfectly) were captured by this game, in which, as Louis XIV explained to his son, "The jealousy of one holds the others in check"[3] and which Norbert Elias has visualized for us as a series of circles from the innermost of which "now one steps forward to whisper into the king's ear how he can harm another, and then a second to tell him how he can harm the first."[4] Emmanuel Le Roy Ladurie has more expansively reified the social network of the court so that we see it laid out in his *Saint-Simon, ou Le système de la cour* as something like the Paris metro map.[5]

As Daniel Roche explains in *France in the Enlightenment,* "A complex system of signs and codes, protocol and ceremony, assigned each person a place and determined who had the stature to be invited to the royal retreat at Marly or share in the king's pleasures or receive certain honors."[6] The rules of competition were the dictates of etiquette, which served to keep ambitions within bounds, making "the many hundreds of courtiers visible at the same time, acting as a kind of signaling device that publicly registered any self-will, any outburst or mistake by an individual, since this impinged on the prestige-claims of others, and were therefore reported through all the intermediate links to the king."[7] The absolutist state, meant to rise above particular interests, was also meant to rise above the passions of its members. Theories of absolutism explained the role of the state in controlling the passions; ambition was understood as one of these powerfully corrosive forces. Jacques-Bénigne Bossuet explained in his *Politique tirée des propres paroles de l'Ecriture Sainte,* written for the edification of the Grand Dauphin in 1679, that "a ruler is required to overcome the confusion stemming from each person's pursuit of personal desires."[8] Nicolas Delamare, author of the *Traité de la police* (1705–19) and a commissary of the Paris police, suggested—with some experience perhaps—that people might try "living cooperatively with their fellows. 'But self-love, the other passions, and error soon throw up trouble and divisions.'" Bossuet and Delamare agreed that "government [was] necessary as 'a brake on the passions'"; it was "the only possible source of stability in a world dominated by the passions."[9]

Absolutism's interest in controlling the passions had a moral cast to it from its beginnings: "A feeling arose in the Renaissance and became firm conviction during the seventeenth century that moralizing philosophy and religious precept could no longer be trusted with restraining the destructive passions of men . . . new ways had to be found."[10] Albert Hirschman notes in *The Passions and the Interest: Political Arguments for Capitalism before Its Triumph* that Augustine and later Calvin had argued that the state should play this role.[11] Hirschman also explains how Augustinian thought left the door open for the recasting of ambition into a noble virtue. For Saint Augustine "the three principal sins of fallen man" were "lust for money and possession," "lust for power," and "sexual lust."[12] Expulsion from the Garden of Eden had released these passions in men, set loose these drives so akin to animal instinct. But Augustine suggested as well that "when combined with a strong desire for praise and glory" the "lust for power" (*libido dominandi*) might become morally acceptable.[13] This possibility allowed for the "chivalric, aristocratic ideal which made the striving for honor and glory into the touchstone of a man's virtue and greatness. What Augustine expressed most cautiously and reluctantly was later triumphantly proclaimed: love of glory, in contrast with the purely private pursuit of riches, can have 'redeeming social value.' "[14]

Is it a surprise, then, that the nobility of old regime France aggressively defended itself against the charge of ambition? Ambition was both ignoble and immoral. As one recent historian of the aristocracy has explained, ambition "epitomized the selfishness and cupidity of roturiers [commoners]. Like lust for wealth, the desire to rise above one's natural station in life betrayed an unseemly acquisitive spirit."[15] This desire was disparaged as "bourgeois"; the attempt to make it acceptable became, as we will see, one of the themes of post-Revolutionary life. Ambition was "the trait of a 'depraved soul.' " Pierre de La Primaudaye "called 'ambition and avarice' the main elements of mischief, and he observed that the two qualities 'are found together for the most part in the same persons.' "[16]

These observations offer a set of ways through which we can understand how absolutism set limits on ambition, if only abstractly. "Even though the institutions of the monarchy ensured that real power was never concentrated in one man's hands," the monarchy, in Roche's words, "was defined by the notion of universal obedience to the will of a single individual."[17] To explain more prosaically: "The relationship of elites to the Crown was predicated on an exchange of loyalty for benefits. The elite abstained from rebellion against the authority of the monarchy, while the king guaranteed the integrity of an hierarchical social order in which elites enjoyed a privileged status."[18] The drive for success was cast in noble life as a quest for glory, a virtue that became a central part of the aristocratic ethos. Ambition, so defined, had redeeming value. It contributed to the general weal. As Montesquieu claimed, anticipating Adam Smith, "The pursuit of honor in a monarchy . . . 'brings life to all the parts of the body politic,' [and] as a result, 'it turns out that everyone contributes to the general welfare while thinking that he works for his own interests.'"[19] More generally, absolutism's approach to ambition was set within the early modern understanding of the state as essential to "harnessing the passions . . . into something socially constructive."[20] As Giambattista Vico explained in his *Scienza nuova* of 1725, "Out of ferocity, avarice, and ambition, the three vices which lead all mankind astray, [society] makes national defense, commerce, and politics, and thereby causes the strength, the wealth, and the wisdom of the republics; out of these great vices which would certainly destroy man on earth society thus causes the civil happiness to emerge. This principle proves the existence of divine providence; through its intelligent laws the passions of men who are entirely occupied by the pursuit of their private utility are transformed into a civil order which permits men to live in human society."[21]

In the 1750s and 1760s, as "French politics broke out of the absolutist mold,"[22] these notions were newly expressed in patriotism. "Economic activity was recast," by some, "as patriotic," along lines drawn above: "Economic agents" (especially of global capitalism) "were represented as acting out of a civic regard for their fellow citizens, or more often, out of a desire for legitimate honor and esteem."[23] More poetically, a "cult of great men" developed, initially supported by the state.[24] The Académie française (wary of ambition, as their lexicon shows) was central to this development, offering "prizes for eloquence" for "eulogies of great men" beginning in 1758.[25] The date was "hardly a coincidence," notes David Bell, it being "the year in which the Seven Years War started to turn desperate for France, and the anti-English propaganda campaign reached it height."[26] These eulogies celebrated French heroes on the model of Plutarch's *Lives,* defined by their "solemn dedication to the common good," along with their "independence, steadfastness, immunity to seduction and luxury, lucre, and sensual pleasure."[27]

The relationship between eulogies of the old regime and those of the Academy of Science in the early nineteenth century will be addressed in chapter 4. Here we note how these qualities were meant to address "the corrupting seductions of an expanding commercial economy" on display in shops and cafés and boulevards as a consumer revolution swept through elite France as it had done across the Channel.[28] "Egoism" was the enemy, and a "polity stirred by the same spirit of civic virtue that characterized the republics of the ancient world" was posited in this discourse, which stood as a "diagnosis" of contemporary ills.[29] The "unstable state of passions," which a modernizing economy was stirring, "could be contained only by a political order in which individual interests were identified with the common good through the inculcation of civic virtue," a project of classical republicanism whose hold on the moral imagination of revolutionaries we note below.[30]

The pursuit of Enlightenment, too, was meant to embrace competition within a harmonious whole, at least as expressed in its well-known social aspects. The Republic of Letters, previously defined by its diffuseness, was tethered in eighteenth-century Paris to the salons, places where conversation superseded letters as the dominant means of intellectual exchange. From seventeenth-century civility a code of conduct was created that rested on civility and the avoidance of personal attacks.[31] Face-to-face encounters within a hierarchical society could be negotiated, and quarrels among the philosophes might be mediated by their hosts.[32] An *homme de lettres* hoped to be counted among *le monde*—as an *homme du monde*—in a formal salon sociability. Egalitarian conventions of politeness and a language of friendship lubricated relationships and helped construct "an imagined community" in which individual ambitions were meant to be subsumed within a greater project of Enlightenment, I suggest, as the desire to succeed was subsumed—formally—in the court society to the goals of the absolutist state. Voltaire's "little church" is a case in point.

Amitié bound the philosophes to their powerful hosts.[33] A "fiction" but not a "lie," in Antoine Lilti's terms, the language of friendship disguised power lines that were otherwise obviously drawn. In return for regular attendance at a salon, its host offered direct aid in the form of gifts, pensions, and, vitally, access to the "fountain of privilege" that spilled out of Versailles. Salons were an "interface" between the court and Parisian networks of power and influence; Lilti has shown how they formed an integral part of the power structure of the old regime.[34] Was a chair open at the Académie française? The philosophe's "friend" could lobby courtiers at Versailles as well as academicians who—like the candidate—were under his or her protection and caught within their own complicated webs of influence.[35] This pretense of sincerity was what so upset Rousseau, whose recoil from the salons set him at odds with Voltaire and the Encyclopédistes and helped shape his argument about the moral value of transparency.[36] The maneuvering for positions and privilege that characterized the world of the salons was satirized in 1788 by Marie-Jean Hérault de Séchelles—then *homme du monde*, noble, and member of the Parlement of Paris, and, later, Montagnard Jacobin. His *Theory of Ambition*, the pre-Revolutionary copies of which were destroyed by friends to protect him, was a mock how-to guide on getting ahead. It recommended duplicity in conversation and superficiality in all intellectual engagement. Who best to know, suggested its editor in 1802. Some would accuse the president of the Convention and member of the Committee of Public Safety "of conforming too closely to these principles." "Those who knew him during the course of the Revolution had seen in effect with what art he knew how to disguise his thoughts, to present himself in different lights according to his audience," to be a political shape-shifter, as it were, as he carefully plotted his objectives: exactly the recommendations to be found in his essay. Hérault was executed in 1794 alongside Danton, and his fate was "a frightening lesson for all those who would be tempted to take in these writings rules for their own conduct."[37]

Friendship failed to contain Enlightenment ambitions within the bounds of its community in ways that shaped the experience of ambition in post-Revolutionary France. As early as 1755, Rousseau was warning about the corrupting influence of competition. In the *Discourse on the Origin of Inequality* he suggested what conflicts between philosophes soon would bear out: "I would point out how much that universal desire for reputation, honors, and preferences which devours us all, trains and compares talents and strengths; how much it stimulates and multiplies passions; and making all men competitors, rivals, or rather enemies, how many reverses, successes and catastrophes of all kinds it causes daily by making so many contenders race the same course."[38] In behalf of corporatism, the advocate-general, Antoine-Louis Séguier, argued in a similarly apocalyptic (and politically adroit) way when he spoke against the abolition of guilds and the liberalization of the economy. At the Lit de Justice in 1776, where Turgot's Edicts were read, Séguier warned against the disorder that the "thirst for gain" would unleash among previously restricted workers. " 'This sort of freedom is nothing other than a true independence,' Séguier said, and 'independence is a vice in the political constitution,' 'this freedom would soon transform into license. . . . This principle of wealth would become a principle of destruction, a source of disorder.' "[39] Rousseau was clear that ambition was destructive of equality. Inequality, he wrote, "spreads without difficulty among ambitious souls, always ready to run the risks of fortune, and to dominate or serve almost indifferently, according to whether it becomes favorable or adverse to them." Ambition furthers oppression: "Citizens let themselves be oppressed only insofar as they are carried away by blind ambition."[40]

The *Encyclopédie*'s remarks on ambition lack the force of Rousseau's critique, but they express an ambivalence that would become more powerful in the new regime. Ambition is defined plainly as "the passion that drives us excessively toward aggrandizement."[41] The section on *ambition* also warns, however, that "one must not confound all those who are ambitious; thus some . . . ambition passes for vice, some other for virtue, some . . . is labeled willfulness and strength of character, some waywardness and baseness."[42] In the essay on *homme*, ambition is met with anxiety. While the pursuit of happiness may be good, when inflected by ambition, it can degrade: "The idea of distinction having once been formed, it becomes dominant, and that secondary passion destroys that which had given it birth." One's true needs are neglected. That desire to win at all costs, which characterizes the victory of Pyrrhus, "wearies still all those ambitious people who want to raise themselves in the world, all those misers who want to amass wealth beyond their needs, all men who, passionate for glory, fear their rivals."[43]

The *Encyclopédie*'s characterization of ambition implies that, if harnessed toward a common goal, ambition is fine. But when it speaks to self-fulfillment, it becomes rogue. As Elisabeth Badinter comments in *Emilie, Emilie: L'ambition féminine au XVIIIe siècle,* "One sees therefore that the major fault of the ambitious person is to work for his [or her] own account. Not only is he guilty of indifference to the fate of others but, worse still, he wants to escape the common run and raise himself above his fellow men."[44]

The texts of the high Enlightenment signaled to contemporaries the difficulty in maintaining community in the face of the drive for self-advancement. Conflicts between the philosophes drove home the point that the impulse to succeed would destabilize a system that depended on informal cooperation. We see this conflict between friendship and ambition in the relationship between the writer and *salonnière* (or host of a salon) Louise d'Epinay and the philosophe Melchior Grimm, her lover, who broke up their collaboration in Geneva (where they were—happily, as she thought—in retreat from Epinay's lunatic husband) to accept a position "as diplomatic representative in Paris for the Free City of Frankfurt-am-Main, at an annual salary of 24,000 livres." "'One must follow one's vocation,' Grimm solemnly explained: 'Our happiness during these past months . . . has been a gift from heaven, and we must be grateful for it. It has been a blissful period in our lives, but we would be wrong to bewail its brevity: our duties call us away.'"[45] The application of the notion of a religious call to God to one's secular self-fulfillment would have a long life in modernity.[46] The chapter on Stendhal in this book will present this claim as its major point. Other conflicts not complicated by gender inequalities—such as Rousseau's with the salon philosophes—also show how friendships among the philosophes were strained by their secular, as it were, ambitions.[47]

In another famous quarrel in the early 1770s, between the genial abbé Galiani and André Morellet (*"Mords les,"* Voltaire punned, "Bite 'em"), we see ambivalence toward ambition being expressed, an uneasiness that would become the hallmark of life in the new regime.[48] On the one hand, ambition was gendered male. As such, it was considered good, rational, and progressive. It was also dysfunctional, a negative quality, monstrous and defective. For the physiocrats, of whom Morellet was a spokesman, freeing the trade in grain from the state's control was equivalent to forwarding the project of Enlightenment. It was a rational, progressive policy of encouraging economic individualism. For Galiani, whose essay "Dialogues sur le commerce des blés" ("Dialogues on the Grain Trade") argues for continuing government control of the rural economy, it was the process of discussion itself, the reasoned exchange of ideas, the conversation of equals on issues of great moment that formed the Enlightenment, as Dena Goodman has argued.[49] For Morellet, competition was virile, collaboration effeminate, the "Dialogues" bewildering: "Morellet's style of refutation was personal: it was hand-to-hand combat; it was the war of the sexes. Morellet relished the fight, and he could not understand why Galiani did not share his pleasure in it."[50] For Galiani, Morellet was a self-serving *"ambitieux,"* himself transparently its opposite, " 'sacrificing myself before a troupe of the most impudent and rude [*malhonnête*] fanatics, in order to unmask them, and to expose their foolish ambition and their seditious views.' "[51]

The Republic of Letters was destroyed by 1788, its demise confirmed by the polarization of "polite society" attendant to the meeting of the Assembly of Notables and the calling of the Estates General. (Though after a hiatus during the radical Republic, salons continued to define high society into the twentieth century.)[52] The rank competition of the male public sphere replaced collaboration to become one of the norms of the new regime. The constitution of 1791 and later the Napoleonic Codes "provided the structure of a new male public sphere of open competition, in which talent and merit were to receive their due and in which property and money would flow freely from hand to hand in response to the pressures of supply and demand, and from which the family and women would be firmly excluded."[53]

Yet the characterization of ambition as pernicious, self-serving, corrupt, and secret that describes old regime concerns about this passion ran through Jacobinism as well. Ambition itself was part of the mixture of "principle, personal calculation, and rivalry" that marked the revolutionary drama and every player from Mirabeau to Robespierre, from 1789 through Thermidor.[54] Robespierre's speech to the Jacobin Club in January 1792, which denounced the impending war with Austria, was also an attack on the Girondins in control of the Legislative Assembly: war "served the interests of the ambitious and greedy, it was 'good for the military officers, for the ambitious, for the speculators.' "[55] In the "Report on the Principles of Political Morality" delivered by Robespierre to the Convention in February 1794, Danton, soon to be eliminated, is presented as that type of *ambitieux* who like "a king, a haughty senate, a Caesar, a Cromwell are obliged above all to cover their plans, to compromise with all the vices, to humor all the parties, to crush the party of the honest folk, to oppress or deceive the people, in order to reach the goal of their perfidious ambition." The enemies of the Republic, now unmasked, revealed the ambition that set them apart: "Hence the defection of so many ambitious or greedy men who since the beginning have abandoned us along the way, because they had not begun the voyage in order to reach the same goal."[56]

Jacobinism's solution to the problem of ambition entailed its transformation from private vice to public virtue as a means toward merging the individualist claims of modernity with communitarian goals, that very mix which defined the Jacobin state.[57] "Fair shares for all" would naturally ensue.[58] "The representative body must begin, then," Robespierre asserted in "Principles of Political Morality," "by submitting all the private passions within it to the general passion for the public welfare." "We seek an order of things in which all the base and cruel passions are enchained, all the beneficent and generous passions are awakened by the laws; where ambition becomes the desire to merit glory and to serve our country; where distinctions are born of equality itself."[59] By offering self-sacrifice to the Republic in place of self-service, Jacobinism showed its debt to classical republicanism and its deep roots in early modern history.[60] The demonizing of ambition calls to mind early modern representations of the cosmic battle between the virtues and the vices. In the city-states of the sixteenth century, the triumph of virtue over the Seven Deadly Sins was visualized in civic processions. At the Festival of the Supreme Being in June 1794, the Tuileries Garden was the site for such a battle. On the Grand Bassin, effigies of the disruptive vices, ambition prominent among them, were floated, then torched by Robespierre, to release the transcendent image of wisdom (*la sagesse*).[61] As Robespierre had argued in his speech in May when he lay the groundwork for the festival, "Vice and virtue shape the destiny of the world. They are two opposing genies in contention for it."[62]

Alas, the "image of wisdom" itself was weak. Neither natural nor civic virtue held.[63] In the disarray of Jacobinism after the fall of Robespierre on 9 Thermidor, "great, unregulated, furious, horrible, execrable, pernicious ambition" was left without official controls, unchecked by the post-Revolutionary state. Individuals were free to make of this passion what they would, to take from the debris of these discarded solutions the means to make the pursuit of self-interest ethical—ways and means, I argue, that would mark thenceforth the modern self.

Ambition as a Cultural Marker

The problem of ambition in post-Revolutionary France has generated surprisingly little attention, though it may be central to our understanding of liberalism. More than thirty years ago Theodore Zeldin wrote about the cultural hesitations shaping French response to the promise of competition. His two-volume work, *France, 1848–1945*, began with a section on ambition that described the expectations and desires of doctors, notaries, industrialists, bankers, bureaucrats, peasants, and workers as a means of explaining the resilience of traditional norms in modern France.[64] Economic historians of the same generation made a similar point, stressing the importance of the family firm and its values of security and safety over the behaviors of risk taking in accounting for the contrast between the French and British econo-mies.[65] In contemporary media we hear echoes of these arguments as commentators cite preferences for leisure over income to explain the apparent weakness of France compared to the United States within the global economy. Nicolas Sarkozy has invariably been described as the *ambitious* Sarkozy, especially during the election and early months of his presidency; the media sometimes denigrate, sometimes celebrate him as Anglo-Saxon in style. Essays published in the mainstream press stressed the shock of Sarkozy's new regime—work more, earn more, was his mantra—as they began to sort out the moral implications of his open celebration of ambition.[66]

Lack of interest on the part of anthropology, so helpful ordinarily for cultural history, is more unexpected. But that indifference is in itself a sign of the importance of our subject. In anthropology's treatment of comparative culture, ambition remains invisible, a given attribute of Euro-American modernity, the corollary to Western individualism, hardly worth a nod from the vantage point of non-Western struc-tures. Even on the part of the growing number of anthropologists and ethnographers who study the subcultures of Europe—Scottish fishermen, the Roma, the Swedish middle class (the last in Frykman and Löfgren's pathbreaking work, *Culture-Builders: A Historical Anthropology of Middle-Class Life*), the problem of ambition—its defi-nition and its role in these societies—either appears as a nonissue in traditional life or as a scarcely registered assumption of modern life.[67]

New work in philosophy points more helpfully in the direction of our project to explain the changing solutions to the problem of ambition in France. Thomas Dixon, writing about the "revival of philosophical interest in the emotions," explains that philosophers are directing their field back to the ambiguities of morality and history and away from the supposed certainties of neuropsychology. Recent work claims that "the experience and expression of the more complex and interesting human emotions are intellectually and culturally conditioned." Their work mines the intellectual history of the eighteenth and early nineteenth centuries, when it was understood that emotions had moral weight and that some passions could be "cognitive and moral mistakes." The problem of the role of ethics within a materialist universe being vetted by philosophers is exactly, as we will see, the essence of the question about ambition with which this book is concerned.[68]

Despite contemporary understanding of ambition as a passion—the liberal passion, par excellence, burnt in effigy as we saw, along with selfishness (egoism), discord, and other disruptive vices spawned by materialism on June 8, 1794, on the very eve of the Great Terror, at the Festival of the Supreme Being—ambition scarcely figures in the histories of the passions that are rejuvenating the cultural history of modernizing Europe. Nonetheless, this work proves very useful in structuring our understanding of this key cultural behavior.[69]

Philip Fisher explains in *The Vehement Passions* that the eighteenth century was a critical moment in the construction of the modern approach to feelings. From midcentury on, English theorists began to detach, as it were, the emotions from the passions, or the fleeting feeling from the driving force, exactly the process that explains, as we will see, the limbo in which the category of ambition rests. An impoverishing distinction was established between the modern experience of anger and grief, newly understood as feeling, and the antique Greek experience of these as passions. A boundary was established between ourselves and Hector and Achilles and the antique world overall, which Fisher's readings are meant to bridge. In this project, we are taken with Fisher's point that "each new moment in the history of culture refilters the passions,"[70] an argument that presumes for humanity, as this work does in its more limited claim for the generations who crossed the Revolutionary divide, a consistent package of desires. The "refiltering" of the passions emphasized by Fisher involves a change in their "template," as he suggests.[71] Here we find this change effected by the state. The formal or legal opportunities offered to the self to forward itself at the expense of others appear in the old regime, as we saw, under the rubric of classical or monarchical glory, and in the nineteenth century under the rubric of self-interest. Could we also note that Fisher's project restates beautifully the humanist apology for the search for ourselves in the historical other?

William Reddy's work is signally important for understanding ambition in its historical context. *The Navigation of Feeling: A Framework for the History of Emotions* describes how a template of emotions might change. Reddy introduces the concept of emotives, a type of speech act that allows for and intensifies the experience of certain emotions at the expense of others. Emotives lay the groundwork for the "emotional regimes" that describe any given culture, which in turn act as "the necessary underpinnings of any stable political regime."[72] Like Fisher, Reddy posits a universal set of human emotions. He speaks of a common "toolbox of emotions" that is employed, variously, to shape cultures in different times and places. Notably, he offers the example of the French Revolution to explain how this toolbox might be employed. Reddy argues that sentimentalism (sensibility, more familiarly, the privileging of the " 'evidence of the heart' ") came to define the emotional regime of pre-Revolutionary France. Though it worked well as a culture of opposition (standing in opposition to the court society), it failed to anchor the Jacobin state, and that failure led to the unraveling of the Republic.[73]

The trajectory of the Revolution from the optimism of 1789 to the cynicism of Empire can be understood, then, in the context of this failed worldview. Sentimentalism recognized "sincere expression [as the] root of virtue," and it undertook to judge that sincerity by the intensity of its expression. "How did you *feel* when you heard the news [of the king's death]?" was the emblematic Jacobin interrogation.[74] An "escalating spiral of suspicion" resulted from the reduction of virtue to feeling, and the "Republic of Virtue" faltered on such an ambiguous foundation. The "normative emotions" of the Jacobin state heightened a disjunction between the feelings of individuals (perhaps unsure of their feelings about the execution of the king and the progress of the Terror) and their official permissive expression.[75] On 9 Thermidor the Terror collapsed and modern French law took self-interest—the lowest common denominator of the general will—as its guiding principle.

It is the experience of those people who survived the collapse of the old regime and the Republic of Virtue that interests us in this book, those whose desires and fears were meant to fit a new template.[76] In the last section of this chapter we review that template and then introduce the patterns of thought that connect the modern liberal self to its traditional moorings.

The "Free Play of Competition" and Its Referees

The new civil order was shaped by property and the "free play of competition," whose principles the Napoleonic Codes would inscribe.[77] As Europe opened wide under French dominance—"after Ulm, after Austerlitz,"[78]—opportunism and individualism triumphed in French law. Civil atomization, though offset to a point by patriarchal "family values," took place within expansive opportunities for gain. It was said that every soldier's cartridge pouch held a marshal's baton. So, too, did a prefect or councilor of state's income (25,000 francs a year in the early Empire) beckon bureaucrats involved in the direction of the Empire at home and abroad.[79]

Ambition, the passion to succeed, was recognized as central to this project of aggrandizement. Recent work reminds us of the influence of the Idéologues—in the orientation of ideas set by the collapse of both the old regime and Jacobinism—during the Directory and into the Empire. Though Napoleon abolished the second class of the Institute of France, which was a stronghold of the Idéologues, the pursuit of "enlightened self-interest"[80]—its elevation to a moral good, liberating men and women from "providential design"[81]—was compatible with Napoleonic opportunism. This was an attitude that would find its motto in Guizot's later (though misunderstood) exhortation, "Enrichissez-vous."[82]

Theorists of capitalism such as Bernard de Mandeville (1670–1733) and Adam Smith (1723–90) had argued that the individual's interest in advancing at the expense of others worked, paradoxically, to the benefit of all. Competitive individualism led to happiness. Nicolas de Condorcet (1743–94) spoke of "civilized competition" as the "normal condition in which men and women are happy, in the midst of 'pain, need, and loss.' "[83] Nineteenth-century liberals would elaborate on this theme of ambition as "a virtuous trait." As Pierre Larousse reported in his *Grand dictionnaire universel du XIXe siècle:* "Ambition is better suited to free states than to absolutism." "Vanity is the desire for honors and distinction, ambition is the desire for power. The first (vanity) [is] the mainspring of absolutism: the second (ambition) the mainspring of liberty." Lucien-Anatole Prévost-Paradol described the positive association of ambition and modern politics: "In a free country ambition is eloquent, active, and of use to the country." As Jules Simon concludes, "The ambitious man in a free country (*un pays libre*) may succeed in life by virtue of his talent or courage; he advances towards success under wide open skies."[84]

Yet doubts lingered throughout the nineteenth century, as this book will also explain. Popular guides to careers urged restraint. So, too, did medical advice books, which warned, "The ambitious man is a sick man." Ambition could make one pale, shaky, blind, and eventually insane. It could also lead to cancer, strokes, and heart attacks, " 'But the most usual end of this passion is melancholy and above all ambitious monomania.' "[85] In the words of Jean-Baptiste-Félix Descuret, author of *La médecine des passions:* "The victim of this passion soon becomes pale and his brow furrows, his eyes withdraw into their sockets, his gaze becomes restless and anxious, his cheekbones become prominent, his temples hollow, and his hair falls out or whitens prematurely."[86]

The critique of ambition turned on the contrast of the old regime with the new. For Etienne Esquirol—whose research helped establish the monomania diagnosis within the developing field of French psychiatry—as "the dominant passions of the era" changed, so, too, did its dysfunctions. The madness of Don Quixote gave way in the Reformation to the madness of religious enthusiasm.[87] In the Restoration and July Monarchy, "lunatics by ambition" were seized by the belief that they were Napoleons, Caesars, and dauphins, "generals, sovereigns, popes, and even God," Descuret warned.[88] "Put in more general terms," Jan Goldstein writes, "the special monomania of the early nineteenth century was overweening ambition of all sorts, stimulated by the more fluid society that was the legacy of the Revolution."[89] Fashionable, bourgeois, and statistically more liable to hit the middle classes, *monomanie ambitieuse* was one of the defining diseases of the age.[90] It is little wonder that a quarter of the inmates in the Bicêtre and a tenth of the patients at the Salpêtrière admitted in 1841–42, for instance, were diagnosed as overly, insanely ambitious.[91]

The great critiques of capitalism that appeared in France in the first half of the century by definition also underlined the dysfunctional qualities of ambition. Saint-Simonian and Fourierist theories were shaped by the attempt to found society on the principle of cooperation rather than competition. More obliquely, historical materialism understood the end of history as the end of competition. The great novels of the nineteenth century also play to this theme. The bankruptcy of César Birotteau, the suicide of Mme Bovary, the putrid rot at the heart of the Second Empire, which even Doctor Pascal could not escape, linger in French culture as the "natural" results of a drive for success.[92] The problem of ambition in an era that was coming to terms with Enlightenment modernity (as formally and legally the French were obliged to do under the Napoleonic Codes) is the subject of this book. How could one person's success in the face of another's loss make moral sense in the absence of a subjective God? How could the privileging of individual over community needs not lead to social disarray?

After the Jacobin goal of "universalist harmony," that is, the construction of a "moral public space where the ancient Christian and Platonic dream of reconciling the rights of the one to the claims of the many might finally be recognized," was abandoned, broken under the weight of the past and the demands of the present, as Patrice Higonnet has explained, the disruptive quality of competition was left to the devices of private lives.[93] But how was this effected? The central part of this book is the examination of individuals caught between the ebb of old regime attitudes toward ambition and the rising tide of a new regime marked by the opportunities of the First Empire and Restoration. I examine the experience of three iconic personalities, famous for their response to this intractable stress: Germaine de Staël (1766–1817), Stendhal (1783–1842), and Georges Cuvier (1769–1832). All three took on the problem of ambition and dramatically cast solutions to its discomforts in their lives and in their signature works. In a series of chapters traversing fiction and history I establish these solutions as plots with powerful and lasting appeal.

Romantic genius is posited as one of these solutions to the problem of ambition. In my discussion of Staël, I trace the appeal of this notion—a type of grace that propels one to be creative at all costs and sets one apart from one's fellows—to this daughter of powerful parents (Jacques Necker, finance minister and hero of 1789, and Suzanne Necker, *salonnière*) whose efforts to influence history were thwarted first by Jacobinism, that band of brothers, then by Napoleonic patriarchy. I show how the links between female genius and doom that define Staël's famous feminist novel, *Corinne,* published in the early years of the Empire, resonated throughout the nineteenth and twentieth centuries and ripple into our own. Yet though Corinne is a suicide, Staël lives, finding more realistic ways to accommodate her striving self, and that is the point that gives weight to the chapter. In the art of living in opposition to Napoleon, in the argument that *was* her life in exile, romantic genius was tempered, shaped into a sociability, a sensibility, in range of us all: rooted in romantic individualism but defined by a heightened awareness of the costs of an unfettered life.

Vocation is another solution to the problem of post-Revolutionary ambition, as I show in the chapter on Stendhal. There I contrast Stendhal's behavior with that of his legendary character Julien Sorel and suggest how vocation plays the same role in Stendhal's life as genius played in Staël's—enabling ambition in an ethically satisfying way. First I read *The Red and the Black* alongside Pinel's studies of *monomanie ambitieuse* in the *Treatise on Madness*. I show that Julien's behavior is consistent with the medical critique of ambition and, arguing against the grain of *stendhaliste* criticism, I claim that Stendhal's understanding of its dangers was consistent with bourgeois views overall. I highlight the importance of the trial of Julien Sorel as the site of Stendhal's open-ended exploration of the problem of ambition in post-Revolutionary life, an exploration that spilled out into Stendhal's other fictional works and shaped his autobiographical fragments. The chapter ends by demonstrating how secular vocation—vocation that is recast from a call to God to a call to a profession—came to stand as an alternative in Stendhal's life to Julien's violent and celebrated rejection of ambition's lure.

In the last of these case studies, I contrast the common image of Cuvier as a ruthlessly ambitious climber—a Napoleon of science—with his own notion of the scientist as a simple man drawn toward his career by destiny. Cuvier's memoirs—"for use by whoever will write my *éloge*"—along with the several dozen widely read *éloges historiques* written by Cuvier on the lives of members of the Academy of Science, offered a stylized answer to the question of his success. Like the fairy tales collected by his contemporaries the brothers Grimm, they are organized by certain set motifs. The famous scientist is born in obscurity. Poverty in some cases would preclude a career in science, but a series of helpers, some animal, some human, some in disguise—like the abbé Tessier in hiding from the Terror in Normandy—launch Cuvier and others on their careers. Destiny—a calling, "an irresistible instinct"—draws him forward. Events that at first seem setbacks—failure to take first place on an exam, having to drop out of school to support a family—become critical steps. And talismans, more elliptically, mark the way.

In exploring these lives we see how ambition was embraced through a kind of subterfuge. Vocation, genius, destiny, or instinct, each allowed its bearer, we will see, to overcome the burdens of ambition—the charge of selfishness, the feeling of oneness with a derelict capitalist society, the disapprobation of one's peers directed toward women, especially, who sought distinctions for their own selves. Each subterfuge, I suggest, is a construct pulled along from a pre-Revolutionary—Christian, antique, barbarian—past, to cover up or contain, as it were, the bristly edges of competitive individualism.

This is distinctly not a study of historical sociology, focusing on a specific generation, or cohort, as Alan Spitzer did in his admirable *French Generation of 1820*.[94] It is interested in broader trends. Indeed, these three people belong to different generations—Staël was seventeen years older than Stendhal, Cuvier was fourteen years older than he. But each one's maturity was defined by Napoleonic Paris. The unhappiness, the sickness, defined by this drive—the liberal passion, as ambition was known—that consumed the lives of these thinkers begs for us to cast a wider net.

I have chosen these people as representative of a culture that came of age during the Empire, with the goal of understanding that culture. This approach reflects renewed interest in the field of cultural studies in the notion of the representative person—the exemplary character who acts as a "cultural synecdoche" who represents the whole by its part, as James Chandler notes in his literary history, *England in 1819*.[95] Or as a practitioner of the New Biography explains, "Cultural politics are most easily examined as well as empathetically imagined in the individual life."[96] This methodology is particularly apt for the study of the early nineteenth century. It was post-Revolutionary—Romantic—Europe, after all, that posed the question of the relationship between individuality—the particular—and culture overall. Goethe's life, for one, was "consumed" by the quest to understand "this whole process whereby an individuality comes to be a unique self, and at the same time a representative of its world."[97] As Chateaubriand more confidently believed, "*Ecce homo, ecce humanitas.*"[98]

We first encounter the representative person via the "represented event"—the fate of Corinne, the trial of Julien Sorel, the fabled story of the scientist hero—and in this way we follow strategies for understanding post-Revolutionary visual art. By explaining the artist Jacques-Louis David's Thermidorian works as constructions of a self, disorganized, disoriented, in dissolution after the fall of Robespierre because of his intense identification as Jacobin, Ewa Lajer-Burcharth, for example, moves from the particular—David—to the general—Jacobinism, and the "broader cultural destabilization" that ensued in France from its failures.[99] As Lajer-Burcharth does for the creations of David, I explain these literary texts as case studies of the self, framed in the post-Revolutionary era by a "normative domain" that simultaneously celebrated competitive individualism—in the Napoleonic Codes—and feared it.[100]

But the emphasis of this book is as much on the lived lives as on works of art. It delights in Staël and Stendhal as much as Corinne and Julien. Indeed, it treats the lives of these people on a par with the works, "as one form of expression among others," indeed, as "a particularly eloquent work of art," as Tzvetan Todorov explains in his luminous essay on Benjamin Constant (the great liberal thinker and friend of Madame de Staël).[101] It is animated as Stephen Greenblatt's work on Shakespeare is, as we all must be, by the "mystery" of the relationship between works and lives. "How is it possible to get from the works to the life and from the life to the works?"[102] This approach directs attention to the disjunction between the lived and invented arguments, between Staël's more supple genius and Corinne's, between Stendhal's self-discovery and Julien's arrested self, between Cuvier's fables and history's traumas, and then back to common themes.

Traversing these (real) lives is the figure of Napoleon. It is one of the obvious ways in which they are connected, albeit tangentially. Stendhal and Staël each entered Paris on the 18 Brumaire. For Stendhal the date was accidental, though propitious. On November 9, 1799, the prize student from Grenoble arrived ostensibly to attend the new Ecole Polytechnique, though instead his plans were for literary success; in the event he joined his cousins—the Darus—at the Ministry of War. Staël, surreptitiously, arrived that day from Coppet with hopes of shaping the coup d'état. In 1803, in 1807, and again in 1812, Staël in exile from Napoleonic France traveled through the Germanic states that Stendhal as provisional assistant to the commissary of war in 1806 was paid to organize. In the 1820s Stendhal was a habitué of Cuvier's salon at the Jardin des Plantes, one of the focal points of Cuvier's vast power, which extended from the Jardin des Plantes to the Academy of Science to the Council of State. It was partly with his experience of those soirées in mind that Stendhal later wrote to Sophie Duvaucel (Cuvier's beloved stepdaughter) that " 'no one has made a great fortune without being a Julien.' "[103]

More important, Napoleon—the literal image of ambition in later caricatures of the Empire[104]—acted on each of these people as a means to organize their thoughts about the ethics of self-interest. In a speech lauding Napoleon's power in the Constitution of Year VIII (1799) Dominique Garat (pre-Revolutionary philosophe, former member of the National Assembly, the Convention, and the Council of Five Hundred, and at that point apologist for the 18 Brumaire—in Isser Woloch's words "an opportunist of the first order"—and surely someone who understood the shifting sands of politics) described the Consulate as " 'an immutable fixed point, around which everything becomes solid and constant.' "[105] So too did arguments about the self take shape in encounters with the politics of empire. What are the limits to one person's desires? Where do my needs end and yours begin? How can they both be reconciled? Article 4 of the "Declaration of the Rights of Man and of the Citizen" of 1789 had clearly stated the answer: "Liberty consists in being able to do anything that does not injure another; thus the only limits upon each man's exercise of his natural rights are those that guarantee enjoyment of these same rights to the other members of society." For later liberals such as John Stuart Mill this would mean that when harm of others begins, my rights end and theirs commence. As Napoleon transparently conflated his own desires with the needs of the state in its expansion at home and abroad, when the model of the man became the model of an age, discussion of this issue among his contemporaries sharpened.

Post-Revolutionaries knew that when speaking about ambition they were talking about modernity. Ambition stood as a code word for liberalism, in its widest sense of the freedom of the individual. This is a reminder to us how very political these issues are. Self-making is always about the relationship of the self to others. It is always political, which is one of the reasons attention paid to these individual lives is so well deserved. And in a new era of empire, when global capitalism raises anew questions about the relationship between talents and rewards, can we afford not to take note of the hesitations and adaptations that marked the advent of modernity? It is to stories of these *ambitieux* that we now turn—plotlines of post-Revolutionary success, and lifelines from the First Empire to our own.

2

GENIUS, MADAME DE STAËL, AND THE SOUL OF PRODIGIOUS SUCCESS

Corinne, or Genius

When *Corinne, or Italy* by Germaine de Staël was published in 1807, five years before Byron's *Childe Harold's Pilgrimage*, it was an overnight success. The romantic hero was initially cast as feminine.[1] Its message about the link between female genius and doom resonated throughout the nineteenth century and echoes into our own, taking on a life of its own. Like Frankenstein's monster, John Isbell suggests, "Corinne has led a mythic life independent of her creator and her text."[2]

Corinne's influence has been traced in George Eliot, Charlotte Brontë, Harriet Beecher Stowe, George Sand, Willa Cather, and Kate Chopin, who "was known as the Corinne of St. Louis."[3] The book launched a plotline, a "master fiction" a "heroic model" of feminine behavior with enormous appeal.[4] Others who "modeled their own lives on Staël's heroine or created Corinne-like characters" include the writers Jane Austen, Mary Godwin Shelley, Fanny Kemble, Elizabeth Barrett Browning, Elizabeth Stuart Phelps, and Lydia Maria Child. She stands as the precursor of Simone de Beauvoir.[5]

Corinne's extraordinariness—her connections to other extraordinary and creative women past and present, her alienation from and rejection by the conventional society that she has been born into—impresses, as does the obvious identification of the author with her character.

Reviewers linked Corinne and Staël on first reading. Their outré personalities were alike: "The need for *distraction* and *applause,* an excessive sensibility, both the heroine and her creator are rebuked for these traits."[6] As Madelyn Gutwirth explains, "People began to call her Corinne, seeing right through the thinness of the fictional gauze draped over this elaborate wish-fulfillment novel."[7] This collapse of identities was fixed visually in Elisabeth Vigée-Lebrun's *Portrait of Madame de Staël as Corinne* of 1808.[8]

Staël's cousin Albertine Necker de Saussure called her "an extraordinary, if not unique, woman, on account of her faculties [of mind]."[9] Benjamin Constant completed his enthusiastic description of his first meeting with Staël in similar (though unwelcome) words to Madame de Charrière, who had earlier been the object of Constant's fascination: "In short, she is a Being apart, a superior Being, such as one encounters perhaps but once in a century."[10] "From childhood on, her family and her entourage constantly asserted Mme de Staël's genius,"[11] Gutwirth explains. " 'The Staël is a genius . . . an extraordinary woman in all she does. She only sleeps during a very few hours, and is uninterruptedly and fearfully busy all the rest of the time.' "[12]

Staël and Corinne use the same language to describe their relationship to others, making it difficult to separate their voices. " I am an exception to the general rule," Corinne says to herself as she wanders alone through Florence.[13] "Heavenly creature, may ordinary women be judged by the ordinary rules," Staël has Oswald say to Corinne, as he echoes her point of view.[14] In *Ten Years of Exile,* Staël's unfinished memoirs, she explains her need to escape Coppet, luxurious but dull; it was not Paris: "All mediocre people are endlessly amazed that the needs of the talented are different from their own."[15] "And must we imitate the instinct of bees, whose swarms follow each other without progress and all alike?" Corinne asks in *her* memoir, the "Histoire de Corinne," "Corinne's Story." "No, Oswald, forgive Corinne's pride, but I thought I was made for another fate."[16]

Corinne complains in her "Histoire" that in Scotland, where she was miserably isolated by fog, loneliness, and her memories of Italy, others would say to her, " '*You ought to be content. You do not lack anything.*' "[17]

Staël will say the same thing later in *Ten Years of Exile* when describing the reaction of others to her unhappiness in exile: "Buzzing around me I heard the platitudes to which everyone succumbs: 'Doesn't she have money? Can't she live well and sleep well in a fine château?' "[18] "What a stupid opinion, based on the externals of life," as she has Corinne say, "while the whole centre of happiness and suffering is in the innermost and most hidden sanctuary of ourselves!"[19]

That Corinne doubled for Staël is never in doubt. Necker de Saussure explained in her "Notice sur le caractère et les écrits de Mme de Staël," which introduced Staël's posthumous *Oeuvres complètes,* that "her works are, in a manner of speaking, an abstraction of her life."[20] In feminism's rediscovery of Germaine de Staël in the 1970s that identification is clear. It is as a "woman of genius" that Staël appeals, the phrase becoming emblematic, as in the titles of works such as Ellen Moers's "Mme de Staël and the Woman of Genius" in 1975.[21] The woman of genius appears timelessly before us as well in an essay by Isabelle Naginski in Madelyn Gutwirth, Avriel Goldberger, and Karyna Szmurlo's *Germaine de Staël: Crossing the Borders* (1991), which traces the Sapphic link between Germaine de Staël and George Sand and which seems to connect us all. Naginski speaks of the "ways in which the model applies to women, particularly to women of genius." She says of Staël's theme of the *décalage* between happiness and genius that it "denounces the catastrophic situation of the exceptional woman" and that Staël speaks to "the inevitable tension between fame and the pursuit of happiness in the lives of women—between the female public persona and the private self," that relationship of public and private self being a continuing theme of this book.[22] Gutwirth (whose early and tenacious work on Staël did much to bring *Corinne* to critical attention—writing a dissertation on Staël in the early 1950s, then publishing it in revised form in the 1970s) is more explicit. In the preface to *Crossing the Borders* she highlights the connections between Corinne (and Delphine, Staël's earlier heroine) and us today: "Staël speaks to the unresolved conundrum of women's aspiration. Fictions from her pen plot the degree of entrapment of will and heart subduing women's powers. . . . Her own discourse in a sense went underground.

It lies there for us to disinter and mine as part of our own ground, the ground of women's seizure of their share of the terrain of culture."[23]

The use of the term *genius* as if it described a timeless category of experience, as if it were resolutely biological, can be traced back to the social scientific and early psychiatric work on the subject in the last half of the nineteenth century. Its ahistorical meaning should give us pause as we consider Corinne and the meaning of her genius. Dr. Edouard Toulouse, for example, took Emile Zola as representative in his study of genius. In his physical and mental exam of Zola, published in the *Enquête médico-psychologique sur la supériorité intellectuelle,* Toulouse found evidence of superiority relevant to other geniuses such as Alphonse Daudet, Puvis de Chavannes, Rodin, Saint-Saëns (and other less familiar names today, such as Dalou and Jules Lemaître). His work sought to measure the distance between these exceptional men and those who were average, and he placed its findings in the context of contemporary studies, especially Cesare Lombroso's French edition of *L'homme de génie.*[24] This approach finds its culmination in the astonishing statement in Havelock Ellis's *Study of British Genius* (1926) that "greater rarity of intellectual ability in women" is proved by the fact that *The Dictionary of National Biography,* that "authoritative and well-balanced scheme of the persons of illustrious genius . . . who have appeared in the British Isles from the beginning of history down to the end of the nineteenth century" includes descriptions of "975 British men of a high degree of intellectual eminence" but only 55 women.[25]

A similar logic prevails in many of the essays in *Genius and the Mind: Studies of Creativity and Temperament,* edited by Andrew Steptoe of St. George's Hospital Medical School. The book's contributors aim for the most part at developing a biological determinist explanation for "genius" and demolishing environmental arguments. The *Times Literary Supplement* justly complained in its review that not one of the essays took as its subject an accomplished woman: Shakespeare, Byron, Mozart, John Stuart Mill, Darwin, Einstein, Ramanujan all covered, but only a mention of Virginia Woolf; no Marie Curie.[26]

A look at Steptoe's essay on Mozart reveals his logic. There, Mozart's sister, Nannerl, appears in the narrative as evidence for the biological determinist argument about the nature of genius. Nannerl, Steptoe argues, was brought up exactly like her brother, Wolfgang. Both were trained and encouraged by their father; "indeed she had the advantage over him, since she was four and a half years older and so was trained without any competition until she was more than nine years old." Steptoe asserts that female musicians in eighteenth-century Europe had the same opportunities for success as males: Maria Theresia von Paradis was a piano virtuoso, Regina Strinasacchi was a violin virtuoso, and Nancy Storace was a famous opera singer. That we know Wolfgang as Mozart and Nannerl as a footnote in the history of music and culture is because Mozart was born a genius and Nannerl was not: "If the environmental stimulation provided by living and training within this musical family was enough, then Nannerl Mozart would also have become a great musician and composer."[27] That none of Nannerl's female contemporaries was famous for composing, however, lies beyond Steptoe's point.

But although the discussion of genius as a category of experience in these books appears at odds with feminist readings of Staël (in their misogynist understanding of genius as male) the arguments align in their assumption of genius as an a priori category of experience.[28] Genius lies outside history except with respect to its adversarial relationship to the society the genius is born into, a binary that proves its universality, a structural constant. As Penelope Murray (a classicist) asserts in the introduction to another collection of essays in this vein, *Genius: The History of an Idea:* "The notion of genius raises questions about the role of the creative individual and his place in society: Nietzsche, as Michael Tanner reminds us, insisted on the 'preposterousness of expecting the exceptional (which alone is valuable) to proceed from someone who leads a model bourgeois existence.' "[29] In both Murray's and Steptoe's books this theme is developed by offering to us Plutarch's description of Archimedes: "For these reasons there is no need to disbelieve the stories told about him—how, continually bewitched by some familiar siren dwelling with him, he forgot his food and neglected the care of his body; and how, when he was dragged by force, as often happened, to the place for bathing and anointing, he would draw geometrical figures in the hearths, and draw lines with his finger in the oil with which his body was anointed, being overcome by great pleasure and in truth inspired of the Muses."[30] Antibourgeois, without a doubt.

Andrew Elfenbein notes in another work on the subject that "genius has become a favorite noun in bourgeois aesthetics because it reinforces a myth of individualism. As a quasi-mystical gift that simply occurs, with no help from society, genius points to pure greatness, divine inspiration in a secularized world." This is an apt description of romantic genius, but is it not the myth that historians are meant to explore?[31]

When Staël speaks through Corinne of the incompatibility of happiness and glory, of the tragic arc of genius, to whom is she speaking? This chapter returns *Corinne* to the moment of its creation, when romantic genius was being shaped from the disparate meanings that genius held in the eighteenth century. It suggests the appeal of this notion of genius to Staël and her alter ego, Corinne, who were privileged and enlightened but restricted by traditional expectations for women's lives. This chapter grounds a discussion of genius in the life experience of Staël, a "hinge" figure whose explorations of the limits of ambition crossed the Revolution to self-consciously help create the norms of the new century.[32]

Romantic genius enabled success, because its drive was irresistible. It was a way of becoming a self that seemed to originate outside oneself—to be outside one's control. It allowed success without the charge of selfishness. The drawbacks, however, were significant. Whereas Staël survives, her heroine dies—like Baudelaire's later albatross, floundering on the deck of a merchant ship:

> The Poet is a kinsman in the clouds
> Who scoffs at archers, loves a stormy day;
> But on the ground, among the hooting crowds
> He cannot walk; his wings are in the way.[33]

By looking past the shadow cast by Corinne's fate, as we will do, we can see pre-Romantic meanings of genius deployed by Staël in her novel.

These muted meanings compete with the elegant binary described by Corinne's combative romantic genius, allowing us to consider the novel from other points of view, including that of its other female characters, ordinary but searching, as Staël generously concedes, for safer solutions to the problem of female ambition. Romantic genius was just one of the ways for Staël to figure herself within competitive individualism, I argue. We might better see *Corinne* as part of an extended essay—Staël's life's work—on the morality of self-interest in post-Revolutionary France. Corinne voices Staël's complaint: "We live in a century when self-interest seems the only motive for all men's actions, but what sympathy, what emotion, what enthusiasm, can ever result from self-interest?"[34]

That Corinne's genius is the presenting theme in *Corinne* is never in doubt. We first encounter her through the eyes of Oswald as she is about to be crowned in Rome for her genius and beauty: "He heard the bells ringing from the many churches in the town; bursts of cannon fire from different places proclaimed some important occasion. . . . He was told that that very morning, at the Capitol, the most famous woman in Italy, Corinne, poetess, writer, and improviser, and one of the most beautiful women in Rome, was to be crowned."[35] That Corinne is as much our fantasy as Oswald's is suggested by the comments of the crowd we overhear and Oswald's reluctance to be enthusiastic about Corinne: "*That's the string of her admirers,* said one Roman. *Yes,* replied another, *she receives homage from everyone, but she gives special preference to no one. She is rich and independent; they even think, and she certainly looks it, that she is a woman of noble birth who wants to remain incognito. Whatever the truth may be,* continued a third, *she is a goddess surrounded by clouds.*"[36] "There was universal enthusiasm," the narrator adds, "but Lord Nelvil did not yet share it."[37] Throughout our encounter with Corinne we find the term *genius* used to describe her, not least of all during the coronation scene, which includes an invitation for us to see ourselves in Corinne: "All of them [the Roman poets] lauded her to the skies, but the praise they gave her made no distinction between her and any other woman of genius. Their verses were a pleasant combination of imagery and mythological allusions which, from Sappho's day to our own, might have been addressed throughout the centuries to all women renowned for their literary talents."[38]

Staël continually stresses the extraordinary nature of Corinne by contrasting her to ordinary female characters. In the story of her life that she gives to Oswald, labeled for us "Corinne's Story," she explains how discordant had been her life with her stepmother in Scotland. She had been forced to go there with her father after the death of her mother in Italy, and social life for the young woman became the experience of deadening repetitions, her new home a place where no intellectual or creative sparks could kindle. Staël has Corinne memorably describe after-dinner conversation among the women, waiting in English fashion for the men to join them after their port: "One woman would say to another: *My dear, do you think the water is boiling enough to put on the tea? My dear,* the other would reply, *I think it would be too soon, for the gentlemen are not yet ready to come. Will they stay at table a long time today?* the third would say. *What do you think, my dear? I do not know,* the fourth would reply. *I think the parliamentary elections are to take place next week and it is possible they will stay to talk about them. No,* the fifth would say, *I think rather they will talk about the fox hunt which they were so busy with last week, and which is to start again next Monday. But I think dinner will soon be over. Oh! I doubt it,* the sixth would say with a sigh. And silence would fall again."[39]

Corinne had longed for success, "I used to like success and fame. My ambition used to be to win the applause even of those who were indifferent," but her stepmother discouraged the exercise of her talents.[40] " 'What is the use of all that?' she would say," explaining to Corinne that "a woman was made to look after her husband's household and her children's health, that all other pretensions only did harm, and the best advice she had to give me was to hide them if I had them."[41] In the cold climate of provincial Britain, Corinne explained, "I felt my talent slipping away."[42] She began to doubt herself, wondering "if it was not I whose way of thinking was crazy."[43]

Communitarian demands speak strongly in *Corinne,* countering the impulses of its heroine. Individualism is contained through domesticity—through the split between the private and the public that the dining habits of the British upper classes describe and that Staël recounts in the scenes of Corinne in Scotland. It is also contained within the atavistic tribal nationalism that Oswald's Scottishness represents. The male political community speaks loudly in *Corinne.* Oswald turns definitively away from his plan to marry Corinne when he reads his dead father's letter to the father of Corinne (then still Miss Edgermond)—a type of cultural *mainmorte:* "If my son married Miss Edgermond, he would certainly love her greatly . . . and then, to please her, he would try to introduce foreign ways into his house. Soon he would lose the national spirit, the prejudices, if you like, which unite us and our nation; we are a group, a community, which is free but indissoluble, and can perish only with the last one of us."[44] Oswald's father goes on to urge Corinne's father to encourage the marriage of Oswald to Lucile, Corinne's father's child by his second wife, a Scotswoman. Oswald feels the draw of Lucile and the domesticity she represents. In Scotland, away from Corinne, they meet. "He would have liked Corinne's genius," Stael tells us, "to bring about the disappearance of the slight figure which took all shapes successively in his eyes."[45]

In this context of disapproval, ambition—subsumed under the rubric of genius—becomes acceptable as it becomes inevitable and as it leads to suffering. Its inevitability is signaled by its expression, that is, by the fact that Corinne is an improvisator who recites her verses without preparation, spontaneously. She is, to a degree, merely the vehicle for the divine to express itself. "The sublime," Corinne tells us on her deathbed, "in every genre is a reflection of the divine."[46] The passivity of genius, its characteristic lack of self-will, of self-construction, is expressed by Staël in her creation of Juliet. Juliet, the daughter of Oswald and Lucile, becomes, as Corinne dies, Corinne's reincarnation. Corinne teaches Juliet to speak Italian and play the harp: "Corinne, in her feeble, wasted state, gave herself very great trouble to teach the child all her talents, as a legacy she wanted to leave while still alive."[47] Oswald was struck by the resemblance: "She was holding a harp shaped like a lyre but proportionate to her size, in a way like Corinne's; her little arms and the look in her pretty eyes were a complete imitation of Corinne's. It was as if you saw a miniature of a beautiful picture, with the addition of a childhood charm which gives an innocent attraction to everything."[48]

For Corinne to succeed she needs to forsake her family and her father's home. Her separation from her half sister, Lucile, is a loss, for Corinne loves her sister deeply. Her abandonment of her father's name, Edgermond, frees her from tradition but alienates her from loving associations. Corinne creates a network of friendships for herself in Italy, but they are all male. Corinne dies, forsaken by Oswald, "struck by destiny"[49] and unable, as Staël explains in "Corinne's Last Song," to reconcile love and talent. Corinne passes her torch to Juliet and genius speaks through the generations—from George Sand to Beauvoir to us.[50]

But of what stuff was Corinne's genius fashioned? Staël's childhood in Enlightenment Paris was far removed from Corinne's youth in rural Scotland with her rigid, unimaginative, and conventional stepmother. Staël was born in a milieu at the cutting edge of modernity, to a family in which the extraordinary was ordinary and talk of genius was commonplace. Yet the emotional realities of Corinne's genius were rooted there, in eighteenth-century Paris, at the frontier between the traditional and the new. Like Corinne's, Staël's options were limited, first by old regime models for feminine behavior, then by the somewhat more limiting models set within the emerging male public sphere. Though Staël never sought full political rights for women, her efforts to manipulate power along the model of a *salonnière's* maneuvering behind the scenes became more difficult in the context of Jacobin and Napoleonic politics. As Jacques Godechot explains in his introduction to Staël's *Considérations sur la Révolution française:* "She wished for [women] to be free to exercise their influence on such or such a statesman, a role that she coveted [*ambitionnait*] to play to the highest degree."[51] This was a goal that, as we will see, Napoleon claimed to have personally, aggressively frustrated.

Both of the Neckers' occupations signaled their status as modern. Jacques Necker, banker and Protestant from Geneva—financial capitalist—was one of the richest and most powerful men in Paris. In 1764, when he married Suzanne Curchod, he was worth 7 million livres, the equivalent of 150 million francs in 1983, or almost 23 million euros today.[52] Director of the Compagnie des Indes, finance minister from 1777 to 1781 and again from 1788 to July 11, 1789, he was wildly celebrated as the savior of the French Revolution when Louis XVI was forced to return him to power after the Fall of the Bastille. Suzanne Necker presided over a late-Enlightenment salon that attracted Diderot, d'Alembert, Grimm, and Buffon and was a help to her husband's career, being a center of the public opinion that sustained it.[53] But when Suzanne expressed hopes of entering the Republic of Letters in a more formal way by publishing a book on the writer and theologian François Fénelon, Jacques asked her to desist: " 'Picture to yourself,' " he explained to his daughter in a double censure "when she began to show similar inclinations, 'how I dared not go to her for fear of tearing her away from an occupation that was more enjoyable to her than my presence. I saw her, in my arms, pursuing an idea.' "[54] As the critic Sainte-Beuve would later advise a friend, "But if you are after any happiness in love at all, never love a muse. Where you think her heart is, you will find only her talent. 'Do not love Corinne—and especially if she has not yet reached the Capitol; for then the Capitol is inside her, and on any pretext, on any subject that arises and even the most intimate ones, she'll mount it.' "[55]

In a parody of liberalism that holds that an individual's freedom to act is limited only when that action harms another, Jacques's point was that his wife, the *salonnière,* was free to think, to create insofar as her intellectual activities did not disturb her husband's sexual or emotional needs, which writing a book surely would do.

Suzanne Necker's response set the stage for her daughter's expression of genius. Unable to publish, she still wrote compulsively. "She lived pen in hand," Ghislain de Diesbach explains, carrying on "a vast correspondence which encompassed relatives, friends, crowned heads, favor-seekers, even Necker himself, since the couple, although rarely apart, had adopted the habit of writing little notes to each other and of sorting out important problems through letters."[56] These letters were extensions of conversations, on the model of the salon, but also reflections, advice, summaries of readings that she would also note down each day in her journals—which after her death her husband would reverentially publish.

Staël's writings, too, were extensions of conversations. It was to observers as if she could not stop talking, as if speaking and writing flowed within the same medium. Her writing was accomplished in the midst of conversations, in the frenzy of family life at Coppet, the Neckers' estate in Switzerland on Lake Geneva where she lived in exile: "The Countess de Boigne records she never did have a study for work and wrote by placing a little writing case of green morocco containing her work and correspondence on her knees, carrying it from room to room, often surrounded by people."[57]

Jane Austen, who would die the same year as Staël,[58] was also famous for writing in the midst of family life, screening, shielding her words from her parents. Fanny Trollope was remarkable for her ability to write no matter what the family crisis, at night keeping vigil at a sick child's bed, for example, working to support the household in the face of bankruptcy. Gutwirth suggests that writing within the interstices of domestic life was one of the ways in which intellectual work on the part of women was and is made respectable. Writing is acceptable if it is somehow part of "leisure time," if it is demonstrably not in conflict with the needs of family life.[59]

But Staël's response to the disapproval shown to her even by her indulgent father—who famously called her Monsieur Saint-Escritoire (Monsieur Saint-Desk),[60] a tease that honored the importance of her writing while questioning its femininity—went far beyond the response of her mother, or of Jane Austen or other writing women to this same conflict. Those women interwove domestic and intellectual life as a means of reconciling femininity and creativity. This strategy covered up the clash implicit in early modern liberalism between the rights of the individual and the demands of the family. It reflected the need for women to adjust their desires to the needs of their families, to accept the proposition that posed the importance of family life over the importance of the particular female self. But by adopting the persona of genius Staël pushed these contradictions of liberalism to the fore—positing an intense, unstoppable force that, despite cultural norms, unfolded itself as it might.

Staël's genius was a demonstration of the force of individualism, a performance of its goals that, as we will see, prompted visceral responses. Her life, "narcotic, erotic and baroque," in Bonnie Smith's terms, was a whirlwind for some to avoid at all costs. In the *mot* of Talleyrand: "To appreciate the value of such repose" (he is referring to his dull marriage) "one must have lived for a month in the same house as Mme de Staël."[61] Genius allowed Staël to pursue her goals in politics and literature. She did not need to "desist," like Suzanne Necker. But her genius was not simply instrumentalist, a means to an end. The genius she played at was also a provocation, a demand that witnesses weigh the costs of individual versus community needs, as Corinne's fate does. It asked questions about individual difference and its place in social life.

What explains the differences in aptitudes or talents between people, and what should the social consequences of difference be? Are we born equal as blank slates, or is there a hierarchy of "natural" difference, whereby some few at the top, as Diderot imagined d'Alembert in *Rêve de d'Alembert,* "emerg[e] from 'material factors, the successive stages of which would be an inert body, a sentient being, a thinking being and then a being who can resolve the problem of the equinoxes, a sublime being, a miraculous being, one who ages, grows infirm, dies, decomposes and returns to humus.' "[62]

Is it agency, God, education, or some other source of privilege that explains success? Is it a matter of will or of fate? To whom do my talents belong, myself or my community? With whom should their benefits be shared?

That these questions generated anxiety among the Neckers is apparent in the upbringing of Staël—baptized Anne-Louise-Germaine Necker but called Louise as a child—which was in the hands of her mother. Staël's own answers to these questions—which frame the liberal-communitarian debate of our own times—define Staël's differences with her mother and her mother's understanding of genius as rational, learned, and resting on rigorous training. They allowed her to revolt from her mother's stifling will. They also led her to ponder different ethical solutions.

A genius seems to have been expected. Certainly, Suzanne Necker was ready from birth to raise her as a prodigy, a Mozart of letters, as it were, in Gutwirth's words a "wonder child."[63] Suzanne Necker immediately assured friends after the birth of her girl that she would raise her like Emile, not Sophie; that is, Gutwirth insists, "she intended to develop the independence of judgment Rousseau in his *Emile* had prescribed be cultivated in boy children, rather than the compliance of character he had recommended to girls." The most important sign of these intentions was Suzanne's decision to take "her daughter into the literary salon to sit alongside her from childhood. . . . [By doing so,] Germaine's mother fostered the girl's ability to learn and speak in a public forum."[64]

But Louise-Germaine's cousin (in marriage) Albertine Necker de Saussure, writing from family memories, pointed out that Suzanne's system "was exactly the opposite of Rousseau's."[65] After paying lip service to the importance of *Emile,* after (in Diesbach's words) this "token offered to public opinion," she raised Louise according to her own deliberate ideas.[66] For Necker, it was essential that "a large number of ideas be forced into a young head, without wasting too much time putting them in order, convinced as she was that intelligence becomes lazy when spared such hard work"[67]—exactly the reverse of Rousseau's pedagogy, Necker de Saussure explained, based as it was on the "principle that ideas only come to us through our senses. [Rousseau] had maintained that one must begin by developing the organs of sensation, if one were to achieve a moral development which was neither irregular nor illusory."[68] Necker, averse to Rousseau's sensationalism, "took therefore the opposing path, and wanted to act directly on the mind by the mind."[69]

Thus, exactly unlike Emile, who was given no formal education until age twelve, Staël received an education, as her cousin believed, "well above her age." She was taught Latin and English and made to copy "long exercises from books." " 'All education consisted in instruction,'" in Christopher Herold's summary of Necker's approach.[70]

Necker zealously organized her daughter's education. She "undertook the education of her daughter with the same zeal which imbued her notion of duty."[71] She worked compulsively, inflexibly, morally, authoritatively: "For Mme Necker, there were no degrees of wrongdoing, whether it be venal or not, any fault constituted an infraction of the established order and placed in jeopardy the Neckerian world."[72] "In a manner fully worthy of a wife of a financier," Diesbach suggests, "she scrupulously kept an account of her losses and gains in a register entitled: '*Journal de mes défauts et des fautes qui en sont la suite avec, à côté, les pensées que je recueille comme remède*' [*Journal of my shortcomings and the errors that ensue from these with, alongside, remedies compiled to correct them*]."[73] Necker's careful record of self-improvement may have been influenced by her husband's habits, as Diesbach believes, though one notes the famous omissions in the *Compte rendu au roi* of 1781. It is more likely that her attitude sprang from the broad source which fed Benjamin Franklin's journal, as well as Boswell's and, earlier, Fénelon's. Necker's Calvinism prepared her perhaps to be especially attuned to the anxiety raised by the profile of genius in the eighteenth century: Was one born or made a genius? How does one become a self? Necker deceptively dismissed her husband's efforts at banking and politics by claiming that his success resulted from a force outside his control: "'M. Necker is certainly a man of genius, but he has no right to any pride in it . . . nature created him as he is.'"[74] But the intensity of Necker's efforts to educate her daughter, the drive to shape her into a miniature adult able to hold her own with the philosophes at her salon—"Always . . . young . . . never a child," in her cousin's words—suggests a lack of confidence in genius's ability to shape itself without help.[75]

Review the well-known vignette of Staël at her mother's salon offered by Catherine Huber—Staël's only childhood friend, presented to her by Necker when she was eleven years old with these impressively self-important words: "Voilà! A friend which I give to you."[76]

> We entered the salon. Next to Madame Necker's armchair was a little wooden stool upon which her daughter was seated, obviously obliged to hold herself very erect. Scarcely had she taken up her accustomed place when three or four elderly personages approached her, and spoke to her affectionately . . . one of them . . . engaging in conversation with her just as if she were twenty-five years old. This man was the Abbé Raynal; the others were MM. Thomas, Marmontel, the Marquis de Pesay and the Baron Grimm . . . .
>
> [After dinner] a crowd of people arrived. Each one, approaching Madame Necker, would say a word to her daughter, by way of a compliment or a witty remark. . . . The very men who were most celebrated for their wit were the ones most apt to draw her out. They asked her to tell them about her readings, suggested new ones to her, and gave her a taste for study by discussing what she knew and what she did not know.[77]

Genius was both natural and shaped by circumstances, but how could that be? What explains individuality, how plastic is the human, who controls her becoming, to whom to credit her success? Of course Staël was a genius, a phenomenon of nature, but one had to admit that hers was a genius aided by circumstance: "At the same time, it is also true that a rare concourse of outside forces favored the early development of her mind," her cousin explained. Necker, as we have seen, took no chances with her daughter's education, playing both to nature and to circumstance. But as Necker de Saussure noted, it was not a system "without drawbacks," for it led to a major depression.[78]

Staël was a prodigy, like Mozart and so many gifted children in that gilded age. Staël's response to her mother's tutelage is what gives her life its lasting significance. Like a later genius, John Stuart Mill, she broke down under the weight of her parent's philosophy. Staël was ordered by the famous Dr. Théodore Tronchin to be sent to the country, to be relieved from her instructions, and to be prevented from reading (though this last proved impossible). Mill and Staël each rebelled against a system seen as sterile and rule-bound. Mill's response was to reject a cold utilitarianism, to call for the importance of the emotions in day-to-day life and in our ethical systems. For Staël, like the later liberal, the solution to parental domination was an ethical emotionalism that offered liberty in place of her mother's rigidity.

Necker de Saussure pointed to the importance of Staël's response to her upbringing in shaping her views, in determining the argument of her life (which, as we will see, came to be set against the authoritarian universalism of Napoleon): "She felt she could be, simply through the élan of a good heart, by the blissful impulsion of a well-born soul, all that her mother had been by force of reason and close supervision, and she wanted to be the representative of natural gifts, because her mother stood for those qualities that were acquired."[79] As Oswald said to Lady Edgermond in Corinne's defense, "'The world would have been very dull, my Lady, if there had never been either genius or enthusiasm and if human nature had been made so regimented and monotonous.'"[80] And, as the voice of Oswald also explained, she was "someone who admitted of no nuances or exceptions and judged everything by general, unsentimental rules."[81] So did Staël posit the problem of Napoleon's universal despotism, as we will see below.[82] The same "strict tyranny" and "contemptuous mediocrity" marked the despotism of the emperor, Staël reflected when trapped in exile at Coppet and hounded by Napoleon's men.[83]

Staël offered intuition and feeling, something irrational to counter her mother's drive. The excitement of escaping her mother's rules, of offering feeling in its place, is caught in another of Huber's vignettes. Catherine's mother suggested taking the two friends on a carriage ride through the Bois de Boulogne. Suzanne Necker hesitated. Her child had never *been* on such an excursion. (Would she hurt herself on the carriage door?) The Hubers prevailed. The party set off. As Catherine explained, Staël ignored the passing woods and displays of people—the ostensible point of the excursion—and spent the time in a kind of trance, in an ecstasy of enjoyment that she would later label "enthusiasm" and define as the "breath of God." The superior state of the inspired, superior person, close to madness, perhaps modeled on Diderot's exposition in *Rameau's Nephew,* clearly expressed the *Encyclopédie*'s point of view that "the man of genius . . . has a way of seeing, of feeling, of thinking which is his alone."[84]

Suzanne Necker's disappointment at the failure of her system was recorded by Staël's cousin. After receiving her compliments on the nearly grown Louise's accomplishments, the mother sighed, "It is nothing, absolutely nothing next to what I wished to make of her."[85] Diesbach suggests that Necker, having been brought up without an education, in service until her marriage, was determined that her daughter would achieve what she had been prevented from attaining.[86] Little Louise sitting at the feet of her mother at the Neckers' salon was the child as duplicate of her mother. Does this not remind us of the relationship between the dying Corinne and Juliet? In the first case, though, genius was fabricated for personal satisfaction, for family pride (as we will also see in the upbringing of Stendhal). Staël imagined her own genius—Corinne's—being passed as a torch through the receptacle of Juliet, toward the goal of progress for all, for the advancement of the human race. It is selfless, not selfish, motivation that explains her behavior. As romantic genius will claim, geniuses help move history forward. Their voices speak to the future, as Staël explains in all her comments on genius. Or, as Baron d'Holbach said of his fellow philosophes: "You are not men of your times; you are men of the future, the precursors of future reason. It is not wealth, nor honour, nor vulgar applause that you should aim for, it is immortality."[87] The genius advances progress by his discoveries, "soaring like an eagle toward a luminous truth," as the essay on genius in the *Encyclopédie* explained.[88]

The young Staël's conception of genius was one with the century. The term had been most commonly used to mean talent and its drive for expression, or simply the reasoned use of the intellect. That seems to have been the Marquis de Condorcet's aim when he argued that the differences between men and women are explained by differences in the way they are brought up. In his *Lettres d'un bourgeois de New-Heaven à un citoyen de Virginie* he argued that " 'a species of constraint put upon the strength and the mind of woman by public opinion as to what custom deems acceptable, from childhood on, and especially at that point where genius begins to unfold, must harm their progress in every sphere.' "[89]

As individualism increased its appeal, genius—meaning talent—came to mean the particular, the unique talents of superior individuals. ("The genius has a way of seeing, of feeling, of thinking which is his alone," the *Encyclopédie* asserted.)[90] For Staël genius enabled success by driving her, willing or not, to her goals. But genius is precisely described by Staël as ethically distinct from ambition. She constructed a Corinne who is propelled by her love for glory, a value that looks backward to aristocratic life and the court society. Staël explained in her *Treatise on the Influence of the Passions* (begun in 1792, completed and published in 1796) that the love of glory distinguishes the truly talented from the mediocre who are profanely ambitious: "In speaking of the love of glory, I have considered it only in its most perfect sublimity, in that character when it springs from real talents, and aspires only to the splendour of fame. By ambition, I understand that passion which has only power for its object, that is to say, the possession of places, of riches, or of honours, which may conduce to its attainment: a passion which mediocrity may likewise indulge, because ordinary talents may obtain the success with which it is attended."[91]

Debate on the origins of genius was implicated in a larger discussion of materialism. For thinkers like the abbé Jean-Baptiste Du Bos, interested in the problem of aesthetics, the starting point was the antique understanding of genius as divinely inspired. In insisting on natural rather than supernatural explanations for great works of art, these thinkers helped launch a project of research into the mechanics of thinking and creativity that absorbs psychologists today and that helped shape Staël's debate on the ethics of ambition.[92]

Du Bos and others, like Montesquieu in *The Spirit of Laws,* explained cultural difference through climate.[93] Genius is explained by geography. It was easier to be extraordinarily creative in southern Europe than in the cold, damp north. The claim that "genius is more likely in southern climates than in northern climates" is an idea that resonates in *Corinne, or Italy* as well as in the thinking of Stendhal. The relationship between climate and temperament would become one of the truisms of European culture in the nineteenth century, both a prejudice and a romanticism, perhaps easily believed because it was a kind of cultural habit, a reference to pre-Christian beliefs in the genius of place. It would lead Staël to the cultural relativism argued for in *On Germany* and in her "groupe de Coppet," which she offered in place of the authoritarianism of the Empire and which I describe in the conclusion of this chapter. The idea that genius broadly describes the culture of a region, the traits of a people, helped shape German nationalism. It helped counter the barbed offer of French universalism. Less understood is its importance in *Corinne:* the binary of Corinne, the romantic genius opposed to the conventional "other," would be undercut when the "others" were found to harbor potential genius as well.

In *Corinne* the British, French, and Italians are found to have their own distinct genius. The Italian language may be unique in this respect, since its component, separate parts each manifests a particular genius: "Italian is the only European language whose different dialects have separate geniuses."[94] Males have a genius that differs from the female genius. Empires have genius, too. "Through her genius Rome conquered the universe and through freedom she became queen."[95]

Genius spoke to difference, and difference to harmony. An early eighteenth-century writer asserted that we all have genius: "Everyone may have his own genius, but the harmony of society comes from the interplay of their differences, like the different instruments and notes that create music."[96] In *Corinne* we see this interplay of differences, this harmony, in the decoration of Corinne's apartment. As Oswald recognizes, the apartment is a representation of Corinne: "In every detail he noticed an agreeable mixture of everything that is most pleasing in the three nations, French, English, and Italian, the taste for social life, the love of literature, and the appreciation of the arts."[97] The disharmony between Oswald and Lucile is due to their similarity, Staël explains: "The more they were like each other . . . the more difficult it was for them to emerge from their constrained situation."[98]

Corinne is Italy, as the title suggests.[99] The book sets southern genius against northern aggression and manipulation.[100] Corinne is also a mélange of European values, and the book, more quietly than its presenting theme of combative genius, is a history of toleration, an invitation for readers to recognize the value of difference. Oswald begins to learn this lesson on his first trip to Italy, when he meets the French count Erfeuil, who has lost not just his father, as has Oswald, but his fortune. Nonetheless, he is charming and gay. Perhaps Oswald's melancholy is simply an illness, a deviance, we might say, an indulgence: " 'An Englishman,' Oswald said to himself, 'would be overwhelmed with sadness in similar circumstances. What is the cause of this Frenchman's strength? . . . Does the Count d'Erfeuil really understand the art of living? When I am superior, am I only sick? Is his frivolous existence better suited to the pace of life than mine?' "[101]

Though he was prepared by "Corinne's Story" to dislike Corinne's stepmother, Oswald's experience of Madame Edgermond invites the reader's sympathy. Corinne found her rigid and cold. Oswald begins to see her as a loving mother, loved by her daughter, generous within her domain. Devoted to her daughter, she herself has frailties and is charming in her own way. When they meet intimately for the first time, when "he looked at her closely, to compare her with the description that Corinne had given him . . . in many ways he found that description true, but it seemed to him that Lady Edgermond's eyes expressed greater sensitivity than Corinne had ascribed to her and he thought she [Corinne] was not as used as he was to reading reserved expressions."[102] Corinne, when in London searching for Oswald, begins to realize she may have misjudged the British: "Lady Edgermond's strictness, the boredom of a little provincial town, had given her a cruel illusion about everything that was good and noble in the country she had renounced, but she linked herself to it again in a situation in which, for her happiness at least, it was perhaps no longer desirable that she should have this feeling."[103]

The protean nature of genius, its dispersal across societies and within societies, suggests that it is something we all have access to, if it only could be allowed to develop. Was Staël thinking of Condorcet's argument in *Lettres d'un bourgeois de New-Heaven à un citoyen de Virginie* about the effect of social restrictions on the development of women's intellect (his reference to " 'that point where genius begins to unfold' ")[104] when she launched Corinne's thoughts about Scottish domesticity, detailed in her description of the Scottish dinner party, the women waiting patiently for the men to join them for tea? There she also mentions meeting several women "who, by temperament and reflection, had developed their minds, and I had discovered a few expressions, a few glances, a few words said in an undertone, which were out of the usual line."[105] Corinne explains that "the petty opinions of this small place, all powerful in its little circle, entirely stifled these seedlings."[106] Corinne's talent was superior, she reassures us, as "it was able to resist the deadly cold."[107]

Corinne, the novel, only obliquely speaks to these women, it is true. It is Corinne's Italian connection and independent wealth that enable her fame. The novel's theme of transcendent genius, of the clash between genius and love, leaves these women behind as surely as Corinne does in returning to Italy. As one of these Scottish acquaintances makes clear, some costs are too high too bear: "While liking poetry and intellectual pleasures, she judged much better than I did the force of circumstances and human obstinacy. . . . Her mind escaped the circle, but her life was enclosed within it. I even think she was a little afraid of reawakening her natural superiority by our conversations. What would she have done with it?"[108]

Staël does have an answer, though, to this question about the possibilities of genius in ordinary life. What if Corinne had returned to Scotland as Oswald's wife? In that same letter to Oswald that contains her life story, Corinne declares, "If you wished to spend your days in the heart of Scotland, I would be happy to live and die there beside you, but far from abdicating my imagination, I would use it, the better to enjoy nature."[109] Talent and love might connect for Corinne, if genius were somehow ordinary, too.

This is the intriguing problem that genius raises. As much as it is a question of liberty—how should a "genius" be treated by conventional society (which is the romantics' way of posing the problem of genius)—it is a question of equality: how should each of us relate to each other within our society, despite our natural differences?[110] It is as a question of equality that Staël addresses these issues, perhaps as much as the more obvious problem of liberty. Are humans at base exactly the same? How does universality—all human beings born free and equal in their rights—relate to originality?[111]

The materialist point of view offered in the eighteenth century was that the genius was cut from the same fabric as the rest of humanity. "The man of genius does not reason *differently,* he simply reasons more *rapidly,*" claimed the abbé Charles Batteaux.[112] Or, as the philosopher Etienne Bonnot de Condillac asserted, "The man of genius has gained his knowledge in the manner common to all men," a claim d'Alembert would also make in his *Discours préliminaire* to the *Encyclopédie:* "There is no qualitative difference between the reasoning of the man of genius and the rest of mankind."[113]

But if we are all alike, how do we explain one person's success and another's failure? How does one explain one's own failures? As Alain de Botton worries in *Status Anxiety,* "If we all started off equal, then it seems that your riches and your brilliant career must be due to your talent and hard work, while my misery, redundance and writer's block are all my fault."[114]

How could one know one was a genius, an extraordinary being, if everyone had genius? The confusion of views about genius—whether it is a talent, perhaps one among many talents, or a defining determinate of one's being—appears in the entries on genius in the *Dictionnaire de l'Académie française.* In 1740 both meanings were offered: "One says that 'A man is a fine, a great genius, a superior genius,' in lieu of saying that 'he has a fine, a great genius.'"[115]

To understand the importance to contemporaries of these discussions on the meaning of genius, it is not enough to note Romanticism's roots in sentimentalism, in the privileging of feeling in moral decisions. Genius raised the question of balance between liberty and equality, the continuing problem of liberalism. On the one hand, genius spoke to liberty, of the freedom of the self to become itself. Charles Taylor, in *Sources of the Self,* explains the importance of what he calls Expressive

Individualism: it became "the basis for a new and fuller individuation . . . [the] late eighteenth-century [belief] that each individual is different and original and that this originality determines how he or she ought to live." The idea of difference is not new in the eighteenth century; "What is new is the idea that this really makes a difference to how we're called on to live." These are not "just unimportant variations within the same basic human nature," "rather they entail that each of us has an original path which we ought to tread; they lay the obligation on each of us to live up to our originality."[116] Taylor paraphrases Johann Gottfried Herder: "Each person is to be measured by a different yardstick, one which is properly his or her own."[117] As Corinne asks in her "Story," posing liberal feminism's question, "Ought not every woman, like every man, to make a way for herself according to her nature and talents?" "Is it true that duty prescribes the same rule to every temperament?"[118]

But Corinne offers yet another image of the self to Oswald. People are like leaves on a tree—each different, each making up a whole, none dominant, all equally important.[119] This image should be held alongside the Janus-faced image of Corinne as genius—genius triumphant, genius doomed—the two images speaking to the instability of the modern self and the moral dilemmas it presents. Beside the bold outline of Corinne's genius lies a solution of respect for difference, of relativism and tolerance, which will outlast Romanticism and the Empire. Isbell notes that when Corinne dies so does the Revolution,[120] but Staël's own survival plots a lifeline from the generosity and liberalism of the Enlightenment to our own dilemma as moderns today, wrestling with the homogeneity and uniformity of globalization (while deploring the cult of personality, the worship of celebrity, that it perhaps spawns).

How does Staël escape the fate of Corinne? That is the subject we turn to next. Romantic genius enabled the young Germaine de Staël to break with her mother and prepared her, as we will soon see, to stand her own against the personalities of the Revolutionary age. Genius was a way for Staël to construe a self, a liberated, liberating self, which found its perfect expression in *Corinne,* where author and hero were confounded. Genius was also a way for Staël to think through the problem of the self, to ponder the ethics of self-assertion. Is the unfolding of selfhood a moral good, as individualism promised? If so, would not the greater expansion of self be a greater moral good? But is a morality based on the self to be trusted? The Marquis de Sade famously explored the morality of following self-interest at the expense of others in his life and works. In an equation that stated that one's sexual pleasure is not to be limited to the point of another's pain, Taylor explains that "Sade at the end of the century showed how the utter rejection of all social limits could be embraced as the most consistent and thoroughgoing liberation from traditional religion and metaphysics."[121] But where does that leave the social order? What if that self unfolding is evil? What if it is destructive? How would we know? By what measure would we judge? Can there be an ethics of the self?

After Brumaire, the problem of the "solipsism latent in modern culture"[122] was depicted by Staël in her word portraits of Napoleon, which stand as counter images to herself. In *Ten Years of Exile* and *On Germany,* competing types of genius are engaged: Napoleon's, constructed from an ethics of materialism, and Staël's own, whose value lies in its offer of "enthusiasm," that "breath of God" that speaks of the selfless self. This binary repeats the struggle between the young Staël and her mother—enthusiasm offered as a counter to "system"—and that between Corinne and her stepmother, Madame Edgermond. These abstractions are captured by Staël's image of herself and Napoleon hovering over their separate maps of Europe in 1812, "struggling over [Revolutionary Europe's] soul."[123]

These are reifications of ideas about the self. In real life, of course, Staël was neither goddess nor doomed poet-queen,[124] though these fantasies would animate her life. Staël, as herself, found more realistic ways to accommodate her striving self, and this is my central point. Hers was a denouement less gothic than Corinne's but more telling to modern ears. In the art of living in opposition to Napoleon—in the argument that *was* her life lived in exile—were realized the promises resting in the background of *Corinne.* At Coppet the power of romantic genius (her genius, Napoleon's) was attenuated, tempered into a sociability, a sensibility, in range of us all: rooted in romantic individualism but defined by a heightened awareness of the costs of an unfettered life.

Madame de Staël

Staël's own story begins with her attempts, as Mary Wollstonecraft said of herself, to "form a new genus" in the circumstances of the French Revolution.[125] As the wealthy daughter of the Neckers pondered marriage prospects in the declining years of the old regime, it was clear that power could be exercised by working behind the scenes as a partner to a great man, and it was this goal that shaped Staël's ambition and sensibility at that time.[126] Suzanne Necker's salon had helped establish the career of the finance minister in 1776 and would enable his return to power in 1788. Staël knew how women could influence policy in this way. As Diesbach explains, "In her mind, love and ambition were so intermingled that she was convinced that there was no greater happiness in the world than to govern men's minds or to be loved by those who do."[127] To review Staël's history from the 1780s to 1803—when she left for Germany in her first exile—is to see how the persona of genius worked for Staël in creating a space for herself as a political being, making plausible, if not true, anecdotes of 1797, when Staël was supposed to have wished to assume with Napoleon the burdens of future rule.

Staël's liaisons provide the set pieces of her biography as a Revolutionary figure—from the summer of 1789, when she joined her father in his exile from Paris on the eve of the Fall of the Bastille and then accompanied him on his triumphal return. Unlike her mother's, however, Staël's access to power was not effected through her husband. " 'True pleasure for me can be found only in love, Paris or power,' " as she once explained to her father,[128] but with the Baron de Staël, these options narrowed to Paris. The Neckers' Protestantism limited their daughter's choices, excluding otherwise eligible Frenchmen. A marriage with William Pitt had been broached by her mother, a marriage that would have kept her close to the machinery of power, albeit the enemy power. Twenty-five years old in 1783, Pitt was the once and future leader of the British Empire. He was both the former chancellor of the Exchequer and the soon-to-be prime minister, a position through which he would direct British response to the Revolution at home and conduct the battle with France (until the Allied debacles of Ulm and Austerlitz "led to [his] complete breakdown" and death).[129] Surely the prospect of a marriage between Staël and Pitt (however unlikely) whets the imagination.

Though the Baron de Staël lacked éclat, he was Protestant and, the essential point for Staël, established in Paris. The marriage contract with the Baron de Staël, signed in 1786 by the royal family, stipulated that the baron, the Swedish ambassador to France, would never insist that Madame de Staël be forced to live in Sweden, and that the protégé of Gustavus III would be ambassador was negotiated in high circles before the marriage would be considered. But the Baron de Staël was a nonentity, and her adored father was already taken and in any case would retire to Switzerland in 1790, so Germaine de Staël's liaisons with power took the form of affairs with powerful men. These began, possibly, with Talleyrand, whose success in politics is so well known. Staël's first great affair was with Louis de Narbonne-Lara. Narbonne, young, handsome (Fanny Burney acidly noted that they were a mismatched couple; he was comely, she was not), was raised in the court culture at Versailles and understood to be an illegitimate son of Louis XV. The course of the affair established a pattern of elation and loss whose themes would be repeated almost to the end of Staël's life. It also established a style of political involvement that was emotional, heroic, and at one with its times, at least until the advent of the Empire. It is on this quasi-Jacobin dimension of Staël's relationships that we dwell.

The affair with Narbonne began in the winter of 1788–89, that is, after Necker had been recalled as finance minister and in the expectation of the meeting of the Estates General in May 1789, a moment of emotional and political turmoil, compounded by the death of Staël's first child. By the fall of 1789 Staël and Narbonne were leaders of the liberal aristocracy. Their power base was her salon at the Swedish

Embassy, where participants helped shape the liberal constitution of 1791. Staël's influence brought Narbonne to the Ministry of War in December, but in the spring of 1792, on the eve of war with Austria, Narbonne was dismissed. At odds now with the radicalizing Revolution, in July Staël and Narbonne worked together to plot a (rejected) plan of escape for the royal family.

After the *journée* of August 10 Narbonne, now outlawed, was helped to safety by Staël, who risked her life again to help friends escape the September Massacres (September 2–7), employing her status as wife of the Swedish ambassador, her money, and her influence to do so. After the birth of her second child in Switzerland, to which she fled during the massacres, Staël joined Narbonne in England at Juniper Hall, a refuge for French émigrés. Then she returned to Switzerland to wait unhappily for Narbonne. Narbonne's rejection led to intense pleas for his return, and in the following we see how much the political was the personal to Staël, and what her merged commitments represented. "I swear to you," she wrote in October 1793, "if you go to Toulon [where Narbonne meant to join the planned British invasion], I'll leave for Paris on the instant, assassinate Robespierre and help you by dying. My God, what a barbarian! Did you have to accept my life only to tyrannize it so?"[130]

Narbonne's suicide mission would be countered by Staël's own, she threatened, along the model of Charlotte Corday's, the Girondin who in July had murdered Marat, practically in full view of his supporters; this suicidal gesture meant to stop the Terror was as unsuccessful as Staël's failure to stop Narbonne from drifting away. The trajectory of Staël's relationship with Narbonne was repeated in her affair with Adolf Ribbing, a Swedish count who had declared himself a revolutionary in March 1792 by assassinating Baron de Staël's benefactor, the king of Sweden. By early 1795 Staël was again threatening to follow Corday's lead: "I will devise something which will both make me famous and put an end to my too odious life. I will avenge myself on you with the last words that I pronounce, and it is not to happiness, to the liberty of your country, that this victim will be sacrificed!"[131]

Staël's intense and failed relationships with men are breezily and often explained away by Staël's personality in accounts that are strangely ahistorical, given her self-conscious involvement in history. She was "a force of nature in her turban and shawls," a recent (2005) biographer repeats.[132] Indeed, she was overeager and demanding. Diesbach explains Staël's problem with relationships by offering the metaphor of a garden. Staël would sow a garden, then pluck the plants as soon as they began to grow, without waiting for them to mature. As Benjamin Constant said, "Staël could rule the world if she could rule herself," but alas she could not.[133]

Madelyn Gutwirth persuasively explains Staël's behavior as a result of her upbringing. She was both a female child in a prefeminist world and the child of particular parents. Her mother was cold and controlling and loved by the man whose love for Staël herself was always secondary. Staël's life was marked by "the search for confirmation through love, with its insistent call for assurance of worth from others. Germaine Necker's hunger for approval was apparently founded in the clash between her intense nature and the remote, dutiful affection of her reproving mother."[134] This conflict was public. Suzanne Necker wrote her harsh *Réflexions sur le divorce* just as Staël was exploring the possibilities of separation from her husband.[135]

Even on her deathbed, and even in the face of Staël's own pain, her mother was censorious (as Napoleon, too, was about Staël's behavior to her husband, accusing her in 1800 of abandoning him to misery and destitution).[136] This hostility on her mother's part suggests how much Staël gained and lost in playing the genius card. " 'My daughter,' " said the unyielding Necker in the spring of 1794, " 'I am dying of the pain which your guilty and public attachment has caused me. You have been punished by the attitude of its object [Narbonne] towards you. It puts an end to what my prayers could not make you abandon. It is through your care for your father that you will obtain my forgiveness in heaven. Say nothing. Leave now. I have no strength to argue at the moment.' "[137] Genius had allowed Staël to break the rules, but at what a price!

Could Staël have played such a hand in the political events of the Revolution as simply the wife of the Swedish ambassador or the daughter of the dismissed finance minister of the absolute monarchy? Manon Philipon Roland, after all, was able to shape Girondin policy because the speeches she wrote were delivered by her husband, the minister of the Interior. Someone who felt as Wordsworth did in 1789 that "bliss was it . . . to be alive, but to be young was very heaven!"—or as Diesbach explains for Staël, "It is wonderful in that springtime of 1789 to be twenty years old, and Mme de Staël, who will soon turn twenty-three, turns back the clock so that her heart might beat in unison with the enthusiasm of the nation"[138]—would seek the means to play a role; it is through her genius, which pushes Staël to act beyond the bounds of propriety, that she does so. Here we may remind ourselves of Staël's ability to make self-insistence seem will-less by quoting from Juliette Récamier's account of her first meeting with Staël. She explained in her memoirs that Staël " 'complimented me on my appearance in a way that might seem too direct and exaggerated had it not seemed to escape her unconsciously, giving her praise an irresistible fascination.' "[139]

Rather than understand Staël's behavior with Narbonne and others in terms of dysfunction or even peculiar excess, can we not see it as a kind of "heroic individualism" typical of the age, part of the Jacobin or revolutionary sensibility, a sacrifice of the self that historians of the Revolution have emphasized in recent years and that is now being explored for the British?[140] In this respect the contrast between Staël and Elisabeth Vigée-Lebrun is clear. Another "exceptional woman," she was Marie Antoinette's most important portraitist and an important society portraitist in exile during the Revolution and in Paris during the Empire and Restoration. She painted *Madame de Staël as Corinne* in 1808. She explained her success in terms of innate talent rather than training, and that places her squarely in her age; but her behavior, her "self-presentation," at least after 1789, was as socially and politically conservative as Staël's was eccentric or heroic.[141]

Linda Colley has described the death by overwork and "compensatory drinking" of Pitt the Younger. Busyness, or "energy," in the French context, was a signature trait of male political behavior. Among many examples of how this worked, one might recall David's 1812 *Napoleon in His Study,* where the lit candle stub and sunlight streaming in from outside tell us that the emperor has been working all night, and the paper headed "Code" explains what he has accomplished. In Staël this energy was a sign of her genius, or, unkindly, her "weirdness." Visitors to Coppet always noted her high energy. She was always working and talking, as we saw earlier. At Juniper Hall a visitor was struck by these traits: " 'Madame de Staël was "an extraordinary, eccentric genius," who only needed a few hours of sleep and who was otherwise constantly busy,' " wrote the amazed Erich [or Justus] Bollman, the Hanoverian doctor who had smuggled Narbonne out of France to England.[142] How distant is Staël's behavior from that of Charles James Fox, who would cap his work as an M.P. by a night of gambling?

Staël's generation was so young to rule the world. Colley refers to the *"sturm-und-drang* quality" of British political life, "a special kind of emotionalism and violence" that marked the intensity of the times. Colley thus describes "the Earl of Chatham collapsing in the House of Lords as he made his last manic and incoherent speech against war with America in 1778, [and] Edmund Burke flinging a dagger onto the floor of the House of Commons in December 1792 as a symbol of his departure from the Foxite Whigs, and . . . Charles James Fox bursting into tears in response."[143] When Staël begged Paul-François-Nicolas Barras in 1797 to bring Talleyrand into the Directory (and out of the political wilderness he had entered in 1792), she was on her knees, in tears. She threatened violence. She convulsed. She clutched his hand and swore not to let go until he promised. We see the more broadly cultural context of her behavior here and in her pleas for him to deploy his "energy" on Talleyrand's account: "Speak forcefully to your colleagues, ride your high horse, assert your will, make Talleyrand a minister, otherwise, I lose all hope, I myself will die, I can do no more."[144]

Extraordinary times and extraordinary behaviors: it is in a context of intensity and tension between the collective purpose of politics—the general good—and the role of individual wills within it that we can understand Staël's at least implicit offers to Napoleon during the Directory that she might join her genius with his so they might change the world. According to the *Mémorial de Sainte-Hélène,* Staël sent Napoleon "many long epistles, full of wit, imagination, and meta-physical erudition" during the conquest of Italy in 1796. "Simply out of affinity for glory," she "instantly professed for him sentiments of enthu-siasm worthy of *Corinne*." It was a perversion of fate, as it were, "an error, she observed, arising only from human institutions, that could have united him with the meek, the tranquil Madame Bonaparte."[145] Or as Louis Antoine Fauvelet de Bourrienne, Napoleon's friend and private secretary from 1797 until 1804, presented Staël's characteriza-tion of Josephine in these now-missing letters, that mistake had given him that " 'insignificant little Creole, quite incapable of understanding or appreciating his heroic qualities.' "[146] Staël supposedly explained, "It was a fiery soul like hers [Stael's] that nature had undoubtedly destined to be the companion of a hero like him."[147] Napoleon is said to have laughed while reading them and exclaimed, "The woman is mad!"[148]

Of course, the *Mémoires* of Bourrienne are unreliable.[149] A misogynist tradition explains the impending conflict between Staël and Napoleon as being rooted in a "sort of *dépit amoureux*," or unrequited love.[150] Napoleon's own comments form part of a general diatribe against Staël in the *Mémorial de Sainte-Hélène*, which suggests how personal and expansive was his antipathy for Staël, while also describing the effect of Staël's overtures toward him from 1796 until the disillusions of the Consulate. For instance, in his first year of exile on Sainte-Hélène, Napoleon reread *Delphine*, which he had hated already in 1802, and whose subject, liberation, clearly haunted him: "Very little pleased him about it. The confusion of mind and imagination which reigned there prompted his critique. Here were the same flaws which had formerly alienated him from the author, despite the most energetic advances and cajoleries on her part."[151] The editors of Staël's *Correspondance générale* believe that the importuning letters from Staël to Napoleon in Italy, which probably are real, "extolled the glory due to heroes and urged a deed worthy of that honor, that is, the liberation of La Fayette and his companions," moldering since 1792 in Austrian prisons.[152]

It is this view of Napoleon as redeemer of Revolutionary ideals that Staël describes in the early pages of her memoir *Ten Years of Exile*, in the expectation of a meeting in Paris in the winter of 1797–98, "in the interval between his departure from Italy and his departure for Egypt" (in effect, as we learn from the meticulous work of Simone Balayé, in the weeks between December 5, 1797, when Napoleon arrived in Paris, and January 6 or 8, when Staël left for Coppet).[153] Napoleon was heralded as the savior of the Revolution, Staël explains. He was the one who might renew the promise of 1789, which had been "dishonored" by the Terror but was not forgotten by people of Staël's generation, who were shaped by the Enlightenment[154] and came of age with the Revolution: "In my generation . . . there are very few young men or women who, at the time, were not filled with the hope the Estates General led France to envisage."[155] Napoleon was that hope. As *Ten Years of Exile* asserts, "When General Bonaparte won renown through the Italian Campaigns, I felt the strongest enthusiasm for him. Republican institutions were losing all dignity in France through the means employed to maintain them. . . . Bonaparte's proclamations from Italy were designed to inspire confidence in him. They were governed by a tone of noble moderation that stood in contrast to the revolutionary harshness of France's civilian leaders. In those days, the warrior spoke like a judge, while the judges used the language of military violence."[156]

Napoleon seemed a man of feeling, a general whose favorite book was said to be the *Ossian* (the specious epic of a Celtic hero who was both warrior and poet),[157] " 'this poem in which the love of war is infused with a feeling of melancholy, which subjects the conqueror and the conquered alike to the same sadness of heart.' "[158] What a contrast with the leaders of the Directory, whose liberalism evaporated into coarse ambition in the events of 18 Fructidor,[159] Staël argued, when "the power of public opinion disappeared entirely in the face of military force, and what good faith there had been in the Republican party gave way to the calculations of ambition. People sensed that the roof was about to come crashing down, and each one sought shelter for himself."[160]

Staël's memoirs are structured around her disintegrating relationship with Napoleon, from those first meetings in Paris to her flight from exile at Coppet, a journey that took her through Russia in the late summer and early autumn of 1812, just a breath ahead of the *grande armée*.

In *Ten Years of Exile* Staël imagines herself and Napoleon simultaneously making plans to go east, each poring over the map of Europe in advance, for herself to plan her escape from Napoleon, for Napoleon to effect his mastery of Europe: "And the goal of my campaign, like his, was always Russia. She was the last refuge of the oppressed, she was to be the power that the sovereign of Europe wanted to strike down."[161]

But in that winter of 1797–98, when Napoleon was in Paris, laying the groundwork for his later political triumph, courted by the Directory, he was in a sense courted by Staël too, who would have welcomed a role in the reconstruction of post-Revolutionary France that she imagined him leading. They first met at "the grand reception held for Bonaparte by Talleyrand,"[162] the new minister for Foreign Affairs, at his headquarters on the Rue du Bac.[163] They also attended a dinner in mid-December at Talleyrand's, which included the abbé Sieyès, Sophie de Condorcet, and Dominique-Joseph Garat. It was at one of these events, according to Balayé, that the famous exchange described in *Mémorial de Sainte Hélène* took place between Staël and Napoleon on the value of women, on the importance of Staël: " 'General, what kind of woman has the greatest merit? . . . Madame, the one who has the most children.' "[164] This remark prefigures Staël's later image of Napoleon's disintegration in the unraveling of the Empire when he was reported as desperately growling at another dinner party that his female companions should "make soldiers for me."[165] Her address to Napoleon also makes credible the appealing and counterfeit story about a visit Staël made to Napoleon's rooms in that early winter of 1798. When told that Napoleon could not receive her—that he was not yet dressed—Staël supposedly urged an audience anyway, explaining, " 'genius has no sex.' "[166]

By 1803 Staël was known for her ambition. In 1804 Frédéric-César de La Harpe, former director of the Helvetic Republic, tutor to the czar of Russia, and enemy of all Neckers,[167] described Madame de Staël to Alexander I as " 'a woman of wit and intelligence, but eaten up by ambition.' "[168] Isabelle de Charrière had warned Benjamin Constant away from her in 1794, ostensibly on this account: she "had criticized

the 'ambassadress' for her too noisy attempts to force the gates of
fame; she had referred to her as a 'talking machine.'"[169] Constant, on
the other hand, claimed that that quality was just what he needed.
Staël made him want to reach for glory again, he wrote to Charrière:
"'The habit of work has come back to me; even the mirage of literary
glory, which you were at such pains to destroy in me, has returned
and makes the future beautiful.'"[170] Constant, Staël's third great love,
remained with Staël for more years than he wished on this account,
or partly on this account; "'She alone understands me,'" he wrote to
himself.[171] As Diesbach argues, "Naturally lazy, worn out quickly by
any sustained effort, he had found in Mme de Staël an energy which
ignited his own."[172]

In the early years of the Consulate, Staël's reopened salon was a
base for the liberal opposition to Napoleon. It was well understood
that Constant's courageous speech in the Tribunate against authoritarianism—delivered eight weeks after the 18 Brumaire, and two weeks
after Napoleon had named him tribune—spoke for both himself and
Staël. In 1803, though, Staël's ambition had lost its outlets. Constant
had been expelled from the Tribunate in early 1802. In February 1803
Staël herself was banished from Paris by Napoleon, and in October it
was made clear she should leave France.

When Staël traveled east under autumn skies, her plans for exerting
her will had been stymied. She had taken the model of powerful women
available to her from the old regime and reshaped it under the pressure
of circumstances to create the mold of romantic genius, but she then
seems to have exhausted its potential for political power. The fate of
Sappho remained real for women like herself who sought "to force
the gates of fame."[173] "'By examining the small number of women
who have a true claim to glory,'" Staël explained in *On the Influence
of the Passions,* which she worked on at Juniper Hall in 1792 as her
relationship with Narbonne collapsed,[174] "'we will see that this striving
of their nature has always been at the expense of their happiness. After
having put into song the sweetest lessons of ethics and philosophy,
Sappho hurled herself from the top of Leucas. . . . Women are forced

to think that, for the sake of glory, they have to give up the happiness and tranquility which constitute the destiny of their sex.' "[175]

Staël's exile in 1803–4 took her to Frankfurt, Weimar, Leipzig, and Berlin. In 1807, again intensely at odds with the Napoleonic regime, she went to Vienna. Napoleon haunted her on these trips through French-occupied or -threatened German Europe. We will see how her response to Napoleonic ambitions in Germany helped her articulate the meaning of *enthusiasm* as the quality that brings moral sense to the expansion of political self. Genius had functioned in Staël's life to enable her to pose as the counterpart to Napoleon (elliptically in *Corinne,* directly in her memoirs and in *On Germany*). In her eyes *enthusiasm* distinguished her genius, her aspirations, her ambitions from Napoleon's, her moral self from Napoleon's amoral one. But how "moral" can an expansionist self—however well-intentioned—be if its limits are not clearly defined? Does not "liberty" have to take into account "equality," however fumbling and earthbound? Staël's conflict with Napoleon would end by offering her (and us) a way out of the imperialism of self (and self-destruction) that genius seemed to threaten alongside its admirable project of liberation.

Ten Years of Exile records Napoleon's acts of aggression against Staël, some of which—the exiles—we have noted already. We can further list the reviews of *Delphine* both written and engineered by Napoleon, the "unprecedented pulping" of the manuscript and proofs of *On Germany,* and the hounding and exile of her friends Juliette Récamier and Mathieu de Montmorency. But the book has as its major subject the character of Napoleon, whose meaning Staël claimed to have grasped before it was manifest to the rest of Europe, and which it was the book's object to reveal: "Emperor Napoléon . . . had persecuted me with meticulous care and inflexible asperity at an ever-increasing pace. And through my relations with him, I came to know what he was long before Europe had found the key to the enigma and, failing to guess what it meant, let herself be devoured by the sphinx."[176]

Begun in 1811, the book was meant to describe the years 1797 to 1804, along with the new period of active conflict with Napoleon that began in 1810 and effectively ended with Staël's asylum in England—though Staël leaves us abruptly on the rough seas between Finland and Sweden in September 1812. Though obviously a memoir, Staël's intention in *Ten Years of Exile* is made plain in the opening paragraph: "It is not to draw attention to myself," she claims, "that I have set out to relate the circumstances of ten years of exile. The misfortunes I have endured, however bitter, count for so little amid the public disasters we confront that it would be shameful to speak of oneself if the events that concern us were not connected to the great cause of endangered humanity."[177]

The threat to humanity who was Napoleon was devoured by his own ambition, at least, he was in 1797, before he began to fatten on his conquests: "His face was less unpleasant then than it is now—he was thin and pale at least, and one could think that his own ambition was devouring him, whereas for the last few years he has seemed to fatten on the unhappiness he causes."[178] Napoleon, "whose character is fully revealed in everything he does," even, as we see, in his very appearance, was a monster created by his age.[179] In her Rankean expression of the relationship between the unique and the universal of history, Staël posed her victimization at the hands of Napoleon as indicative of the nature of Napoleonic tyranny ("the events . . . connected to the great cause of endangered humanity").[180] So, too, was Napoleon representative of his age—like Goethe, who, Staël explains in the banned *On Germany,* "possessed in himself alone all the principal features of German genius; they are all . . . found in him to an eminent degree."[181]

Though Staël's Goethe demonstrated the best of German traits, "a great depth of ideas, that grace which springs from imagination,"[182] in Napoleon were all the tendencies of a utilitarian, materialist epoch exaggerated. "No man can act with great effect except in the spirit of his century," Staël explains in *Ten Years of Exile,* "and if you examine the story of all those who have changed the face of the world you will see that, for the most part, they have merely seized for their own advantage the trend of minds already in place."[183] In the case of Napoleon, it was the inclination of the materialist sector of the Enlightenment that found its bent in him and was shaping their age: "The bad philosophy of the end of the eighteenth century derided all cults of the soul. Bonaparte put this philosophy into practice. Bonaparte knows that force, as long as it is unrelenting, can never be ridiculous."[184]

People were a means to an end for Napoleon, not an end in themselves, Staël claimed. He saw in people only the use he could make of them: "You would think [that like a hunting dog] he sniffs men out to make them his instruments or his prey."[185] And Napoleon believed that everyone was like him in this regard. All people were hypocrites, virtue was a facade that masked ambition and self-interest: "Bonaparte thinks that when someone says he loves liberty, believes in God, prefers his conscience to self-interest, he is a man who conforms to convention and follows accepted practice to explain his ambitious pretensions or selfish schemes."[186] Napoleon's egoism explains his coldness, a trait Staël notices time and again for us: "He hates no more than he loves, since for him there is only himself, and men act on his soul only as facts or as objects, never as his fellows. His strength lies in an imperturbable egoism that neither pity, nor charm, nor religion, nor morality can for an instant divert from its course."[187]

For Staël, as for many others in Europe, the execution of the duc d'Enghien in 1804 (on the eve of the Empire) was understood as a crime, a political murder, which more than any other measure linked Napoleon with the Jacobins of the year II of the Republic. Truly he was "Robespierre on horseback," as she had quipped after the 18 Brumaire. As Napoleon himself explained the day after Enghien's execution at the Château de Vincennes, "I have spilled blood and I would spill still more, not in anger but simply because a bloody deed enters into the combinations of my political medicine. I am a statesman. I am the French revolution. I say it again and I stick by it."[188]

The duc d'Enghien was a relation of the prince de Condé, well known as a leader of the counterrevolution abroad. Enghien, himself a cousin of Louis XVI, was suspected of being involved in a royalist plot that involved some person of stature acting as the front man who would head France in anticipation of the arrival of Louis XVIII, the brother of the executed king.[189] Whether Enghien was involved in the Cadoudal conspiracy is unclear, though he probably was not.[190] But what is certain is that his arrest was illegal—he was seized in a neutral Germanic territory and his trial was a sham.[191] The same night he was brought by French troops to Vincennes (a fortress on the eastern border of Paris where in 1749 Diderot was imprisoned by *lettre de cachet*),[192] he was court-martialed and executed.[193]

The Enghien affair appalled because it was so clearly an example of the principle that the ends justify the means—even murder and lack of due process—but also because those in Napoleon's entourage who opposed it did so for reasons of expediency. This, for Staël, laid bare the roots of the regime: "Fouché himself," Staël tells us in *Ten Years of Exile,* "disapproved the deed; he had used those words so characteristic of the present regime: 'This death is worse than a crime, it is an error.' "[194] Balayé argues that it was not Joseph Fouché, a former Jacobin and terrorist, at the time Napoleon's minister of Police,[195] who made these comments (often attributed to Talleyrand, as well), but rather another Bonapartist, Boulay de la Meurthe, but, of course, for the point being made, it does not really matter.[196]

Staël blamed the materialist strand of the Enlightenment—C'est la faute à Helvétius, so to speak.[197] " 'The philosophes of this school . . . make use of the word "fault" not "crime," because, according to their way thinking, there is nothing in the conduct of life but skillful or unskillful contrivance.' "[198] As she argues in *On Germany:* "The French writers were absolutely correct to consider that a morality based on interest is a result of that metaphysics which attributes all our ideas to sensation. If there is nothing in the soul but what sensation has introduced, then what is agreeable or disagreeable must be the sole engine of our will. Helvétius, Diderot, Saint-Lambert have not deviated from this line, and have explained all actions (including self-sacrifice) by self-love."[199]

Staël's response to Napoleonic ethics—understood to be based on a materialist self-interest—was to elaborate a spiritualist theory of selflessness that was based on the interconnectedness of the particular self with the "infinite." This she labels "Enthusiasm." As she explains, " 'Enthusiasm rallies itself to the harmony of the Universe, it is love of the beautiful, elevation of the soul, the delight in unselfishness all united into one and the same feeling.' "[200] It is "God within us."[201] It is, at times, a kind of rapture.

Especially in the draft versions of *On Germany* we find "veiled political allusions"[202] to the Empire as Staël discusses enthusiasm, making it clear how directly her theory is hewn out of her experience with post-Revolutionary politics. "What is salient," Staël tells us, "what is manifest in the human race is a fawning attitude towards the warrior, a constant craving for the fortune, the success which surrounds him."[203] Staël grants the appeal of living solipsistically: egoism is comforting; "it is like being in a warm nest where one feels sheltered from the storms, and there is on the part of many people a vulgar but real satisfaction in not letting themselves be 'duped' or 'seduced' by ideas which might lead to sacrifice."[204]

But what a bleak value system egoism leads to. In effect, it takes us to the one described openly in *Ten Years of Exile* as Napoleonic—where individuals pride themselves on the realization that all motives are venal and where the reasoning of an egoist allows him to see himself as "the center of his existence and to take care of others only out of prudence [never by *entraînement* (in the sense of enthusiasm)]."[205] *Egoïsme* takes us to the Europe of 1810, dominated by a state from which enthusiasm has disappeared and left only itself. "Eliminate for a moment all enthusiasm from the world," she says hypothetically in a draft version of her chapter on enthusiasm in *On Germany;* "suppose no affinity between moral good and man, what justification would then exist for not taking oneself as the sole goal."[206]

Staël's hypothesis is then recast from the personal to the national in the last stirring lines of *On Germany.* They bear repeating in full because their meaning pertains both to the French First Empire and to the problems of modern empires generally. As did Gibbon's *Decline and Fall,* which spoke to the Roman Empire and elliptically to the British Empire, Staël's image of France in 1810 conjures up ruins and speaks to the fugacity of temporal power. It takes a romantic view of time and history, which readers of Staël find easy to notice.

But Staël is striking out at a more perplexing paradox. It places at the heart of the modern expansive—universalist—empire the problem of the individual, meant to be protected by universalist principles that legitimate imperial rule but are overwhelmed by empire's "personality," that knot of liberalism that Staël tries to sort out: "Oh, France! Land of glory and of love! If the day should ever come when enthusiasm shall be extinct upon your soil, when all shall be governed and disposed upon calculation [in version A, personal calculation] and even the contempt of danger shall be prompted by reason alone, to what will avail your beautiful skies, your so brilliant minds, your so fruitful nature? An active intelligence, a clever impetuosity may return to you the mastery of the world; but the sole traces you will leave in that world will be like torrents of sand, terrible as the waves, arid as the desert!"[207] Enthusiasm gives meaning to life—to Staël's life, to all lives—"by taking us outside of ourselves": "enthusiasm finds in the heart's reverie and in the extension of thought that which fanaticism and passion confines to a single idea or object."[208] This is to say that enthusiasm saves us from the consequences of our passions, since the passions, Staël claims, derive from *égoïsme*. The very physicality of life, our drives, can overwhelm our souls—our bits of immortality—"if something of pride and vitality does not detach us from the vulgar ascendancy of egoism."[209] Enthusiasm, like justice, is "a sentiment which rallies us to the universal order."[210]

Even for genius, Staël stresses, maybe especially for genius, is enthusiasm critical. "This sentiment is by its universality, even, very favorable to thought and imagination."[211] Enthusiasm animates genius. And not only does it give it life, it gives that life "moral dignity."[212] For genius is not immune to the pull of *égoïsme,* as the description of Napoleon implies. "Having superior talents," as Staël says, "is not a guarantee against that degradation of character which would secretly dispose of the lives of others. Enthusiasm alone might counterbalance the tendency toward egoism, and it is by that sign of the divine that one recognizes the immortals."[213]

Ten Years of Exile thus depicts the clash between Staël and Napoleon as a titanic, romantic struggle between two geniuses, one good, one evil, whose master image is of the author and her nemesis hovering over their maps of Europe, like God and Lucifer, "struggling over

[Revolutionary Europe's] soul."[214] Napoleon is literally demonized. He is "the genius of ardent egoism," Necker de Saussure, Staël's cousin and confidante, explained to readers of Staël's collected works.[215] He is also the "genius of evil," Satan, as well as Attila the Hun, accused in *On Germany* of ruling over a state that by giving itself over to self-interest has lost its soul: " 'If a State's policy is to follow only its own interests, then the nation is no more than an infernal 'legion,' the name the devil gave to his troops.' "[216] Staël brings to bear on her subject Napoleon's own words. " 'I am the god of war and fortune. Follow me.' "[217] And to the duc de Broglie over the bishop's qualms about the exercise of French power in Belgium: " 'Don't you know that if God reigns in heaven, I am the one who commands on earth?' "[218]

It is this image of binaries, with its romantic cast, that has been bequeathed to Staël scholarship, on both sides. The books by Paul Gautier and Henri Guillemin on the relationship between Staël and Napoleon demonize Staël while deifying her other.[219] This reification explains the only intuitively plausible *mot* of 1814, irresistibly quoted by critics, that "Bonaparte had so persecuted her that in Europe one had to count three Great Powers: England, Russia, and Madame de Staël"—as if this could in any way be true. The less dramatic original is more to the point. On her second trip to Germany, a new acquaintance noted that there were only three free powers in Europe: England, Russia, and Madame de Staël.[220]

The Staël portrayed here seems to soar above the complicated mess of Enlightenment thought, picking and choosing bits to digest. Indeed, Paul Bénichou, in *The Consecration of the Writer, 1750–1830*, suggests we notice the counterrevolutionary aspect of Staël's arguments against Napoleon in this respect (although he will also argue for their essential humanism and links to Enlightenment thought): "This image of a negationist, abasing eighteenth century that reduces man to a material mechanism, and morality to an interplay of interests, will be, for half a century, spiritualism's target and the background against which writers will aim to advance contrasting views."[221] The arguments of Constant, too, in tandem, "seem to come from some contemporary counterrevolutionary pen. Thus Constant defines the men of the eighteenth century as 'men of the moment who limit their existence and their influence to that moment and write only to push toward egoism and self-abasement the subsequent generation, which indeed paid heed to their counsels.' "[222]

Presenting Staël as a goddess lifts her from her time and place and makes her experience seem irrelevant, as Bonnie Smith's argument verges on doing in her essay on Staël as historian, "History and Genius: The Narcotic, Erotic, and Baroque Life of Germaine de Staël."[223] The title echoes the famous statement about Byron, who spent time at Coppet during the Restoration but whose destructive sociability is exactly not Staël's legacy, as I will be at pains to show below.[224]

The merging of the self with the infinite, which Staël labels "enthusiasm," is one way to make moral the assertion of self licensed by the Empire (and seen as rogue from the moment of its discovery—"I am myself alone," says the murdering future Richard III in Shakespeare's disapproving *Henry VI, part 3*). But it lacks a practical dimension. Her encounters with German culture offered a more tangible way out of the modern dilemma by grounding an ethics of self in social life, rather than in the self alone and its intentions—as is implied by both Napoleonic ambition in Staël's understanding of it and in Staël's counternotion of enthusiasm. This social approach has purchase today. In *On Germany* we find the self defined in terms of individuality—"I'm myself, and my society benefits from my uniqueness," rather than in terms of individualism—"I'm out for myself," in that sense that materialism in the Empire found unavoidable and which, in the formula of Irshad Manji, stands axiomatic for the modern Western state.[225]

It is the contrast that she found between universalism and particularism that allowed Staël to develop this line of reasoning. The imperialism of the Empire was preceded by the cultural expansion of the old regime when most of Europe sought its "self-esteem in the imitation of the French."[226] Whether as absolutism or Enlightenment, French language, fashion, ideas, and practices held sway. The Revolution intensified this power. The emperor insisted that this was a positive good: "What is good for the French, Napoleon will say, is good for all," especially, perhaps, because to speak of the French was to speak of himself, as a projection of himself. This imperialism of the self was clear as early as the 18 Brumaire, Staël claimed in *Ten Years of Exile:* "This was the first time since the Revolution [began] that I had heard a proper name on every tongue. Until then, they would say the Constituent Assembly did such and such, the King, the people, the Convention. Now there was talk only about the man who would take the place of them all and reduce the human race to anonymity, either by seizing a great deal of fame for himself, or by keeping everyone else on earth from acquiring any."[227]

The authoritarian Empire expanded its power so that even distinctions between individuals lost their value. What Tocqueville would ascribe to centralization, thus modernity, Staël blamed on Napoleon. His regime led to uniformity: "'There is in unlimited power a sort of vertigo which seizes the genius as well as the fool and destroys the one as much as the other,'" Staël claimed in *Considerations on the French Revolution,* which she began in 1812 as the Empire started to fall.[228] She made the same point pictorially in *On Germany:* "A man of wit described how one evening at a masked ball, he passed in front of a mirror and, not knowing how otherwise to distinguish himself in the midst of everyone else wearing the same domino, he nodded. One can say as much about the way in which our minds are dressed up to face the world. One person blends into the other, so that the true character of each scarcely shows."[229] The Empire reduced our humanity.

How to fight the reduction of self, which is in effect the collapse into another's self, a reduction of many wills into one will? The first step is to realize that imitation is harmful. The "despotism even" of French style allows for "no originality."[230] Do not try to be another person, or another people. "A foreign language is always in many respects a dead language," Staël explains, speaking against the practice of a lingua franca and a universal intellectual style.[231]

The more profound challenge is to stop seeing the world solipsistically. This is Napoleon's crime. It reduces even the nation to the self and all interest to self-interest. "'From the moment one first says that morality be sacrificed to the national interest, one is close to contracting the meaning of the word nation, day by day, first to partisans, then to friends, then to family, which is simply a euphemism for oneself.'" As Balayé explains, this statement is "the clearest of allusions to Napoleon Bonaparte."[232]

The way out of solipsism is to recognize the value of others. This can happen on the level of states—"free nations have need of each other." For individuals it is what learning about another culture will do, or help us do. To adopt a foreign language for the purpose of imitation is to reduce oneself, but to understand another culture through its language is to stretch oneself. It is to reach outside oneself.[233] Language learning should be part of education: "One is all too fortunate in being able to turn the flexible memory of a child toward this type of knowledge, without which he would be constricted all his life to the circle of his own nation, as limiting as any other exclusive group."[234]

Staël's argument against mathematics should be seen in light of her argument against solipsism. The new schools of the Empire, which replaced the *écoles centrales,* had science and math at their core. The Ecole Polytechnique (to which her son was refused admittance and, as we will see in the following chapter, Stendhal declined to enter) is an example of the higher education the Empire applauded. Unlike language training, the study of math leads toward a reduction of viewpoint. Relativity is absent. So, too, are nuance and viewpoint. "A proposition couched in numbers is definitely true or false; in all other relations the true and the false are so intermingled that often it is by instinct alone that we can decide between different motives."[235] Math's universal language shadows absolutism.

Staël holds up the German states as a model of the diversity that allows for the expression of individual genius: "This division of Germany, fatal to its political power, was very conducive, however, to all sorts of expressions which were able to tempt genius and the imagination."[236] In a particularistic system—of hundreds of big and small, secular and religious states[237]—"there was a sort of mild and peaceful anarchy with respect to literary and metaphysical opinions, which allowed each man to fully develop his own way of looking at things."[238]

In Germany difference had value: "Any trace of the ascendancy of fashion in Germany can be explained by the desire on the part of each person to show that he is completely different from everyone else." In France, "to the contrary, each person aspires to merit that which Montesquieu said of Voltaire: 'He has that quality of mind that all [Frenchmen] have, just more of it.'"[239] The German approach lent a kind of thickness to culture. It resulted in an accretion of thought that we find as we explore its depth. As Cuvier and others were discovering for natural history (as we will also see below), so in German literature one finds "traces of different cultures, just as one sees in mountains layers of diverse minerals deposited by the revolutions of the globe."[240]

Staël offers us an image of Vienna as a way of describing the "*Aufklärung* concept of unity in diversity, each reflecting the macrocosm from an individual perspective,"[241] which, of course, her work was promoting. In Vienna, returning at night from an excursion outside the walls, she reports seeing "in the midst of that crowd . . . Oriental, Hungarian, and Polish costumes which enliven the imagination, and, at intervals, [hearing] harmonious music which gave to the assembly the air of a peaceful fête, in which each person enjoys himself without troubling his neighbor."[242] John Isbell argues that Herder is Staël's source for her ideas about "unity in diversity": "Herder's growing laments 'that the drive for power of great warlike peoples suppresses small nationalities, notably the Slavs,' . . . offers Herder, not Leibniz, as a source for ideas of unity in diversity."[243] But Staël does offer a very Leibnizian view, which she draws from Alexander von Humboldt, who, with his brother Wilhelm, was loosely a member of the Groupe de Coppet. "The inhabitants of Mexico," Humboldt noted in 1804, "while passing along the grand highway, each add a small stone to the great pyramid being erected in the middle of their country. No one of them will give his name to it, but all will have contributed to this monument which must outlive them all."[244] Is this not essentially the image offered by Corinne to Oswald to explain their relationship, though Corinne will describe their lives as leaves on a tree?[245]

Toward Coppet

The romanticism Staël introduces us to (the word was coined at Coppet) has as much to do with sociability as with the loneliness of the self—that loneliness described in Heinrich von Kleist's famous anecdote about the Franciscan friar imagining walking back down the hill from the scaffold after the execution of the criminal he had charge of: "A Franciscan, one very rainy day, was accompanying a Swabian prisoner to the gallows. The man complained to Heaven all the way of having to walk so gloomy a path in such wet and unfriendly weather. The Franciscan, wishing to offer some Christian solace, replied: 'Lout that you are! How can *you* complain? You have only to get there, but I, in all this rain, must walk all the way back again.'—Whoever has felt the desolation, even on a nice day, of the walk back from the scaffold, will not find the monk's words so unfeeling."[246]

Staël finds a way of solving the problem of Sappho and Corinne (and Kleist, too, whose suicide in 1811 helped prompt Staël's *Reflections on Suicide*).[247] Theirs is the problem of inhabiting a self that is necessarily alone but that craves companionship—the problem, as Balayé says in another context, of being both "a social being and a singular being," in the sense of *singulier* as extraordinary, as genius, but also in the way we are all singular, that is, individual.[248] We all share the plight of genius.

The sociability created at Coppet is a solution to this self, which must face the ethics that its solo nature implies. It recognizes that rampant *égoïsme,* the logic of self interest, paradoxically destroys genius, its own and others, and it wants also to be at peace with the world. As Staël would claim in *Considerations on the French Revolution,* " 'Napoléon's genius only occasionally pierced through the envelope of *égoïsme* in his last days.' "[249] Napoleon's restless ambition destroyed him. There on Lake Geneva, with the Alps in the background, Staël created the "social space" for genius that eluded Corinne and contained *égoïsme* and ambition.[250] A model of sociability was constructed that mirrored the laissez-faire diversity Staël saw in the Germanys. It functioned on the principle of the acceptance of difference, of tolerance of the other, and in the belief that there was something to learn from others, that one could take from others "without chauvinism," as Balayé explains: "The relationship was not that of colonizers and colonized but was rather a rapport among civilizations which shared in the patrimony of Europe."[251]

The Groupe de Coppet began as Staël's salon in exile. Banished from Paris, Staël "became European,"[252] as she explained in 1814, and her gatherings took on an international cast.[253] Besides Benjamin Constant, still Swiss in 1794, Narbonne, and Montmorency, the Groupe de Coppet included the German-Swiss Karl Viktor von Bonstetten and Henri Meister, as well as Wilhelm von Humboldt and August Wilhelm Schlegel, who were Germans, and Jean-Charles-Léonard Simonde de Sismondi, the economist and future author of *The History of the Italian Republics*. The Groupe also included Prosper de Barante, son of the prefect of Léman, whose duties included surveillance of Coppet. The younger Barante would be Staël's lover from 1805 to 1811, as Staël's relationship with Constant soured. This core group was enhanced by visitors from all over Europe, from London to St. Petersburg, including Byron in 1816, that other sort of exile, who had sneered when he met the aging Staël in London in 1813 but recognized her as a comrade at Coppet.[254]

The sociability of Coppet is captured in an anecdote recounted by Jean Roussel in his "L'ambiguïté des lumières à Coppet." "One is reminded," Roussel notes, "of the walk taken by Benjamin Constant with Schlegel and Sismondi: 'they looked at each other as if the others were fools. The French philosopher who "knew" only experience, and the new German philosophy, which reasoned only a priori, could not, I do not say as much as understand each other, but could not even explain themselves to each other.'"[255] It was as if the Groupe thought in different languages, which even the universalism of the lingua franca could not transcend. But their differences were tolerated, and pace Roussel, whose point is to stress the divide, these may have been welcomed. Coppet was "one of those rare places in Europe where Protestants and Catholics were able to enter into a dialogue," Balayé explains.[256] It was a "privileged circle" within which dramatically different responses to Napoleon were embraced.[257] Montmorency was a royalist and Constant a liberal. As Sismondi explained in a letter, " 'We have so many points of opposition and disagreement among us that the word friendship here speaks only of a well-established and very intimate set of habits.' "²⁵⁸ But this *amitié* was held up as a model for Europe.

Stendhal recognized its significance. In *Rome, Naples et Florence* he described it as "the estates general of European opinion."²⁵⁹ It was also a "refuge," a "crossroads," a "home" for all sides.²⁶⁰ So, too, did Napoleon watch its proceedings keenly. Staël's servant, Uginet, called Eugène, was also employed by the Empire.²⁶¹ Coppet was watched by the prefect of Léman, tolerantly when this was Barante, rigorously from 1811, when this was the baron Capelle. It was fear of being arrested at Coppet by Capelle that spurred Staël's flight in 1812.

The ways in which Coppet speaks to us today are obvious. Insofar as it stands for opposition to the Napoleonic Empire in its homogenizing project, it might stand in defense of regions throughout the world against globalization. Might we also recognize in it an alternative model for French citizenship that could encompass the difference of French-Arab and French-African communities—perhaps shifting the meaning of the word *communautarisme* from its pejorative sense of ghettoization toward something more positive?²⁶²

Of course, this is a delicate subject in France today, where the governing classes might welcome the first proposition and be wary of the second. But revisionist work on the Enlightenment suggests that "a discourse of difference" might stand alongside the "universalist discourse of individualism" as the legacy of that age.²⁶³ The salon culture of the Enlightenment, as Dena Goodman has argued, was based on notions of "gender complementarity" as it presented a model of an egalitarian society bound together through conversation, in common purpose, at least hypothetically effacing individual ambitions to the common goal. Revolutionary salons, on the other hand, became partisan affairs, promoting one political vision over another.²⁶⁴ Staël criticized them to Constant for becoming "labyrinth[s] of interests and ambition."²⁶⁵

Coppet stands, then, as the institution that connects us through its sociability to the promises of the eighteenth century, which the

Empire had broken. It squares the circle, so to speak, of individualism and community, allowing, as Rousseau had hoped for in the *Social Contract,* that we might be both equal and free. In the new sociability of Coppet competitive individualism was tamed and differences were tolerated, never effaced. Sismondi and Constant were never to understand each other.

In 1811 Staël defended her last great love from her companions' derision, in a way that makes this same point, to our salutary surprise. John Rocca, twenty-two years her junior, an army officer disabled from wounds sustained in the debacle of Spain, was badly educated and a failure at the conversation that was the lifeblood of Coppet and her own signature behavior. In explaining away that failure, she merely noted, "Words are not his language."[266] Is it too far-fetched to imagine Staël's gesture of love (or resignation, as our feminism leads us to see) as a completion of the half fantasy of Corinne to return to Scotland as Oswald's wife?

Bénichou speaks of Staël's humanism, which saves her from counter-revolutionary spirituality. Staël's life overall implies an ethics founded neither on the supernatural—a divine will—nor on the radical materialism of "*l'homme machine*"—driven by an involuntary will—but on a sense of the human as social being. This is a humanism, then, we conclude, which takes Staël (and us) to an ethics of self, a sensibility that despite her (and our own) *égoïsme* and domineering ways recognizes its limits in the often peculiar genius, or individuality, of the other.

A proxy for post-Revolutionary concerns about ambition established so vividly in fiction as to take on a life of it own, a private life engaged in the same struggle to fit an expansive self within ethical concerns for community (and by so doing defining our neoromantic sensibility), such is the meaning we take from Stendhal, too, whose story we turn to next.

3

VOCATION, STENDHAL, AND THE ART OF LIVING ETHICALLY

Julien Sorel

The most audacious act in French literature may be the most misunderstood. To be sure, Julien Sorel's attempted murder of Mme de Rênal—at the elevation of the host, at the sacrifice of the Mass—was an act of passion, the act of a man maddened by ambition, thwarted at the moment of its climax by the woman he had loved. The story of "*un ambitieux*" presents itself in *The Red and the Black* as a nightmare of democracy, of aspirations grasped and lost. Julien stands in the chapel, at his trial as, in the words of Michel Crouzet, "witness and victim of the egalitarian passion, and the resentment that is its constituent part."[1] It is the negativity, not the savagery, of Julien's crime that arrests readers of *The Red and the Black* and introduces him into the pantheon of French heroes who choose liberty, if even of the tomb, against bourgeois mediocrity and materialism: "In shooting Mme de Rênal, he turns his back on power, 'he saves himself, forever, to the point of death, one might say, from ambition.'"[2]

But how much in discord with nineteenth-century values was Julien's violent withdrawal from society? This chapter plucks Julien from the history of rebel intellectuals and sets him down within the earthier field of post-Revolutionary culture, which viewed ambition as a perversion that (like masturbation), as guides to conduct explained, typically ends in insanity.[3] We read the novel alongside a medical critique of ambition that could baldly assert that "lunacy by ambition" was the disease of overachievers. This broad reading of *The Red and the Black* rehistoricizes Stendhal, repositions him within a multivocal society in which, on many levels of culture, the attractions of competition were balanced by the sureness of their folly.

The power of Stendhal's fantasy partially parallels the drama of the alienist's case study. What accounts for the continuing appeal of Julien's crime is its power to describe the tension between the promise of Enlightenment thought and its threats, but without offering a satisfactory resolution to its stress. It is the incompleteness of Stendhal's critique of ambition that explains its appeal, which begs its resolution as liberal, fascist, or socialist myth. But in an oeuvre riddled with unfinished novels and autobiography, and abrupt abandonment of purpose, is not the key to its importance its unfinished state, which the intensely visual Stendhal might have described as a broken arc?

The circumstances of Julien's life are well known. The son of a carpenter—a peasant operating a sawmill on the outskirts of Verrières—he hates his brutal, male, and mean family. The intelligent and delicate Julien—he has a pale, feminine face marked by luminous eyes, topped by thick, dark hair—is patronized by the elderly, loving Father Chélan, who teaches him to read Latin. Julien memorizes the New Testament. On the sly, he reads Rousseau and Napoleon (the *Mémorial de Sainte-Hélène*) and dreams of escaping from Verrières.

With the recommendation of Father Chélan, Julien, then nineteen years old, becomes tutor to the three sons of the mayor of Verrières. He seduces their mother, Mme de Rênal, who falls in love with him. When scandal about the affair breaks out, Father Chélan's influence gains him entry into the *grand séminaire* at Besançon. There, the abbé Pirard, a Jansenist like Father Chélan (a thinker against the grain), becomes his patron. When both Pirard and Julien are to be forced out of the seminary at Besançon, Pirard's influence lands him the position of private secretary in Paris to the marquis de la Mole, a member of one of the oldest aristocratic families. Julien seduces the daughter of the marquis, Mathilde, who falls in love with him. They engage to marry. Mathilde being pregnant, the marquis de la Mole agrees. He changes Julien's surname to the Chevalier de La Vernaye, buys him a commission in the cavalry, and begins to arrange for the marriage settlement.

As Julien is congratulating himself and plotting his further advancement, the marquis receives a letter from Mme de Rênal denouncing Julien as a seducer and adventurer. "Poor and covetous," Mme de Rênal writes to the father of Mathilde, "it was by means of the most consummate hypocrisy and through the seduction of a weak, unhappy woman that that man sought to further himself and become somebody."[4] Advised by Mathilde that "all is lost," Julien travels to Verrières and shoots Mme de Rênal at church.[5]

The passion to succeed propels Julien from one point in the story to the other, as readers will notice. Ambition dominates his thoughts. It is the most striking aspect of his personality, from the moment we are introduced to him in chapter 4. There, Julien has just set aside his dreams of military success, as he begins his studies with Chélan: "One fine day," the narrator tells us, "Julien stopped talking about Napoleon; he announced his intention of becoming a priest and was to be seen constantly in his father's sawmill, busy memorizing the Latin Bible the curé had loaned him."[6]

Julien is keen on taking holy orders because he calculates that in the context of the Restoration, the priesthood will reward him most. Julien reflects: "When people began to talk about Bonaparte, France was afraid of being invaded; military talent was badly needed and in fashion. But today, you see priests at forty with incomes of one hundred thousand francs; that is, getting three times as much as the most famous generals in Napoleon's divisions."[7] But the idea that, like Napoleon, he could rise from nothing to greatness—"that Bonaparte, an unknown and penniless lieutenant, had made himself master of the world by his sword"[8]—continues to absorb his thoughts even during sexual encounters with Mme de Rênal. Stendhal allows Julien only briefly to forget his obsession with success, as he does in the memorably dark garden at Vergy in the aftermath of kissing the naked arm of Mme de

Rênal: "Julien gave no further thought to his dark ambition, or to his scheme, so difficult of execution. For the first time in his life, he was swept away by the power of beauty. . . . But this emotion was pleasure and not passion. On the way back to his room, he had but one delight in mind, that of returning to his favorite book [the *Mémorial de Sainte Hélène*]; at twenty, one's idea of the world and the impression one intends to make on it prevail over everything else."[9]

Stendhal continually allows Julien to be stimulated by the sight of worldly success, as when the bishop comes to Verrières: "His ambition [was] roused again by the example of the bishop's youth. . . . So young . . . to be Bishop of Agde!" Julien exclaims. "And what does the living come to? Two or three hundred thousand francs, perhaps."[10]

Indeed, ambition drives Julien's lust. Again in the dark garden at Vergy, when, for the first time, Mme de Rênal secretly takes his hand and holds it, Julien's ambition again dominates his feelings. "This action roused the ambitious youth; he wished it could be witnessed by all those proud nobles who, at table, when he was sitting at the lower end with the children, would look at him with such a patronizing smile."[11]

Julien is in love with ambition, not Mme de Rênal, or he is unaware of his love for Mme de Rênal because of the power ambition has over him. The narrator is explicit, telling us in chapter 16 ("Next Day") of his seduction of Mme de Rênal: "He was still in love with ambition."[12]

That Julien's ambition is diseased is revealed in the course it shapes in his life. The narrator asks us to imagine that Julien has been mad with ambition intermittently since his youth. "From his earliest childhood on," the narrator tells us, "he had had moments of exaltation." Then he would see himself in Paris, "as Napoleon had one day done, attracting beautiful women by his glamorous feats."[13] From the age of fourteen, when he realized that the liberal justice of the peace had been corrupted by the legitimists, his ambition became a monomania: "The building of the church and the justice of the peace's decisions suddenly made things clear to him. A notion came to his mind that drove him almost crazy for weeks, and finally took hold of him with the overwhelming force of the first idea that a passionate soul imagines it has discovered."[14] As Shoshana Felman points out in her book on madness in the novels of Stendhal, *La 'folie' dans l'oeuvre romanesque de Stendhal*, the word *folie* and its variants appear 209 times in *The Red and the Black*. As in the other completed novels, *Armance* and *Charterhouse of Parma*, "the frequency increases from one section to another. A pattern, a schema, of frequency emerges as a *constant* that seems to mark a structural tendency of the Stendhalian novel—that of a *growing frequency*, of a *crescendo of 'folie*.'"[15]

The breaking point for Julien, the moment when monomania becomes madness (*démence*), comes at the exact moment he is within reach of his goals: "Julien was drunk with ambition," the narrator tells us when describing him at the camp of the Fifteenth Regiment of Hussars. "Lieutenant for barely two days and through a favor," he is dreaming of becoming a commander in chief. He is in the "middle of a rapture of the most unbridled ambition" when Mathilde's message reaches him.[16] And he sets off to kill.

Julien's behavior—his determination to succeed, his suicidal violence when thwarted—would not surprise a French psychiatrist in the 1820s—certainly not Jean-Etienne-Dominique Esquirol, whose role in developing the profession of psychiatry is equaled only by that of his mentor, Philippe Pinel. In his 1819 *Dictionary of Medicine* entry on monomania, Esquirol described the monomaniacal temperament in ways that remind us of Julien's own: "Their ideas are exaggerated. Their passions are very strong. They are dominated by ambition and pride. These individuals will become monomaniacs when stimulated by thoughts of greatness, of riches, of bliss."[17] Like Julien, monomaniacs are alienated—that is, distanced from family, hard to get close to, and emotionally labile; "they express little affection for their friends and relations or else their attachments are extreme. Often they treat with disdain the people they cherish the most." They are quick to anger, "easily offended, extremely irritable . . . highly impressionable, strong-willed, and defiant toward restraint; easily angered, they slip quickly into fury."[18] Is this not Julien, whose anger Jules Alciatore has shown in his essay "Stendhal and Pinel" to fit the description of angry lunatics drawn by Pinel in the *Traité médico-philosophique sur l'aliénation mentale, ou La manie (Treatise on Madness)*?[19]

The shape of Julien's life fits the pathology of lunacy clearly described in the *Dictionary of Medicine.* There Esquirol explains that certain people, "more than others," are predisposed to monomania by "self-esteem, vanity, pride, ambition; they abandon themselves to their ideas, to their exaggerated hopes, to their outrageous pretensions." Disease sets in, typically, only after a reversal of fortune; "it is remarkable, however, that almost always those individuals who fall into monomania have been stricken by some reversal of fortune, stripped of their hopes, before becoming sick."[20]

Esquirol explains as well that before the lunatic's final step into madness, he behaves reasonably, retaining his grip on reality: "He reasons and makes decisions very well."[21] Is this not Julien, whose whole life up to the moment of the crime is marked by a series of successes checked by failure, but always guided forward by cold, effective logic?

Esquirol abstracts the monomaniacal personality in the *Dictionary of Medicine,* but it is more typically through the presentation of case studies of lunatics that Pinel and Esquirol describe the disease. *Historiettes* (little stories), Pinel called them in his *Treatise on Madness,* such as the following, for the most part are gathered under the rubric "stifled ambition," that is, "*ambition rentrée.*"[22] We meet a law student friend of Pinel's youth who was so obsessed with succeeding at his studies in Paris that he spent his days and nights studying—to the exclusion of eating and sleeping. Naturally, his health suffered. His alarmed and loving parents returned him to the provinces, thus precluding his success at law. Distraught, inconsolable at his failure to succeed, he walked into the woods and fatally shot himself.

Pinel also presents the case of a "hero of the Bastille," a soldier who had participated in the attack on the Bastille but who went insane because his heroism was not rewarded by a promotion to colonel. We also read about a sixteenth-century merchant whose case Pinel encountered; he suffered a commercial setback and became mad—a madness marked by his conviction that he was bankrupt despite patent evidence to the contrary.

Pinel argued that madness often had a "moral" cause. Some illnesses were brought on by organic lesions, brain tumors, and the like, but some were triggered by emotional shock, by a disequilibrium of the emotions.[23] The human passions lie on a spectrum, and madness lies at one end. As Esquirol explained in *Des passions considérées comme causes, symptômes et moyens curatifs de l'aliénation mentale*, "the passions and madness stem from the same source."[24] It is only (as Alciatore quotes Pinel) in "the super-intensity of a single idea" where madness lies.[25]

That Stendhal shared this interest in Pinel is well known. Victor Del Litto explains that in January 1805 he went to the medical school to read Pinel's *Treatise on Madness*, but the doors were closed and he could not. A year later, after being urged to by his friend Jacques Félix-Faure, "whose sister was showing signs of mental illness," Stendhal read the book, recommending it as well to his sister, Pauline. In 1810 he read it again.[26]

What particularly impressed Stendhal was Pinel's chapter "Art of Counterbalancing the Human Passions by Others of Equal or Superior Force, an Important Part of Medicine," where he explains that the doctor (alienist) "often sees no other remedy than to not restrain the patient's natural inclinations, or to counterbalance them by even stronger impulses."[27] We know this insight of Pinel's impressed Stendhal. Del Litto explains that "shortly after reading [Pinel], Stendhal makes allusion in a letter to Pauline to a corollary of these ideas," writing that " 'it is a question of forming new habits, that is the most important thing—read *La manie* by Pinel, and you will perceive the importance of this principle.' "[28] Del Litto shows as well that "in anticipation of applying the principles taken from *La manie* he had particularly made note of the section which addressed the problem of treating the passions. These were in some important way, he saw, an extension of the arguments of Mme de Staël."[29] Stendhal had begun Staël's *Treatise on the Influence of the Passions upon the Happiness of Individuals and Nations*, which she composed, as we noted in the previous chapter, during the Terror and in the midst of the wreck of her love for Narbonne. Or, rather than reading it, he had "translated it into French," as he claimed, finding her exaggerations of language unreadable—a way of expression suitable enough for informal conversation—*causeries*—but inappropriate for the essay form. She "missed her mark" with such a style: "If Mme de Staël had not sought to be more passionate than nature and her early education had made her, she would have produced masterpieces." And what reader of Staël today could not agree with his judgment?[30]

Stendhal "translated into French" Staël's argument about the pernicious effects of the passions, as his journal details: "The happiness of personalities who lack passion is always based on the same assumption, that is, that they will never be controlled by feelings stronger than themselves. Their unhappiness is produced by the reversal of their fortune, the loss of their health etc., etc., and not by the agitation of feelings, not by that which happens inside of them. . . . A man may propose, as a definition for happiness, an absolute moral independence, that is to say, the submission of all his passions."[31] Finally, Del Litto notes Stendhal's January 1806 journal entry: "I observed yesterday evening . . . 'the storms of passions,' in the phrase of Staël, 'those grand passions which may be healed only by the means indicated by Pinel in *La manie*.' "[32]

What Stendhal read in Pinel's *Treatise on Madness* was Pinel's method for curing lunacy. In the case of the soldier at the Bastille, this would mean, Pinel explained, satisfying his ambition by giving him a commission in the army. In the case of the sixteenth-century merchant, this meant replacing one passion for another. In that long-ago case, Pinel found "a fortuitous operation of the strategy of counterbalancing."[33] The merchant, not cured by being shown that his coffers were indeed full of gold, was cured when he began to defend Catholicism from arguments of the Reformation, when the passion for religion replaced his passion for commercial success.[34]

The cure of "lunacy by ambition"—*monomanie ambitieuse*—entailed either the satisfaction of ambition or its replacement by other passions. In the curing of monomania, Pinel argued that the dramatic element is very important. The staging of "pious frauds" or "innocent ruses," that is, the setting up of a fictive event in order to "strongly jolt the imagination," was a lesson Pinel had learned from the practices of English charlatans.[35] As Goldstein shows, "An insanity viewed as imagination gone awry can be countered by a procedure that 'shakes up' the imagination in order to dislodge the erroneous idea that has taken hold or to rupture the 'vicious chain of ideas.' "[36]

Pinel reported the case of a tailor convinced during the Terror that he was to be taken before the Revolutionary Tribunal for having made an unpatriotic remark. No longer working, no longer eating, he had been spending his days prostrate on the pavement outside his home, waiting for his arrest, when he was placed in the asylum. Pinel devised for him the following cure. He staged an interrogation by members of the tribunal whose parts were played by young doctors being trained by Pinel. They came to the Bicêtre dressed in black robes and with all the trappings of their office to examine the tailor on his business, his activities, the journals he had been reading, his patriotism in general. Afterward—in Pinel's words—"in order to shake his imagination even more strongly," the chair of the committee made a formal, loud, and long declaration of his innocence.[37]

I see Julien Sorel's attack on Mme de Rênal as a type of therapeutic theater, one that Stendhal uses to cure Julien of his ambition, a kind of shock therapy like that performed on the tailor in the Terror, which jolts Julien out of his ambition and allows it to be replaced by the passion of love. The sparsely described church, tinted red in our imagination, our expectancy as we hear the three bells announcing the start of Mass, our concern when we see the bowed head of Mme de Rênal and the elevated host, the tinkling of the bells; in its compression, this scene more than others is a stage set for Julien's transformation.[38]

We know Julien is mad at the point when he shoots Mme de Rênal because afterward he is dramatically sane.[39] When chapter 35, "Un Orage," gives way to the next, as other critics have noticed, "Stendhal speaks three times . . . of Julien's coming back to himself."[40] We should note here the same terms used by Pinel to denote a lunatic's cure. For Pinel, a cure is a "return to one's true self, a *retour sur lui-même*," and an act of being *"ramené à lui-même."* In the narrator's terms, after shots were fired, "Julien stood motionless; he saw nothing."[41] "*Quand il revint un peu à lui*,"[42] literally, when he had returned a bit to himself, "when he had somewhat recovered his senses, he noted that all the faithful were running out of the church."[43]

" 'By George! The game's up,' he said aloud as he came to"—"*en revenant à lui*."[44] Later, after sending off a farewell letter to Mathilde, Julien feels "somewhat recovered," though "thoroughly wretched for the first time."[45] When he is told Mme de Rênal lives, Julien begins to repent. "By a coincidence that saved him from despair, in the very same instant, the state of physical irritation and near madness into which he had been plunged ever since his departure for Verrières came to an end."[46] In prison, Julien experiences his epiphany: "He saw everything from a new angle," the narrator explains. "His ambition was gone."[47]

The Red and the Black shares with the medical critique of ambition an awareness of the social hazards of ambition, while refraining from offering an ideological cure. Rather, what Stendhal is accomplishing in his novel is the opening up of a broad "angle of access"[48] on the trials—as tribulations—of ambition in post-Revolutionary France. He is making a case—but not a legal or moral one for or against Julien Sorel that already has been established in the plot. Julien admits his guilt in pretrial formalities. He refuses to offer a defense of jealous rage and insists his crime was premeditated: "His lawyer, a man of rules and formalities, thought he was crazy and, like the public, was convinced that jealousy had shoved the gun into his hand. One day he ventured to let Julien know that this allegation, true or false, would make an excellent plea for the defense. But in the wink of an eye, the accused became his incisive and passionate self once more."[49] Julien's trial, described in chapter 41, "Le Jugement," stands in contrast to the trial of Antoine Berthet (the center of a real-life scandal on which the novel is thought to have been based), who offered in defense of his prototypical crime the "irresistible derangements of love" and whose prosecutor successfully rested his case by establishing that he was motivated by "disappointed ambition": "disabused of his ambitious dreams, understanding too late that he could not reach the goal that his pride proposed, Berthet, stripped of his hopes, would perish; but rage would drag a victim along with him to the tomb that he dug for himself!"[50]

Stendhal "almost certainly" (in the view of Pierre-Georges Castex and others) read about Berthet's trial in the *Gazette des tribunaux,* which reported on the trial and execution as they occurred, and in *Le pirate,* which published an article on the Berthet affair in May 1830, the very moment Stendhal was completing his novel.[51] Here was a plot ready-made for one who thought that anecdotes were the kernel of understanding, Castex notes. As Stendhal's good friend Prosper Mérimée explained for his own *Chronique du règne de Charles IX* (during whose reign occurred the St. Bartholomew's Day Massacre), so would Stendhal more subtly in his novel of the era of Charles X, his *Chronicle of 1830,* as he subtitled *The Red and the Black* during the Revolution of 1830. "In history, it is the anecdotes that appeal to me," Mérimée explained, "and among anecdotes I prefer those where I fancy I can find a true picture of the customs and personalities of any given epoch."[52]

For Stendhal the anecdote or little history (like the *historiettes* of the alienists), perhaps accidentally encountered, comes to stand for the larger narrative of time, the pathology of history. But what wounds— adapting the metaphor offered in *Le pirate* for Berthet ("*une plaie de notre civilisation*")[53]—were sustained in Stendhal's epoch, and how might they be healed? Castex reproduces the news articles on Berthet in his edition of *The Red and the Black.* To review what the *Gazette des tribunaux* and *Le pirate* had to say about Berthet, frustrated in his ambitions by his social standing, is to see how Stendhal transposed Berthet's story into one of the most salient statements of the problem of the individual in modern life, by rejecting its facile resolutions.

Like Julien, Berthet was a poor and talented boy from the provinces.[54] His father was a blacksmith. Berthet, too, was marked as a breed apart by his physique—" 'I was weak and delicate; I wasn't able to work at the forge,' "[55] he explained at his trial—and his intelligence. "A frail constitution, ill-suited to physical labor, an intelligence above his position in life, an elevated taste for learning manifested early on," as the prosecutor described him. Moreover, he attracted the attention of mentors who, through "charity more keen than inspired," enticed "the young Berthet from the modest rank where the luck of birth had placed him and led him to enter the priesthood."[56]

The curé was the most important of these: "The curé . . . adopted him as a cherished child."[57] Through his influence he entered the petit seminary at Grenoble (for lower orders) but left after several years. Then followed a fatal stint as tutor in a family of local notables, the Michouds, which ended prematurely since, Berthet claimed at his trial, his affair with Mme Michoud was coming to light. His patrons found him a place in another seminary, but again things did not work out. Finally, he was admitted to the grand seminary at Grenoble, where his dreams of success seemed about to come true. (He would be a bishop, perhaps!) Abruptly, however, he was expelled. The path to a clerical career was closed.

Returned to his village, he was banished from the family home by his angry father. He was refused entry to three other seminaries. The Michouds then found him a place as tutor with the de Cordons, a rich and noble family,[58] when rumors of a relationship between Berthet and the young daughter of the house led again to a dismissal. The Michouds found Berthet yet another place, this time with poor relations. Berthet objected to his position, "to be nothing in life but a *schoolmaster with a salary of 200 francs a year.*"[59] (By contrast, Julien's wage at the Rênal's was 400 a year, raised from a proposed 300 a year in negotiations with his father.) He began executing those plans for revenge already laid out in a series of letters to the Michouds, for it was Mme Michoud, he charged, who had been thwarting his career. With pistols purchased and borrowed he shot Mme Michoud and himself at the parish church at the sacred moment of the Mass.

For Berthet, each rising prospect folded. Possibilities opened up only to mysteriously close. Theodore Dreiser explained for later generations the murderous effects of these disappointments returned by a formally meritocratic society in his *An American Tragedy* of 1925, itself based on a similar real-life case in New York state. The temptations of upward mobility lead to crime and misery in a world where the real chances of success are slim. To step out of one's class is to court tragedy, and better avoided, as Berthet explained to the court at his sentencing: "It is thus at the foot of the guillotine that it must end, this horrible dream which has so thoroughly disrupted my youth. Ah! Evil was the day that I left the house of my father and his humble employment to try my fatal fate! There, that is what doomed me."[60]

In the stories of Julien and Berthet it is easy to see how implicated their imaginations are in the course of their tragedies. Each admits as much. Julien's ambition led him to a fantasyland, an imaginary country, as he explains remorsefully to Mme de Rênal while awaiting the day of his execution: " 'In the old days . . . when I might have been so happy during our walks in the wood at Vergy, a wild ambition would drag my soul off to imaginary countries.' "[61] As *Le pirate* reported about Berthet, "This young man, gifted by nature with physical advantages and of a distinguished mind, too flattered by everyone around him, led astray by success itself even, had created a brilliant future for himself in his imagination, much more glorious than would be due to his talents alone. The son of the blacksmith from Brangues had built up visions of a perhaps limitless horizon."[62]

Goldstein's recent work on the post-Revolutionary self explores the problem of the wayward imagination. The abandonment of corporatism, which had grounded the self in its group, the legal personality of the old regime, led to anxiety about where that "freestanding individual" might go.[63] The "discourse on imagination typically served as proxy" for this anxiety, Goldstein shows, with "vagabond" and "wandering imagination" its key phrases.[64]

For Goldstein the solution of the post-Revolutionary elite to the problem of the post-corporate self is to ground it in Cousinian psychology. The sensationalist (or materialist) strand of Enlightenment thought had freed the self to construct itself from its environment with all the ethical problems—as we have seen—that would ensue and all the challenges to social stability that Goldstein stresses. Victor Cousin posited instead an a priori, stable *moi,* which would become axiomatic for the bourgeois state, a hegemonic concept grounded in the educational system and institutionalized in state administration. "The Cousinian *moi*," Goldstein strongly argues, "effectively supplanted the structuring principle of Old Regime society: the corporate order that the Revolution had abolished."[65]

But Stendhal must have been on to something else. Could the Cousinian *moi* appeal to one who could relate to the state only in an ironic or cynical way? In 1827, shortly before conceiving his "chronicle of the nineteenth century" that became *The Red and the Black,* Stendhal commented on the "inanity" of a philosophy that rejected "*tout court*" the lessons of the Enlightenment: "If these gentlemen did not hide behind the obscurity of their style, everyone would see the inanity of their thought. While they interrogate their consciousnesses, in which they read so many fine things, they shut their eyes to the realities established by Locke and Condillac and replace facts and experiences with ideal speculations."[66]

A wrong so described at the trials of Berthet and Julien has obvious social solutions, which the reporters of Berthet's story are quick to insist, and most reviewers of *The Red and the Black* have seized on, as Stendhal casts his spell. Berthet could be made to stay in his class, or the Berthets of the world could collectively fight back against the system that stacks the cards in its favor, as Julien's own statement to his jury implies (the famous boast: "In me you see a peasant in revolt against the baseness of his lot"). But Julien's tragedy is different from that of the blacksmith's son. Even after being denounced by Mme de Rênal, Julien could have succeeded. The attack on Mme de Rênal—the crime itself—is gratuitous for an *ambitieux,* since he could still have made his fortune in exile, even after her damning letter to the marquis. The marquis de la Mole offered Julien an income of ten thousand [livres] a year if he would leave the country, abandoning the deceived Mathilde: "If he is willing to live far away, beyond the frontiers of France, or better still, in America."[67] It was a generous sum. Charton's guide to careers tells us that a bishop (which Julien had once dreamed of becoming) could expect to make ten thousand livres a year in 1842.[68] Stendhal himself made eight thousand a year as an auditor of the Council of State.[69] Nothing really prevented Julien from succeeding. He could have been a success in the church, army, or nobility, as Crouzet points out.[70]

The trial of Julien is a case in the terms fashioned by English romantics in which "anomalous combinations of circumstances," in the words of Thomas De Quincey, are presented not to pose solutions but to "catch the conscience" of his age.[71] For what casuistry ensues in this novel in which Jesuits lurking in the background effect the dismissal of the good Father Chélan and other machinations of the plot that, while anchoring us in the ultra-Restoration, lurch us from old regime concerns to new?

Julien's defense, "I have not the honor of belonging to your class," is suicidal when presented to a jury packed in his favor through the agency of Mathilde.[72] The completion of his thought—"in me you see a peasant in revolt against the baseness of his lot"—captures the modern political imagination by shifting his problem from the particular—his murder of Mme de Rênal (who "had been like a mother to me")—to the collective guilt of the jurors who, in Julien's words, "would like to punish through me and discourage forever a whole class of young men who, born to an inferior position in society and, so to speak, oppressed by poverty, have had the luck to obtain a good education and the audacity to mingle with what the rich in their pride call society."[73]

Julien's bold statement about class is a false lead, however, and this is the striking point. No solution to the social question is effected in the plot of *The Red and the Black*. Julien, "decapitated by the bourgeoisie," to paraphrase Maxim Gorki, meets the fate of all Stendhal's heroes.[74] In the words of the mid-nineteenth-century critic Hippolyte Babou: "Octave settles the question with suicide, Julian with murder, and Fabrice, too cruelly stricken to have the energy either to kill or to die, gives in to the suffering which, little by little, spreads through him like a deadly chill."[75] All his heroes, "to take up the expression of Stendhal, end as 'fiasco'"[76]—as is the case as well with Lamiel (unknown to Babou), abruptly left by Stendhal in Paris in chapter 25, independent but uncertain after her successful translation from the provinces.[77] Naomi Schor ascribes the "incompletion" of *Lamiel* to "the fundamental impossibility of representing, or representing in any sustained sort of fashion, a mobile, fully empowered female protagonist within the limits of realism, at least in its French modality."[78] But the stories of all of Stendhal's characters end abruptly, their arguments withdrawn.

For the left and right in the interwar period, "lunacy by ambition" would find its reversal in the sanity of collectivism. The nationalist right in France celebrated in the early twentieth century the violent withdrawal of the Stendhalian hero from society as a sign of his author's "anti-bourgeois," "anti-republican," "anti-democratic" "aristocratic elitism." The March 1913 issue of the *Revue critique,* the literary organ of the protofascist Action française, was a special number dedicated to Stendhal. As Eugen Weber explains in his early book on the Action française, even before this "their first encomiums of Stendhal referred to the aristocratic elitism they discerned in his work, his clear-sighted egotism, his realism, and the anti-democratic nature of his views."[79]

For the Stalinist left, Stendhal's failure to solve the social problem posed in his plots is due to his regrettable myopia, to the fact that "he did not understand or recognize which new class was the true inheritor of the revolutionary tradition."[80] The fate of his heroes is "the manifestation of that absence of historical perspective."[81] Nonetheless, Soviet youth were encouraged to read Stendhal, "as an adversary of bourgeois society and the capitalist regime," in the words of Maxim Gorki, who was "especially seduced by Julian Sorel,"[82] and of Viktor Vinogradov, who saw Stendhal's oeuvre as "imbued with the great revolutionary ideas, which form a precious part of the inheritance that the proletariat receives and develops solicitously."[83] It is no surprise to read then that in the calculation of Vinogradov, by 1938, "in one quarter of a century the number of books by Stendhal published in the U.S.S.R. more than doubled the number of those printed throughout the entire world in one hundred years."[84]

Julien deflects our attention from particular to social concerns in his address to the jury, but the weight of the novel lies in its exploration of the individual. Indeed, Julien is classless—nowhere and therefore everywhere—throughout most of his story, not only in the way that Berthet describes himself unable to return to his blacksmith family after his forays in the upper classes: "I dared not return to my parents' home. I was too weak; how to take up hammer and tongs again when one has spent one's life in a seminary and in the houses of the nobility and the bourgeoisie. I had ahead of me only shame and futility."[85] Significantly, Julien's father is both wilier and potentially richer than M. de Rênal. Sorel bests him at bargaining and at accumulating land. Indeed, he is on his way to riches.[86] Moreover, Julien's return from "lunacy," his recognition that his ambition has left him emotionally hollow, is the prelude to his understanding that life with Mme de Rênal, happiness in her (bourgeois) company, is where the moral center of his (aristocratic) life rests.

That Julien as a social being is nowhere, and therefore everywhere, universalizes his trajectory, that is, it presents it as a problem of our trajectory, too. What are the limits of individual desires, where might they end and we attain moral rest, given their self-referential premises? This is the same problem Perry Anderson defined for liberalism in his celebrated essay on post-Marxist French thought. Neo-liberalism, he complains, presents us with an "atomistic individualism with no logical stopping-place."[87] Here we see Stendhal posing that critique for early liberalism, presenting his hero (ourselves) with literally no place to go. The trajectory of his life lands him in prison. A "happy prison" it might be (in the absence of self-expansion, life is contracted to essentials), but it is the antechamber to death.[88] It leads him to his execution, after which his severed head is cradled to its grave in the arms of Mathilde, acting out her romantic daydream of a medieval, fantasy past. His was a phantasmagorical end.

Goldstein notes in her study of the making of French psychiatry that monomania easily slipped into the "ordinary discourse" of intellectuals. It "was so quickly assimilated into the early nineteenth-century vocabulary because of its special relevance at that historical moment. It corresponded to—indeed, it magnified and even caricatured—a salient mind-set and behavioral pattern of early bourgeois society, with its new possibilities for 'self-making': a single-mindedness and goal directedness."[89] Here we see in Stendhal's novel a description of this single-mindedness, but no solution is offered in its critique except a poetic abandonment of its promise.

To see Julien as embodying generally feared ambition—and not simply opposition to class—is to step out of the binary opposition of rebel intellectual and complacent bourgeois society that has been institutionalized in the right- and left-wing interpretations of the novel. It is also to see post-Revolutionary France in broader cultural terms, as caught between a traditional resistance to individualism and the appeal of modernity, with no easy options in sight. In the next part of this chapter I review the life of Stendhal with the goal of understanding how he could escape the impasse of his alter ego, Julien (as we have seen Staël transcend the fate of Corinne). How could ambition not lead to the ethical plane shared by the elder Sorel, M. de Rênal, the abbé de Frilair, the bishop of Agde, members of Julien's jury, and almost everyone in Stendhal's "Chronicle of 1830," including Julien himself, for a time?

Consider the map of contemporary life sketched out twice by Stendhal in his unfinished autobiography, *The Life of Henry Brulard* (fig. 1).[90] With *A* being the moment of birth, *R* the "route to riches," *P* the "route of good prefects and members of the Council of State," and *L* the "route to getting oneself read," Stendhal describes the ambitions of his generation. Del Litto suggests that the "road to madness," route *F,* is the route with which Stendhal most closely identified.[91] Perhaps. But it is the inflection, *B*, the "roads taken at age seven, often without our knowing it"—to borrow Stendhal's word used elsewhere, one's "vocation,"[92] which he invokes to save himself from the ambiguities of his considerable success, as we will see below.

Henri, Henry, Julien

Stendhal's life is as emblematic as Julien's: "Born in 1783 a few years before the Revolution, he grew up during a period of intense upheaval, went to school under the Directory, became an adolescent with the Consulate, reached manhood under the Empire, participated in the Napoleonic débâcle in Russia, wrote half of his books under the Restoration and the other half during the July Monarchy, and

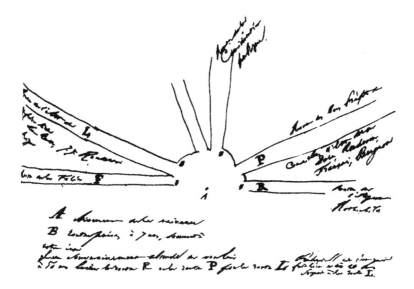

Figure 1. Stendhal's sketch of life choices.

died, in 1842, only a few years before another Revolution."[93] As Henri Beyle, Stendhal grew up in the provincial Enlightenment, a cultural world punctured not by the outbreak of revolution—his beloved grandfather was a "patriot" in 1788, five votes short of being elected to the Estates General[94]—but by Jacobinism. Henri's ecstatic reaction to the news of the execution of Louis XVI—"I was gripped by one of the most intense feelings of joy I have ever felt in my life"—illustrates the gulf between his ten-year-old self and the older generation. In *The Life of Henry Brulard* Stendhal famously describes his detested father's sigh as he reported the news of what those "monsters" had done: " 'It's all over,' he said with a deep sigh, 'They've murdered him.' "[95]

In his unfinished *Mémoires sur Napoléon* (1836–37) Stendhal laments another chasm—that between his generation, shaped in childhood by "enthusiasm for Republican virtues," and those men who were born after the Revolution began, "who were fifteen years old in 1805 as they began to look around and see as their first object of interest the plumed caps of the dukes and counts recently created by Napoleon," that is, who were shaped simply by the outward signs of material success and their "puerile ambition."[96]

Stendhal's place in history within this hinge generation allows us to explore through him the trials faced by those whose "inherited values" were shaken or dissolved by the trajectory of the French Revolution.[97] But how are new cultural habits formed? On the 18 Brumaire, November 9, 1799, Henri Beyle was sixteen years old and on the road close to Paris, to his freedom, as he thought, from Grenoble and a stifling family life. What baggage did he carry with him? What did he leave behind? In this section we encounter Stendhal through the autobiographical fragments that are the *Souvenirs d'égotisme* (1832) and *The Life of Henry Brulard* (1835–36), where we see a performance of selves, or possible selves (*masks* in the term of the *Stendhaliens*),[98] as he experimented with the choices open to his generation.

Should he be a lawyer like his father or a great writer like Molière? The law is the choice his *parlementaire* father would have made for him. An engineer, or mathematician, career goals of a graduate of the Ecole Polytechnique?[99] No, but as Grenoble's top candidate for admission, Stendhal's failure to matriculate in Paris was surprising to his friends and relations. An officer in Napoleon's army? He resigned his commission though his powerful relations, the Darus, had had him promoted, without cause—"through patronage and influence"[100]— to a lieutenancy in the 6th Dragoons. Perhaps Stendhal should be a capitalist? His venture as an importer-exporter of colonial goods in Marseilles also went awry. He considered trying his fortune in Louisiana.[101] A government official? A prefect? A peer of France, like his old friend Félix-Faure? Stendhal was a provisional commissary of wars in 1806, auditor of the Council of State, and inspector general of Imperial Crown Furniture from 1810, but, as he famously said, "he fell with Napoleon."[102]

That ambition focused the imagination of Stendhal is clear from his earliest writings. In Paris in 1802 he began and abandoned several great projects, including a reworking of the *Odyssey, Hamlet,* and Lucan's *The Civil Wars*. Stendhal's *Odyssey* would have centered on Antinöus, an "*ambitieux parfait,*" in Stendhal's words, understood as one who uses his friends and lover to further his own dreams of power.[103] He worked on *Hamlet* for several weeks, *The Civil Wars* as well. Stendhal's project for *The Civil Wars* is lost. But Lucan's story of the fall of the Roman republic was well known, esteemed "among the philosophes and their circles," according to Del Litto.[104] Gaspard Dubois-Fontanelle, Stendhal's professor of literature at the *école centrale,* wrote in 1799 that it provided "a great lesson." In explaining its place in the curriculum, he noted that "its subject is the struggle of liberty against ambition and the defeat of the former."[105]

But Stendhal was also worried about a corollary issue. Why do some people succeed and some fail? Why had so many of Stendhal's fellow Grenoblois—Jacques Félix-Faure, but also Casimir Périer, Louis Crozet, and Edouard Mounier[106]—flourished in the novel conditions of the new regime, and why had he, the cynosure of his family's hopes, landed as consul in Civitavecchia, the only ugly city in Italy, as filthy as Grenoble,[107] and bullied by his assistant?

These are the questions that flow through Stendhal's unfinished memoirs. The self revealed in *The Life of Henry Brulard,* especially, seems to dovetail with that invented for Julien. The lives of both are driven by ambition, this way and that. Stendhal reflects in *Henry Brulard* that although when young he "was or believed [he] was ambitious; what worried [him] about that supposition was that [he] didn't know what to hope for."[108] What gives the lives of Julien and Stendhal their meaning is their arrest of that drive to succeed.

Both Julien's father and M. Rênal seem derived from Chérubin Beyle, or his son's experience of him. Chérubin was deputy mayor of Grenoble in 1804. So, too, was Rênal mayor of Verrières.[109] Each was upwardly mobile. Chérubin, "ambitious for himself and his family," was a lawyer.[110] A *procureur* at first, he soon became an *avocat,*[111] an office he hoped to pass on to his only son.[112] His eyes were on the *consistoire:* "He was on the point of being made a consistorial; this was an ennobling distinction among lawyers which he spoke of in the way a young grenadier lieutenant speaks of the cross," Stendhal noted critically.[113] As Crouzet explains in his life of Stendhal, for Chérubin

Beyle that success would mean a great deal. On Henri's baptismal certificate his father is described as "noble Chérubin Beyle"; the new position would give that nobility greater security.[114]

Like Rênal, Henri's father hired a tutor for him, the repellant M. Raillane, the model, perhaps, for the abbé Frilair. "My father took him on seemingly out of vanity," Stendhal complained in *Henry Brulard*. "What an honour for a lawyer in the Parlement to take on for his own son the tutor who had come from M. Périer's house!"[115] "His family, becoming more and more ambitious, hired a tutor for him," Crouzet explains, the father's decision "mimicking in advance M. de Rênal['s]."[116] Stendhal describes his father's interest in property as a mania: "My father was a memorable example of this mania which stems at once from avarice, vainglory and the mania for nobility."[117] His "passion for wheeling and dealing" became, Crouzet notes, "the principal trait of M. de Rênal."[118]

The alienation between Stendhal and his father was as profound as that between Julien and M. Sorel. Stendhal believed his father had never loved him for himself. "He did not love me as an individual," he complained, but only as the conduit of the family name, of the father's hopes for the future.[119] Julien's father, Stendhal imagined, could not love him. He was so different from his brothers, so unsuited for carrying out the work of a prosperous sawmill. Stendhal's description of himself is apt for Julien: "an 'orange tree sprouting by the strength of its own germ in the middle of a frozen pond, in Iceland.'"[120] Forced while in prison to accept a visit from his avaricious father—"who never loved me"[121]—Julien is brought for the first time in his ordeal to the brink of despair.[122]

Incidents of reading serve to mark the distance of the sons from their families. Julien, perched atop a beam of his father's sawmill, is caught reading by his father and assaulted. Sorel père could have forgiven Julien his "slender build," "so different from that of his brothers,"[123] but not his penchant for reading. In *Henry Brulard*, Stendhal is scolded by his father for laughing while reading *Don Quixote*. The household established after the death of Henri's mother was in permanent mourning: "Judge of the effect of *Don Quixote* in the midst of such awful joylessness!"[124] When he finished it, secreted within a grove of trees at the Beyle estate outside Grenoble, "it's already Julien Sorel beaten for reading," Crouzet explains.[125]

When Julien falls on the Rue du Bac while riding with de la Mole's son, readers recognize in the passage the description of Henry Brulard in Geneva, preparing to cross into Italy with the army of reserve, being mounted "for the second or third time in his life" on a horse, which bolts. "Consistently opposed to seeing me ride a horse, fence, etc.,"[126] his family had overprotected him. Crossing the Alps, he was unprepared; he had the "physique of a girl."[127] Henry describes himself as feminine—"Nature had given me the delicate nerves and sensitive skin of a woman."[128] A similar description marks the otherness of Julien.

And the disappointment with which Julien concludes his first sexual encounter with Mme de Rênal—"My God! To be happy, to be loved, is that all there is to it?"—concludes Stendhal's successful descent from the Alps—"the Saint-Bernard, is that all there is to it?"[129]—and is itself an echo of his first response to Paris, in 1799.[130] As he explains in *Henry Brulard*, that "rather simple-minded astonishment and that exclamation have followed me all my life."[131] "That state of astonishment and uneasiness into which a man who has just obtained what he has long desired may lapse," the narrator of *The Red and the Black* explains for Julien.[132]

When Julien writes *cella* instead of *cela* in a letter dictated by the marquis de la Mole, this echoes the mistake made by Stendhal in 1800 as a new clerk to Pierre Daru, secretary for War, described by Napoleon as "a regular workhorse, a man of rare capacities, my best administrator."[133] In each case the humiliation is double-weighted. It comes not just from such a mistake being made in front of an important person but by being made by a youth touted by his protectors as a paragon of learning, a prodigy certain to succeed. Stendhal imagined his important cousin to be thinking, "So this was the man of letters, the brilliant *humanist* who queried the merits of Racine and had carried off all the prizes in Grenoble!!!"[134]

It is reasonable as well to emphasize the differences between Julien and the young author. Stendhal himself, as we saw, suggested in his *Mémoires sur Napoléon* that the generation that came of age in the Empire lacked the emotional depth of those who grew up with the Jacobins. Julien was younger still. His brief maturity was shaped by the Restoration. Alciatore has argued that "chance determined the destiny of Julien. All his misfortune comes from not having been born twenty years earlier."[135] The accident that he did not come of age with Henri Beyle determines his plot.

But the woes of Julien and Stendhal are accidental to the post-Revolutionary context that each shares. Martin Turnell suggests that the "fact that [Julien] belongs socially to the proletariat simply provides a particular setting for the study of a much wider problem and creates an additional obstacle to Julien's success."[136] For Turnell, writing in 1962, the wider problem is Julien's status as an "outsider": "Julien would have been an 'outsider' in any class of society, and he is equally out of place in the world of his father, of the Rênals, and the La Moles."[137]

We can suggest something broader still, about the tensions within post-Revolutionary France, tensions that stem from the challenges of competition, regardless of class. Julien and Stendhal are versions of the same post-Revolutionary self. According to Jean Starobinski's influential description: "In the reveries of metamorphosis in which he becomes Julien, Fabrice, Lucien, Lamiel, he changes face, body, social status, even sex, but it is always to tell his own life story while introducing greater fortune and greater misfortune. . . . He begins his life anew in another body, the way one starts a card game with a new deal."[138] Each deal is guided by the same conventions. The principles that shape Stendhal's world are the same—for a time—as Julien's. Self-interest makes the world go around, passions shape our ideas, and we are who we are by virtue of our environment. These ideas were introduced to Stendhal in a general way at the *école centrale*.[139] They became more specific through his reading of Helvétius's *De l'esprit* and *De l'homme* in 1802–5 and his association with the Idéologues in Paris.[140]

In letters to his sister, Pauline, he quotes from Helvétius. "The passions are the sole motor of human behavior," he wrote in January 1803.[141] The next day he continued with a list of "general principles" taken from *De l'homme,* including those that "all our ideas come from the senses" and that "education alone makes great men; consequently, one has only to want to do so to become a genius."[142] And, Del Litto explains, "it is again following Helvétius, one suspects, that he champions the 'shining principle' that self-interest is the determinant of all human behavior," as he urged Pauline to understand in February of the same year.[143] Del Litto describes him as "steeped in the principles of Helvétius."[144] Brombert, less approvingly, suggests for him "serious indigestion from his consumption of Helvétius, Maine de Biran, Cabanis, Pinel, Destutt de Tracy."[145]

These ideas clearly shape the character of Julien Sorel. They ostensibly shaped Stendhal's behavior as well.[146] In a letter to the stepdaughter of Georges Cuvier, whose salon he had frequented in the 1820s, Stendhal says, " 'I assure you that no one has made a great fortune without being Julien' "[147]—as we noted in chapter 1. Stendhal had had practice. In 1806, after failing to succeed in his friend's business in Marseilles, he and his family begged the Darus to help him again. The Beyles wanted Henri to be made one of Napoleon's auditors of the Council of State, a position created in 1803 that would bring prestige, access to the emperor, and entry to a lucrative career.[148] "Nothing generous or heroic in that decision to tap the influence of the all-powerful Daru and to play to the limit the family connection," says Crouzet, as earlier Stendhal allowed himself to be promoted in Italy on the basis of a lie: "To legitimate that incredible string-pulling [*coup de piston*], the regiment falsely certified that he was already engaged in July 1800 and had served as sergeant at arms."[149]

How did Stendhal escape the sacrifice of Julien, "fiasco-ed," brought to a dead end, as Julien embraced these principles, then dramatically jettisoned them? After being condemned to death for attempted murder, Julien contemplates the future he could have expected as the husband of Mathilde de la Mole: "Colonel in the Hussars, had we gone to war; secretary of a legation in peacetime; after that, ambassador . . . for I would soon know the ropes. . . . All my blunders would be pardoned, or rather, set down as accomplishments. A man of accomplishments, enjoying the best life has to offer, in Vienna or in London."[150]

When Stendhal died, he had achieved something of Julien's dreams. He was a chevalier of the Legion of Honor, a former officer in the Grande Armée, a former auditor of the Council of State during the Empire, and the current French consul in Civitavecchia in the Papal States—which, though an undesirable posting, afforded extended leaves in Paris for writing and socializing. Stendhal's different course draws us into the patterns of thought of someone who has worried deeply about the problem of ambition—that "'thirst for posts and high-ranking positions,'" in his own definition[151]—whose critique of competitive individualism has become his signature theme, but who has found within himself a way to reconcile his achievements to his residual old regime morality.

Stendhal's reconciliation began with an examination of conscience, a habit drawn from his Catholic past. Both *Souvenirs d'égotisme* and *Henry Brulard* are introduced as such. "Let us see if, in making my examination of conscience, pen in hand, I will arrive at something *real* and that remains *consistently true* for me"; this is the explanation he gave in 1832 for writing the *Souvenirs*.[152] In chapter 1 of *Henry Brulard*, three years later, he prepared "to make a thorough examination of conscience."[153] As Brombert (and others) have argued, these were written "not to justify a man, but to discover him,"[154] distinguishing his exercise from Catholic, Rousseauesque, and Jacobin confessions. "What counts here is the *manner* of the exploration, the state of innocence with which Stendhal faces himself, the problematical nature of his approach," Brombert says in comparing Stendhal's texts to Rousseau's *Confessions,* itself informed by Augustine's. Mutatis mutandis: they differ as well from the Jacobin "moments of moral self-exposure reminiscent of prerevolutionary Catholic confessions" described by Patrice Higonnet: "They often availed themselves of such occasions [in the National Assemblies and the clubs] to recount their entire personal history, including their prerevolutionary life, which became in these personalized narratives, the long prologue to the intense, third, and triumphal act of revolutionary drama."[155]

Each of Stendhal's autobiographies is a search for a coherent self, a unity of purpose, a definition, an answer to the question "What kind of man am I?" when the answer is not already clear or comfortable.[156] "What have I been? What am I?"[157] "What eye can see itself?" he provocatively asks.[158] These are the questions that trouble his sleep at the age of fifty, as Georges Blin emphasizes: " 'I do not know myself at all, and it is that which, sometimes, in the night, when I think about it, brings me pain.' "[159]

His answers begin to reassure him. "In 1835," Stendhal writes in *Henry Brulard,* "I'm discovering the physiognomy of, and the reason for events."[160] He finds the shape and character of himself. "The reader will perhaps think me cruel, but such I was at the age of ten and such I am at fifty-two," he tells himself, and us, when describing his happy reaction to the execution of the king.[161] "From this memory, so present to my gaze, I conclude that in 1793 . . . I was engaged in the pursuit of happiness exactly as I am today; in other, more common terms: my character was absolutely the same as today."[162] The way he loved his mother at age six—she would die in childbirth when Stendhal was seven—was the way he loved women as an adult, he argued.[163] That as a child he never spoke about what really mattered to him explains his reserve today: "I feel this as keenly in 1835 as I felt it in 1794."[164] Describing his first stay in Paris, he quips, "I adored Saint Simon in 1800 as in 1836. Spinach and Saint Simon have been my only enduring tastes, at least after that of living in Paris on a hundred *louis* a year, writing books. Félix Faure reminded me in 1829 that I was talking to him in these terms in 1798."[165] Paths in life are set early, and firmly, in the visual metaphors of *Henry Brulard.*

Writing from the "desert" of Civitavecchia,[166] Stendhal was able to find the sublime in the pattern of his life. "Once and for all I give warning to the brave man, the only one, perhaps, who has the courage to read me, that all the fine reflections of this sort belong to 1836," he explains while recounting his experience of entering Italy loosely attached to Napoleon's army, being stunned by the beauty of the countryside and the music, and being reborn by it. "I would have been greatly astonished by them in 1800; well-versed as I was in Helvétius and Shakespeare, I wouldn't perhaps have understood them."[167]

A sloughing off of Helvétius, like molting skin, allowed him to reexperience the important moments of his life as a process of regeneration.[168] The self of 1835–36 sees himself "born again," reborn while reading Shakespeare. He "returned to life" when his adolescent infatuation for the actress Mlle Kubly ended. "I am about to be born, as Tristram Shandy says," he explains as his story takes him to work at the Ministry of War in the midst of the excitement and secrecy of the planning for the Battle of Marengo.[169]

Stendhal's recovery of his self allows him to see, as Julien's does, the folly of ambition. "I have never been ambitious," he claims in *Vie de Henry Brulard,* "but in 1811, I thought I was ambitious." The cure for that "true fever of the passions . . . [that in 1806] he spoke of as ambition" was the discovery of his vocation, his calling. This, memory reveals, happened when he was eleven, while reading forbidden novels belonging to his uncle: "From that moment on, my vocation was settled: to live in Paris writing comedies like Molière."[170]

Stendhal's vocation, like Julien's recovery of self, allows him to "outnarrate"[171] the accidents of post-Revolutionary life and give them order and sense. That self is "prior to calculation,"[172] fixed, and so aloof from circumstance. But whereas Julien's recovery allows him this autonomy, it allows him that and nothing more. It leaves him morally cleansed but with only one option, death. His return to his self encloses him. He finds freedom only in prison, as critics often note for both Julien and Fabrice, the hero of *The Charterhouse of Parma.*[173]

Vocation is more enabling. Pierre Larousse caught its nineteenth-century meaning in his *Grand dictionnaire universel,* while disclaiming it. Vocation was a word in common use, but real vocations were rare, he warned, and typically directed by fathers, not the self. Mozart is an example of a child whose vocation was prepared for by his father. Madame de Staël is another. "That which is commonly called *vocation* is in reality just a strategy lit upon by the imagination of a child searching for a way to leave his papa and mama, excellent for him. . . . The father cries, the mother weeps."[174] The child, bored with home and school, finds a way to sanction his independence by invoking his vocation. In the autobiographies presented in Denis Bertholet's *Les Français par eux-mêmes, 1815–1885*, we find *vocation* used in this familiar sense. Auguste de Vanssay, born in 1785, served seven years as an officer in the Dragoons. Released in 1811, he set off for Saint-Domingue to repair the family fortune: "If I had taken up arms, it was in submission to her [his mother's] will: my vocation called me to another career. I was destined to go to Saint-Domingue."[175] For Etienne-Maurice Deschamps, also born in 1785, vocation took him away from his village in the Franche-Comté to the wars and a filial devotion to Napoleon: " 'Destiny had spoken: my vocation was totally military.' "[176]

Stendhal implicitly contrasts vocation—"powerful and irresistible" in the words of Sainte-Beuve[177]—to *métier*. Pierre Daru, Napoleon's secretary for War and Stendhal's taskmaster, was also a *poète de métier*, celebrated for his alexandrines, a man who "approached literature with a bureaucratic mentality."[178] Stendhal describes his own work as consul in Civitavecchia as his *"métier gagne-pain"*[179]—something he is very, very good at (a job that pays his bills) but which eludes his deeper self.

This plunge into the self on the part of Stendhal is the cure for his struggles with ambition, as was Julien's assault on Mme de Rênal. It helps him see his life as guided by something outside will or circumstance. One has only to wish it to become a genius, he had written to his sister in 1803. But in 1835–36 he was speaking of fate, luck, and destiny: "I shouldn't bemoan my fate, therefore."[180] "But chance has guided me by the hand in five or six great circumstances of my life. I really owe *Fortune* a small statue."[181]

Stendhal's vocation also stands in contrast with genius. His *Life of Henry Brulard* deplores the allure of genius that led him to waste ten years of his life: "Had I spoken around 1795 of my intention of writing, some man of good sense would have told me: 'Write for two hours a day, genius or no,' a remark that would have led to my making use of ten years of my life fatuously spent waiting for genius."[182] "I always waited for the moment of genius," he explained of his young self, "I was only cured of this mania belatedly. . . . Even in 1806, I was waiting for the moment of genius before writing."[183] He could be a great poet, he imagined himself thinking in 1799, if only he could find "a *flue* for my *genius* to escape through."[184]

Like vocation, genius might enable success,[185] but more intensely, erratically, in a way Stendhal signals as uncongenial to his disciplined self and his desire to achieve. That "quasi-mystical gift that simply occurs, with no help from society," that is romantic genius,[186] would obviate the need for ambition by creating its own reason for being, for succeeding at a task, but it is associated from the start of its cultural life with madness and doom—with route *F* on Stendhal's map of life, perhaps. It is striking that Stendhal's dismissal of genius began at the very moment when it was being heralded by Madame de Staël (in *Corinne, or Italy,* as we have seen) and Lord Byron (in *Childe Harold's Pilgrimage*), when romantic genius was finding its niche in post-Revolutionary culture. It is even more remarkable because of the affinity between romantic genius and the characteristics of the Stendhalian persona. The exceptional person, misunderstood and misanthropic, who creates brilliant works of art that speak to the future rather than to one's own purblind generation, would seem to describe Stendhal and his address to readers of the future, to the "happy few" who might appreciate his novels. Clearly his stand against genius is one to which we need to attend.

Stendhal's "calling" helps him come to terms with competition in a more workaday way than genius would, especially his competition with Félix-Faure in early Napoleonic France, when "a boundless glory seem[ed] to await all those who would join the great enterprise"[187] and into which Stendhal had thrown his lot along with Félix-Faure. Criticism of Félix-Faure—"the most worthless of all my friends and the one who has made the largest fortune"[188]—runs throughout his work. Casimir Périer—"a minister, and celebrated, and in my opinion the dupe of Louis-Philippe"[189]—was cast in the same mold. Félix-Faure, in turn, suggested that "'if Henri had 'remained in the class to which he adhered for some time, if he had followed a path to the Council of State, he would be more fair in his judgments about those who hold power.'"[190]

But Stendhal did not stay the course that Félix-Faure remained on—route *P*, as sketched in *Henry Brulard,* the "route of good prefects and members of the Council of State," or as labeled in an earlier sketch, route *C,* the "road to consideration: F. Faure makes himself a peer of France." Nor did he stay on route *R,* the "path to riches," as described on the diagram above. He claimed, nonetheless, "not to have had such a bad life." "Will the reader believe me if I dare to add that I wouldn't want to change places with Messrs Félix Faure and Mounier, peers of France and once my friends?"[191]

Stendhal's cure is effected in part by a recovery of Rousseauesque ideas about the need to listen to one's inner self. This was a recovery on his part but also on the part of post-Revolutionary culture overall, where we find their translation into romanticism. *La nouvelle Héloïse* is a key text for Stendhal as it was for Julien: "*âme sensible,* imbued with Rousseau," as Del Litto explains.[192]

Critics have argued over the extent to which the appeal of *Idéologie* for Stendhal overwhelmed the influence of Rousseau. Brombert discusses Stendhal's hopes for a cure for that "exaltation" of sensibility that came to him in reading Rousseau (and which he hated so much in his moments of "genius")—"which according to him has become his 'habitual state' and of which he would like to cure himself."[193] But Stendhal never abandoned Rousseau, Brombert shows. As Romantic Expressivism—the term is Charles Taylor's—became an important mood of the new regime, Stendhal's mood fluently turned with it.[194] To discover oneself is to become that self, as Stendhal's work on his autobiographies tells us.

Taylor also describes the importance of Rousseau's "Profession of Faith of a Savoyard Vicar" in secularizing the concept of conscience, or the inner voice that speaks to the truth about oneself. Rousseau's influence, he writes, helped shape a "radical autonomy," definitively modern.[195] "The source of unity and wholeness which Augustine found only in God is now to be found within the self,"[196] Taylor claims for the post-Revolutionary soul.[196] Stendhal's grandfather discussed *Emile* and its "Profession of Faith of a Savoyard Vicar" with him, though Stendhal was not enthusiastic: he "didn't understand any of it."[197] But that "knowledge of the human heart" was one of life's goals was a lesson his grandfather had always urged on him: "My grandfather was endlessly dinning the great saying into me: *knowledge of the human heart.*"[198]

The Savoyard vicar speaks of the time "when I myself shall suffice for my own happiness." Stendhal, Brombert argues, "already in [1804] . . . is meditating on the lesson of Rousseau who taught him the right to seek 'happiness' in accordance with one's individual temperament. 'The tyranny of derision has diminished nowadays; we owe this to Jean-Jacques. A person can freely say, "You find pleasure in going to the bois de Boulogne in a carriage and I in going there on foot." He will seem eccentric but not ridiculous.'"[199]

Vocation is cast from these notions. It is an inner voice, like the call by God that one might hear in an examination of conscience, which from Saint Paul through the Puritans gave meaning to one's life work and witnessed the resonance of God's will within one's own. "What the late eighteenth century adds is the notion of originality," Taylor explains. "It goes beyond a fixed set of callings to the notion that each human being has some original and unrepeatable 'measure.' We are all called to live up to our originality."[200] The "inner gesture by which God calls a person to whatsoever genre of life, to serve and honor him,"[201] as the *Dictionnaire de l'Académie française* explained in 1694, became "an inner impulse or conviction which tells us of the importance of our own natural fulfillment and of solidarity with our fellow creatures in theirs."[202]

Vocation became a practical solution to the ethical crisis posed by capitalism to those for whom, like Stendhal, self-interest alone and the materialist basis for it seemed inadequate, socialism held no interest, and the aristocratic, nostalgic Catholicism of Chateaubriand was repugnant. Reddy notes that Chateaubriand's "*Essai sur les révolutions* (1797) and *Le génie du christianisme* (1802) denounced the self-interest of the new age and glorified the honor and selflessness of the past."[203] But what appeal could Chateaubriand's solution have to the grandson of the enlightened Henri Gagnon, who, Stendhal remembered, often repeated the following exchange at his tutor's expense:

> "But *M[onsieur]*, why teach this child the Ptolemaic system when you know it to be false?" [his grandfather needled].

"*M[onsieu]r*, it explains everything and anyway it is approved by the Church."[204]

A kind of subterfuge, perhaps, a belief in vocation allowed for a compromise with liberalism. Competition was more acceptable to some as the unfolding of self—a poetics of self—than the pursuit of self-interest.[205]

Can Stendhal's experience be read as representative? Stendhal made the claim himself, at least with respect to the search for self-meaning that defines his memoirs: "What consoles me a little for the impertinence of writing so many *I*'s and *me*'s, is that I assume that many very ordinary people in this nineteenth century are doing as I am."[206] Bertholet agrees: the Napoleonic Wars had created "an unprecedented individual . . . a sort of 'new man,' which history may sum up in two words: march, then tell." March with the army, then recount one's story.[207] Pierre Pachet in *Les baromètres de l'âme: Naissance du journal intime* credits Stendhal (along with Maine de Biran and Benjamin Constant) with modernizing the *journal intime*, the diary. But is not that mirror of the modern self a reflection of all our selves?[208]

Pachet argues that by applying the Christian practice of the examination of self, as we have seen Stendhal do, on a soul now understood as existing "without God," or at least, "in the absence of grace," we see that self revealed as lone, unstable, shifting with its environment, chameleon-like—perfectly suited, we might add, to the demands of the market economy.[209] " 'Our existence is serial and cannot be understood otherwise,' " as Maine de Biran put it.[210] A self is merely " 'one unit among the thousands and thousands of beings who are and who were,' " as Anton Reiser says in the eponymous novel by Karl Moritz.[211] But does not Stendhal's understanding of vocation offer escape from this "suite" of selves by grounding self-expression and self-advancement in a humanist ethics?[212]

The argument forwarded here of Stendhal as a man at one with his age will not be welcome, perhaps, to those of us in whom Julien's rebellion strikes a welcome chord. Indeed, the contrast between Stendhal's solution to the problem of ambition and Julien's may be too boldly hailed. Yet the emphasis placed on the ordinary in Stendhal's life may celebrate the man whose Legion of Honor, he felt, should have been awarded for his day-to-day work as a consul, rather than for his writings. Moreover, what Stendhal created with his life was a plotline with as great a contemporary resonance as the story of Julien came to have in later European culture. The "master fiction" of Julien Sorel[213] was paralleled by the quieter resolutions of vocation, "too pervasive to be noticed," as Taylor suggests more generally about "the affirmation of ordinary life" in modernizing Europe.[214]

The next chapter takes up the case of Georges Cuvier. Celebrated for establishing the fields of paleontology and comparative anatomy—he could "reconstruct worlds from a whitened bone," Balzac marveled[215]—Cuvier was notorious for his ambition: a man "always prostrate in front of power," in Stendhal's estimation.[216] Cuvier's memoirs and his influential *Eloges historiques* constructed an alternative scenario to this charge by recasting biography as fable, careerism as destiny. Erased from biography, ambition could also be denied for the aspiring classes. History would stop with the bourgeois state.

4

DESTINY, CUVIER, AND
POST-REVOLUTIONARY POLITICS

The Fabled Scientist

Georges Cuvier was called the "Napoleon of the intellect" (if not the "Napoleon of science") for his success in riding the revolutionary tide to power.[1] In 1795 he was a poor tutor in Normandy. By the time of his death in 1832, he was professor at the Museum of Natural History, professor of the Collège de France, grand officer of the Legion of Honor, chancellor of the University of France, and permanent secretary of the Academy of Science. He was also a member of the Council of State, the Académie française, and "every other scientific association in the world,"[2] as well as a former inspector general of Public Instruction and a peer of France. He died as Baron Cuvier.[3]

How could "un simple citizen"—in the words of one of his admirers—achieve such success?[4] This section explores the path taken by Cuvier to his preeminent place in French science in the golden age of natural history, and to a prestigious and above all lucrative role in the administration of the First Empire and Bourbon Restoration. Our map is the fragment Cuvier left for posterity in his autobiography—written, as he says, in pencil (that tool invented we recall, by his colleague Nicolas Jacques Conté),[5] while commuting from his house at the Jardin des Plantes to the Council of State on Tuesdays, Thursdays, and Saturdays, to the university on Wednesdays and Fridays, to the Institut de France on Mondays, and elsewhere on business of state. As Georges Duvernoy adds, Cuvier always made good use of his time; "one never found him lazy,"[6] though his *Memoirs for Use by Whoever Will Write My Eulogy, Written in Pencil in My Carriage While Out on Business in 1822 and 1823: However the Dates are Drawn from Authentic Documents* breaks off in 1817.[7]

As we read Cuvier's *memoirs* and the graveside orations and other necrologies they helped prepare, we find a stylized answer to the question of Cuvier's success. Like the fairy tales collected by his contemporaries the brothers Grimm, they are structured by certain motifs, recognizable to students of Vladimir Propp.[8] The hero's family is troubled, the child's position precarious. Poverty would seem to preclude a career in science, but a series of helpers, some animal, some human, some in disguise—like the abbé Henri Tessier, in hiding from the Terror in Normandy—launch Cuvier on his path to success. Destiny—a calling—"an irresistible instinct"[9] pulls the scientist forward. Events that at first seem setbacks—failure to take first place on an exam, having to drop out of school to work to support his family—become the critical steps in his career. And talismans, more elliptically, mark his way.

The first element Cuvier's biography shares with the formulaic folktale is that of his problematic birth. The family lived in straitened circumstances in a "modest home," supported by a precarious income that collapsed as he grew up. "My poor parents fell further and further into ruin," he explains in his autobiographical fragment, his *Mémoires.*[10] His family was suspect in other ways, too. As Dorinda Outram and other recent biographers relate, Cuvier's father and grandfather were iconoclasts. Typically, the Cuvier men became pastors or "municipal officials."[11] The great-grandfather, however, became a surgeon and, less fortunately, the father was a soldier fighting for the French in a Swiss mercenary unit in the Seven Years' War.[12] In 1769 he had been pensioned off, but in the fiscal crises of the old regime, payments dwindled. By 1788, in the bankruptcy of the old regime, they had stopped.[13]

This is the "problem" of Cuvier's life, as a folktale hero would experience it, a problem of a family no longer able to provide for its children. Repercussions from that situation established the course of his life, or at least the legend of his life. But was Cuvier's situation so dire? It was certainly not calamitous, especially when compared to that of others whose lives he would present in the *Eloges historiques,* whose detail we explore in the second half of this chapter. Claude-Louis Richard (1754–1821), for instance, was the son and grandson of royal gardeners whose house we see at the Petit Trianon. The family was well placed for patronage, but poor; Claude-Louis was one of ten children. When the archbishop of Paris—impressed by Claude-Louis's intelligence and knowledge in a chance meeting at the gardens at Auteuil—offered to take charge of the boy, "promised to advance him in life if he were given to the Church," he refused, determined to work with flowers, not souls, thereby closing the door to "the sole career where talent without birth could lead to honor and comfort." Angered, the father expelled his fourteen-year-old child from their home, abandoning him to a makeshift existence in Paris, providing a pittance (ten francs) a month for his food.[14] How he survived to become one of France's foremost botanists will be explained below. The contrast with Cuvier's life is clear, as is the contrast between Cuvier and other savants, orphaned and left to themselves in the city.

These men truly began their lives as if in a contemporary folktale. In Stith Thompson's *Motif-Index of Folk-Literature,* which established the typology of tales worldwide, types Lo to L395 begin with a hero faced with a problem, typically grounded in his poverty. His parents are poor and can no longer support him, so he is abandoned. Or he sets off to find the means to fix his family's fortunes, or he is orphaned, or he is left to die by a wicked stepmother. Or he is a prince in disguise—switched or bewitched—but always in a limbo between abilities and rewards.[15]

Of course, we know these problems issue from the precariousness of premodern life. Children often were orphaned or unwanted by stepmothers. Babies were abandoned. In a predivorce world, families were broken by poverty and parental death. Robert Darnton's classic essay, "Peasants Tell Tales," exposed the social and economic realities behind the old regime folktale, arguing against ahistorical, universal explanations, especially the psychoanalytic.[16] Cuvier himself, though baptized Jean-Léopold-Nicholas-Frédéric, was known as Georges, the name of an older brother who died at age four shortly before our Cuvier was born. That Cuvier was a replacement child speaks directly to this fragility.[17]

But what pattern to make of these elements is the question. Darnton argued that for a peasant audience folktales offered a basic strategy for getting by. They lauded scheming and trickery. They showed the "high" bested by the "low" through cunning, as in "Jack and the Beanstalk." Could other patterns be shaped from these same elements, at least as they have been introduced so far in this chapter? The life of the painter Jacques-Louis David offers an intriguing answer. The great neoclassicist and revolutionary (later supporter of the First Empire and Napoleon's court painter) was rich and well connected but orphaned at age nine. Thomas Crow describes in *Emulation: Making Artists for Revolutionary France* how David's early studio attracted other orphans or rich floaters[18] who formed, as it were, a band of brothers—homosocial, certainly, and politicized eventually, which was represented in these multiple terms as early as 1785 in David's painting *The Oath of the Horatii*. This was a configuration that from 1789 began to empower the idea of a republic—a fatherless state from the fall of absolutism, it was patricidal from 1793 and fraternal throughout. For David and his circle Jacobinism (as an "imagination of life") was at first situational, then, in the studio, figural, and finally ideological.[19] Theirs was a way of using personal narrative, psychologists would more prosaically explain, "as a resource and a tool," "part of a continuing effort . . . we all engage in . . . to make sense of life," "to create and maintain meaning over time."[20]

We know that Cuvier meant his life to be understood as grounded in the fact of his family's impoverishment. That was the essential fact that gave it shape in the way the essential bone in a fossil skeleton would determine for him the place of all others, in the method that captured his world's imagination.[21] This "problem" would determine the key turning points of his life, as he wrote it for posterity. We can assume its importance because it is to a large degree an invention. The members of Cuvier's family lived in a well-knit community of relatives and associates. They were town officials and pastors, in a region overwhelmingly Lutheran. His career prospects might have been limited, but he was not about to starve and was hardly abandoned.[22] According to a cousin, who published his reminiscences as part of a fund-raising effort in support of the erection of a statue in Cuvier's honor in his hometown of Montbéliard, Georges Cuvier was privileged. "Our cousin," he explained by way of coming to terms with the savant's precocity, "moreover, never lacked help in his studies: books of all kinds, almost daily conversations with various educated people, emulation, that goad that is so powerful in the education of the public, etc.; there, such were the advantages he had and of which we were deprived."[23] One learns of a doting mother, too, from the 1833 biography by Sarah Lee.

What story is Cuvier telling with his life? Charles-Léopold Laurillard, his colleague from the Cabinet d'Anatomie at the museum, explained to an audience at Besançon that Cuvier's life history stood as a model of success for young people. "We have not yet spoken," he began, "of the position his brilliant accomplishments gave him in the world; that is the example offered most often to youth to incite them to work, and to forswear discouragement," a basic plot of misfortune overcome.[24] Is Cuvier's theme that of the nabobs returning to England from British India, rich and reformed—like William Hickey—who wrote their memoirs to explain to their progeny the redemptive value of work?[25] Biographies of another important scientist, Gaspard Monge, offer yet other explanatory models. François Arago, the astronomer (perpetual secretary of the Academy of Science alongside Cuvier from 1830), explained in his 1853 biography of Monge that the inventor of descriptive geometry, the minister of the Marine in the early First Republic, member of the Commission of Weight and Measures (which gave France the meter), and of the Armaments Section of the Committee of Public Safety (which armed the Republic), founder of the Ecole Polytechnique, and confidant of Napoleon was the son of an itinerant knife sharpener. We now know that Monge père was a textile merchant in Beaune (in Burgundy) who raised his family in a house on the principal street of the town. Monge's most recent biographer suggests about Arago that "the author would have it that his former professor came from below by depicting him as the son of a simple knife sharpener, trapped in a life of hunger and misery, in order more easily to celebrate his success as something out of the ordinary."[26] We might add that Arago, republican, member of the provincial government of 1848 who heroically hid the proscribed Monge in the weeks following Waterloo, would have been likely to read in Monge's life a plebian background as well as to applaud the distance he had traveled from Beaune.[27]

The rewards of hard work and determination are far from Cuvier's major themes, however. Cuvier's life history stands for the power of talent to reveal itself, no matter how deeply hidden, to propel itself— oneself—toward a predestined end, by a "sort of instinct for the truth," rather than the drive of a self overcoming adversity.[28] The eulogies of scientists in the old regime occasionally mention "destiny" and suggest that "nature not sufficiently consulted is likely to overturn the best-laid plans with one blow." But as Charles B. Paul explains in his book on the eighteenth-century *éloges* of the Academy of Sciences, Cuvier's *éloges* succeeded at what those of Bernard le Bovier de Fontanelle and Jean-Paul Grandjean de Fouchy, especially, only reached toward. Eighteenth-century scientists such as the young Joseph Banks may have been romantic heroes, as Richard Holmes suggests in *The Age of Wonder*, or republicans and patriots like Condorcet and Lavoisier, but the old regime eulogies stress the advancement of science over heroics (or, in the case of Condorcet's *éloges*, reason over prejudice and superstition).[29] This distinction emerges as we follow the path between Cuvier's modest birth and the equally fabulous elements that ensued.

The first of these is the revelation of unexpected greatness. Cuvier was like "a pearl [found] in the dung hill of Normandy," to anticipate the abbé Tessier's words,[30] discussed below. The second is the agency of "helpers" (animal and other) to effect this recognition. We see this pattern established in Cuvier's life in Montbéliard and repeated during his training in Stuttgart and his first job as a tutor in Normandy.

Throughout, we also find a third element of the folktale, the twist of disaster become salvation, the mystery of obscure paths exposed as highway, the detour, the direct line. "It is thus," as Laurillard explains about Cuvier's early life, "that without our knowing it, destiny leads us to success on the path that would seem to us must most exactly lead us away from it."[31]

That Cuvier was a prodigy was clear by the time he was six years old. At first he appeared to be a typical child overachiever, advanced in verbal and motor skills, but then we find him transcendent, like the boy Jesus expounding truths to the elders. Our sources include the recollections of friends and relatives, such as that of a M. Rossel, "his companion in study, his friend from school," who spoke at the dedication of Cuvier's statue in Montbéliard about "the first small steps of a man of genius in the career he was yet unaware of, the first essays of an intelligence which did not know itself, that instinct for glory which mingles with the lessons and games of an early age, all those biographical details which friendship alone remembers"—which, summed up floridly by the representative of the Académie française, reprises our theme about destiny.[32] One of Cuvier's cousins described the effect of Cuvier's abilities on his family. He explained that on a visit Cuvier made to their house in a nearby village, their grandfather shamed the cousin and his brother by asking them to consider what it would be like at the gymnasium to be outshone by their younger cousin. In any case, the cousins themselves were impressed: "We were both amazed, my brother and I, to hear how he read and declaimed poetry as if he were twenty years old, to see how clear and beautiful was his handwriting, his ability to draw, his skill at constructing playthings from paper and card, etc."[33]

Later in that visit the family was even more astonished. The uncle, one of the Cuviers who had entered the ministry, invited a traveling magician to entertain them one night, and he opened the vicarage to neighbors to enjoy the show. "Our man presented us with all sorts of legerdemain," we learn: "various and subtle card tricks; a 'heron's fountain' which ran and stopped at the sound of his words, a type of knife which he appeared to plunge into his arm and pull out dripping with blood, which particularly amazed the audience, even those who doubtlessly had already seen other travelling conjurors." Cuvier—"my little cousin"—watched carefully, expressed no surprise, and went on to explain to his audience how the tricks worked. To expose the trick with the dagger, the six-year-old constructed a device out of paper and demonstrated its mechanism to the crowd. His audience was impressed: "he had his good share of the admiration and applause of the assembly."[34]

"Here," Dorinda Outram claims, "one sees clearly back-projections of Cuvier's later reputation as the enemy of charlatanism, illusion and grandiose claims in science. It also conforms to a Romantic tendency to locate innate wisdom in children, women and the untutored elements of society generally; it was a tendency which crept into the ethos of science itself; talent was innate from childhood onwards, the 'naive vision' of nature an absolute gift unaltered by the impact of the social world."[35] The case of Cuvier is congruous to the genius of Staël, which worked to enable her ambitions, as we saw above, and to Stendhal's understanding of vocation. But whereas romantic genius appears as a push to action, an irrepressible imposition of will on the world, and vocation, as Stendhal experienced it, impresses as a process of self-discovery, the emphasis in Cuvier's life history is even more obviously on passivity, not growth or change but timeless being. Cuvier's stance is to a degree will-less, which again calls into question our expectations about the hyper-individuality, the super-individuality, associated with the era's understanding of "genius" and which the child prodigy (Staël, Stendhal, Cuvier) represents.[36]

Cuvier's passivity was raised in his defense by supporters who confronted the very reasonable charge of his ambition. "We will say to those who would be tempted to think along those lines," explained Laurillard, "that several times he refused the position of Director of the Jardin du Roi, made so illustrious by the greatness of Buffon, and that, shortly before the death of M. de Richelieu, he refused the portfolio of Minister of the Interior." "Far from having solicited positions and honors," we are told, "several of them were conferred on him in his absence": he was in Marseilles when elected permanent secretary of the first class of the Institute of France, in Rome when made master of requests for the Council of State, in London when elected to the Académie française, in Holland when given a subsidy from Napoleon, and "it was a spontaneous gesture on the part of Louis XVIII which made him a baron."[37]

Cuvier's inertness in the face of advancement was back-written (to echo Outram's "back-projections") in his biography to show that the key turning points of his early career were not in his control. The first of these concerns the scholarship he received to the Academy of Stuttgart, a training ground for administrators of the Holy Roman Empire founded by the Duke of Württemberg, Montbéliard's over-lord.[38] In this episode, as Cuvier explains, he had been cheated out of a scholarship to the University of Tübingen that would have allowed him to train as a pastor. Each year the scholarships to Tübingen were awarded on the basis of class rank, and Cuvier should have been selected. The decision was made by a regent who "in my childish conceit I let . . . see too clearly that I judged him to be quite igno-rant," however, and the scholarship went to two cousins who went to Tübingen and duly (and dully) became Lutheran ministers.[39] But what looked like disaster—the route to a secure career blocked—was in actuality the way forward to success.

Stymied, Cuvier made a visit to the wife of the Stadthouder of Montbéliard, who was the sister-in-law of the Grand Duke of Württemberg and the grandniece of Frederick the Great. At the nearby palace, the fourteen-year-old Cuvier showed the princess drawings he had made from Buffon. Impressed, she "spoke of him to the Duke," who happened to be visiting, and in Cuvier's words, he "at once granted me a scholarship to the Academy of Stuttgart." Cuvier tells us in his *Mémoires* that in just a matter of hours he was whisked off in the duke's carriage on his way to Stuttgart, squished between the duke's chamberlain and his secretary: "To learn of my nomination and to set off in the carriage of his chamberlain was the affair of an hour."[40] Clearly time is compressed here, since we learn from Outram's biography that two years ensued between the duke's offer of a place in 1782 and Cuvier's entering the school.[41]

"Heavy social guns were in fact mobilised by Cuvier's family" to send Cuvier to the Academy of Stuttgart. "The journey to Stuttgart [was] magically made possible by the carefully cultivated patronage networks of Montbéliard," Outram shows.[42] To read Cuvier's account, however, the magic seems elsewhere—in the fortuitous events, in the turning points that mysteriously worked out in Cuvier's favor, with surprisingly little agency. "He was thus, unawares," Cuvier said of the unfair headmaster, "the cause of all my [good] fortune. Without his act of injustice, I would have become, like my two poor cousins, a country minister and I would have led an obscure life. In lieu of that, I entered into another career, and I was even able to be helpful to them and to their children. But yet to come," as we will see below, "were a long series of other such chance encounters which brought me into that career and which led me to the distinguished posts that I have filled."[43]

At Stuttgart, Cuvier again was impressive. Overcoming the obstacle of language—he explains that part of the discomfort of his journey to Stuttgart was that the duke's chamberlain and secretary spoke only in German, the language of Württemberg and the Academy of Stuttgart—he became a top student in the school. At graduation in 1788, an impasse again arose. Though expecting to step into the bureaucracy of the Duchy of Württemberg, he found the ranks closed. Others in his cohort could afford to wait for better times, but Cuvier's family could no longer support him. He was offered a position as tutor in a Protestant family living in Normandy. Again the meaning of this apparent setback was made explicit by Cuvier himself: "The disorder in the finances of France meant that even the small pension due to my father was no longer paid. I had to do something to help my family and myself, such as by taking a position in a private house as tutor, a step which appeared desperate to all my comrades but which was, however, the origin of my fortune."[44] This he did, setting out for Caen in April 1789, that is, on the eve of the French Revolution, to join the d'Héricy family.

In these two cases of setbacks-become-advancements, an additional element of the folktale appears, one that subtly heightens their magical effect. In the first case, when Cuvier, the oppressed schoolboy, is offered a golden path to success by the local princess, his acquaintance with the animals in Buffon's *Histoire naturelle* was the means to this end. Cuvier had encountered this phenomenally successful multivolume description of the world's living creatures at his uncle's house, where he and his cousins at first enjoyed simply looking at the pictures. As the children grew older, Cuvier began copying the engravings, then coloring them, and finally drawing those animals that Buffon had only described. The work became the means by which Cuvier became adept at depicting the natural world.[45]

Again, time is oddly compressed in the friendly accounts of Cuvier's life. "At the age of ten, a copy of Buffon having fallen into his hands, he read it avidly," says Laurillard, "and then did not rest until he had copied all the figures in order to color them according to the descriptions given [in the text]."[46] This was quite a task, since the uncle's subscription had given him dozens of volumes by 1779. The importance of Buffon to Cuvier (who would take Buffon's place as head of the Jardin des Plantes and supplant his influence on natural history in France), however, is beyond doubt. As imaged for us by his cousin, the Buffon *Histoire naturelle* seems talismanic. He carried it everywhere; it was the vehicle of his success. "He would secret a volume in his pocket so that he might give to the French Pliny as many moments as possible, even during lessons," his cousin explains. "More than once he was surprised furtively reading [Buffon] while the class was meant to be translating Virgil or Cicero, and more than once again these thefts against a venerable antiquity brought down upon him the reprimands of the Rector."[47] At Stuttgart he was given a copy of Linnaeus's *Systema naturae,* which he carried with him to Caen, again as a kind of metaphorical friend (though on the subject of plants). It "was for ten years my companion and guide through my solitary labors," he explained.[48]

All these elements come together in the critical episode of his early life when he met the abbé Tessier in Normandy. Cuvier indicates its importance in his *Mémoires:* "At the height of the Terror, the abbé Tessier had come to find refuge as doctor in chief of the military hospital at Fécamp, and we will soon see the influence that his sojourn in that region had on my ulterior destinies."[49] Cuvier had been living with the d'Héricy family at their country house near Fécamp on the Norman coast since 1791, where the noble family felt safer than in Caen. There, Cuvier claims, he was left to his own devices. He was alone; he had only the sea and its creatures for company: "The Revolution having trapped and isolated us, I was left with no other distractions, and I suspect that never has anyone so completely dedicated his time to study as had I in that era (from '91 to '94), in the midst always of objects [from the sea], almost without books, and having no one to whom I could communicate my thoughts."[50]

In 1793, at a meeting of an agricultural society in Fécamp that Cuvier perhaps had organized, the disguised Tessier spoke and was recognized by Cuvier. He often heard the story, Flourens adds in a footnote to Cuvier's testament of Tessier's importance, "that the abbé Tessier, believing himself safe behind his borrowed name [and in secular clothes] was able to 'open up' in an agricultural society where he went each evening and share his knowledge about rural economics. He betrayed, however, by that same knowledge, the incognito that he wished to maintain. The young secretary, recognizing the author of articles on agriculture in the *Dictionnaire encyclopédique,* softly greeted the poor abbé by his true name, who then cried out in terror: Ha! I am lost!—Lost! Replied M. Cuvier. To the contrary, be assured that you are going to become the object of all my care and regard."[51]

Tessier, in turn, recognized Cuvier's genius. In Flourens's account, appended to Cuvier's memoirs, we learn that "on 10 February 1795, the abbé Tessier wrote to M. Laurent de Jussieu. 'At first sight of this young man I experienced the delight of that philosopher who, cast upon an unknown shore, finds geometric diagrams traced in the sand.'" In another version, Tessier wrote to A. A. Parmentier about his finding a "pearl in a dung heap." In each version the scientific world was alerted, à la John the Baptist, as it were, to the coming of Cuvier.[52] As a result, Etienne Geoffroy Saint-Hilaire wrote excitedly to Cuvier, urging him to "come to Paris immediately" and work with him, whereas Geoffroy's colleagues warned him to be careful.[53] Cuvier "might become a rival to Geoffroy," they presciently warned.[54]

Louis-Jean-Marie Daubenton, Buffon's former assistant and Geoffroy's powerful patron, supposedly tried to get Geoffroy to understand the danger Cuvier posed by offering him a warning from the fables of La Fontaine. At a dinner at Daubenton's house, Geoffroy found at his place "La lice et sa compagne" ("The Bitch and Her Friend"), "which ends, 'Laissez leur prendre un pied chez vous/Ils en auront bientôt pris quatre'" ("Let them get one foot in your door/They'll take everything in sight").[55]

The next chapter discusses the deteriorating relationship between Cuvier and Geoffroy—"the most famous of scientific rivals"[56]—whose tensions climaxed in the famous debate before the Academy of Science in 1830, as Geoffroy's rival arguments became the focus for a debate about competition and the meaning of friendship, as Geoffroy's generosity was posited against Cuvier's ambition. Here we mention one final element in common between the story of Cuvier's youth and the folktale, and that is the importance of watery motifs. In the structure of folktales, voyage over water is often the means by which the hero is carried to his triumph. This travel can be reduced, in the economy of the tale, to objects from the sea—pearls and shells, for example, in types D1520.29.1 and D452.2.1.[57] Can we not see the pearl that stands in for Cuvier in Tessier's message to Paris and the mollusks that form the object of Cuvier's work in Normandy and which lead to the ideas that would reshape his field—"the seeds of my two most important works go back to 1792"—as being a part of this structure that took Cuvier home to Paris, that is, to his spiritual and intellectual home, where he would spend the next forty years of his life (except for official traveling) and die?

Fanciful? Of course. But that the story of Cuvier and Tessier is a fiction, or at least that there "are only nuggets of fact extractable"[58] from it, which is true as well for the episodes of Cuvier's life in Montbéliard, is a twist that encourages us to use devices reserved for literary study in their interpretation. Who could fully believe the details offered at his funeral, for another example, about the last lecture he gave at the Collège de France? Moments before the onset of his terminal illness, he outlined the future of his work in words, Etienne

Denis, duc de Pasquier explained, "which would be difficult not to read as presentiment," "so grand, moving, and prophetic" they were. It was as if he sensed his end was coming and needed to reassure his disciples that the project of science would continue. This lecture, in the imagery offered by his colleague, was a kind of scientific last supper. Pasquier describes a "scene of remarkable beauty . . . which was the termination of his teaching life," in which he offered assurance to the assembled that "science would continue to reveal its eternal wisdom."[59] His death itself was a sacrifice, the magnanimous Geoffroy argued, after confessing his sorrow that on his deathbed his former friend was not able to know how much Geoffroy's thoughts dwelt on "that life in common of our young years, on those relations between us so intimate and so devoted, on that community of work so dear to us both!"[60] The ailing and tired Cuvier had been warned to slow down. The cholera epidemic was intensifying. "But passionate for the science to which he had devoted his life, Cuvier refused to rest," Geoffroy explained.[61] In dying he was hallowed: "His face was calm, at rest, and never did his noble and powerful head appear to me more beautiful and deserving of admiration," unchanged as yet by the paroxysms of death.[62]

Untouched by time, his life seems to have been lived out of time. Even cholera passed him by. In the cholera epidemic of 1832 he died of something else, though obviously that cannot be laid to his account. Outram argues that Cuvier's strangely ahistorical biography functioned to "set him outside the highly charged political field of the Revolution,"[63] though the record shows he was a player. Notably, during the Terror, while Cuvier was working as a tutor in Normandy, he was "appointed secretary-clerk to the tiny Norman commune of Bec-aux-Cauchois, a position which he occupied from 10 November 1793 until 19 February 1795. Not only was he responsible for maintaining contact with the Parisian authorities and keeping the village records, but he was also obliged," as William Coleman sarcastically explains, "to deliver pious Republican patriotic addresses, to help collect saltpeter, and to 'maintain liberty and equality or to die at his post.'"[64] He and his contemporaries were quiet about those details of history that anchored his early working life.[65]

Eloges "Historiques"?

The *Eloges historiques,* short biographies of deceased members of the Academy of Science written by Cuvier by virtue of his position as secretary, are shaped to the pattern of the Cuvier biographies and have the same fey feel. Composed between 1800 and 1832, they are largely silent on the details of history, as are the stories of Cuvier's own drama-filled life. References to the Terror appear but more often euphemistically, and the period overall is met with allusions. This aporia should give us pause. Other thinkers, too, were worried, as we have seen throughout this book, about the power the passions have to drive people forward in search of self-advancement, but these passion-driven people always were understood in their historical context. Lucien Jaume offers the example of an argument launched in support of Napoleon in July 1800 in the *Journal des débats,* which had as its target Germaine de Staël (whose work was suggesting that Enlightenment perfectibility could be redeemed from the despair the Terror had wrought): " 'The genius who presides now over the destiny of France is the genius of wisdom. . . . He never loses himself in vain theories and has no ambition to achieve glory through systems; he knows that men have always been the same, that nothing can change their nature, and it is from the past that he will draw lessons in order to rule the present.' "[66]

Cuvier's lack of interest in history in the *éloges* is also surprising because he was famous for associating the practice of geology (in which paleontology, not yet named, was still subsumed) with history. Geology was a "*historical* science" he argued, in which "the reality or historicity of the events themselves had first to be established."[67] The influential "Discours préliminaire" to his *Recherches sur les ossemens fossiles de quadrupèdes* of 1812 (later published separately as *Discours sur les révolutions de la surface du globe*)[68] opens with the claim that he was a "new species of antiquarian." See how Cuvier imagined himself walking alone toward a new understanding of time: "I shall try to travel a road on which only a few steps have so far been ventured, and to make known a kind of monument that is almost always neglected, although it is indispensable for the history of the globe. As a new species of antiquarian, I have had to learn to decipher and restore these monuments, and to recognize and reassemble in their original order the scattered and mutilated fragments of which they are composed; to reconstruct the ancient beings to which these fragments belonged; to reproduce them in their proportions and characters; and finally to compare them to those that live today at the earth's surface."[69]

Martin Rudwick points out that "Cuvier ended the 'Discourse,' as he had begun it, with the analogy with human history. For geologists to focus attention—as they did—on the old Primary rocks, which contained no fossils, was as if scholars were to lose interest in French history at just the point when the arrival of the literate Romans first provided documentation for that history." "Above all, however," Rudwick continues, "Cuvier's work fleshed out the metaphor that had become almost a cliché: the naturalist was to use fossils as the historian used documents, to piece together an authentic *history* of the earth, and of life at its surface. To 'burst the limits of time,' as he had put it at the start, was to write a *prehuman* history."[70]

We also know that Cuvier enthusiastically welcomed the Revolution on the basis of its being the fulfillment of modern history. Though Cuvier's memoirs claim that on the eve of his move to Normandy in 1789, he "had only the 'vaguest ideas' of the internal affairs of France,"[71] his correspondence suggests otherwise.[72] After the establishment of the National Assembly, he explained to his good friend from Stuttgart, Christian Pfaff, that "the struggle is therefore now only between despotism and liberty." That summer he lauded the " 'men of 1789' ": "The Abbé Sieyès is 'the most sensible political thinker in the entire Assembly'; Mirabeau, despite his execrable morals, is 'perhaps the greatest genius in France'; the Abbé Grégoire 'has shown the greatest political genius and the most noble character.' "[73] In 1792 he decried the nobility as an " 'ignorant and often contemptible class. . . . To see them every day causes one to find good in whatever may befall them.' "[74]

A secret memorandum written in January 1820 to Elie Decazes, Louis XVIII's minister of the Interior (whose liberal Doctrinaire policies were being jettisoned in the face of Ultra-Royalist, reactionary pressures and who would be pushed out of power after the assassination of the duc de Berry in February), fills out the narrative that his earlier observations implied. The friend of Guizot explained the Revolution in terms of the frustrated ambitions of the bourgeoisie. In a speech before the Chamber of Deputies in 1817, Cuvier addressed this explicitly. As Negrin summarizes while quoting Cuvier: "Thus 'ambition,' 'jealousy,' and 'pride' invaded all classes . . . 'the great were jealous of the learned; the provincial nobles of the court nobles; . . . the bourgeois of those who had been ennobled.'" In his scientific writings as well, Negrin explains, Cuvier suggested that the development of private property and a modern economy led to the accumulation of wealth; it allowed for "the inequality of fortunes to develop," and "aspirations for a better life to be fulfilled." Yet "along with such imposing progress came the debilitating effects of indolence and the evils of a 'savage ambition.'"[75] The causes were profound, the effects irreversible. "What happened in France is what will happen 'sooner or later in every nation which becomes wealthy and enlightened,'" Cuvier explained. It was the "passage from one social state to [another], from the feudal and ecclesiastical hierarchy to constitutional equality." Far from being triggered by a "'slight financial embarrassment'" of the Crown—by an "'accident of history'"—it was the built-up frustrations of "'new families' [who] wanted to have a share of the honors and high position to which their talent entitled them, rather than to remain underlings for incapable superiors.'" Although Louis XIV had opened up the elite to new men, the Regency had closed it, and the frustrations of this group led to the events of 1789.[76]

Why, then, are the subjects of the *Eloges historiques,* which we turn to below, not placed in the context of this history? Why does Cuvier's own autobiography elide it? The drive of ambition and of the passions in general was explicitly denied for Cuvier (a challenging position to maintain, as we have noticed: "Such a long list of employments would seem to indicate ambition," one elegist acknowledged, as he went on to refute the charge).[77] But so, too, do other deceased members of the Academy of Science appear at a safe remove from the vortex of opportunism and self-promotion that was public life when

Cuvier wrote their *éloges,* in anticipation of his own. It was quite a feat to make the chemist Antoine François de Fourcroy (1755–1809) an innocent of politics. He was a member of Napoleon's Council of State and former Conventional; it was whispered that his pusillanimity damned Lavoisier, who was executed by the Terror in 1794.[78] But that innocence of history, too, was Cuvier's theme in his collected *éloges* and even more daringly attempted in his life of the naturalist Bernard-Germain-Etienne de Lacépède (1756–1825), former head of the Legislative Assembly, later Napoleon's "slavishly devoted follower," in Isser Woloch's words,[79] whose list of positions and honors in the Empire second Cuvier's own.

Cuvier was clear in his report to Decazes about what moves history forward. The bourgeoisie was motivated not by "abstractions" (theories, ideas, arguments, the tools of the philosophes) but by "real needs" and aspirations.[80] Its ambitions were blocked by the laws of the old regime. It was "these actions [those laws] which, linked to the 'daring' of some men, led to the Revolution."[81] For Cuvier, ambition was the motor of history. But, as previous chapters have made clear, ambition was troubling. On the one hand, it was associated with civilization. The "origins of civilization" lay in the development of private property, which was understood as good. Yet progress was allied to inequality and aspiration and "furious ambition," as he said in the secret report to Decazes, a theme of vicious competition that he describes in an *éloge historique* of 1800 (of the botanist Louis-Guillaume Lemonnier) as marking the animal world as well: "Moreover we find among them the same sights as our world displays; despite what our moralists say, they are scarcely less evil or less unhappy than we; the arrogance of the strong, the baseness of the weak, vile rapacity, brief pleasure purchased by great effort, death following extended pain; voilà, what rules the lives of animals rules our own."[82]

To be sure, talent should be rewarded, not thwarted by the nobility, but the bourgeois Revolution had led to popular violence and the Terror. The Revolution mobilized the lower classes and unleashed their own aspirations. Cuvier described to his friend Christian Pfaff his feelings of shock after the murder of the vicomte de Belzunce in

1789 in Caen, for which some members of the crowd stood accused of cannibalism. He claimed to have seen one woman "invite her four year old son to see the decapitated head," an observation he repeats in his autobiography.[83] The effect was disorienting—as historians of the Terror have explained for Cuvier's generation in general, placing post-Revolutionary sensibility in the same context as post-traumatic stress syndrome.[84] It may also have oriented Cuvier's gaze to the present.

Like that of the Doctrinaires, Cuvier's liberalism rested on the freedom of property, not labor. If a stable social order was more likely without the license of ambition, then we should be quiet about its power. By erasing ambition from biography, concerns over the democratic future would be relieved. History would stall with the bourgeois state. As Foucault's introduction to *The Archaeology of Knowledge* implies, post-Revolutionaries were "force[d] . . . to enter a new time, cut . . . off from its empirical origin and its original motivations."[85] Was the philosopher of discontinuity inspired by Cuvier? We know he paused over this second important statement about history in Cuvier's *Discours sur les révolutions de la surface du globe:*

> Let us now examine what takes place on earth today; let us analyze the causes that still operate at its surface and determine the possible extent of their effects. This part of the [natural] history of the earth is all the more important, since it has long been thought possible to explain earlier revolutions by these present causes, just as past events in political history are easily explained when one knows well the passions and intrigues of our times. But we shall see that unhappily this is not so in physical history. The thread of operations is broken; nature has changed course, and none of the agents she employs today would have been sufficient to produce her former works.[86]

"The thread of operations is broken." Foucault signaled Cuvier's importance to modern thought for having separated—with this statement—human history from nature.[87] But cannot we also see Cuvier's "thread of operations" as the thread linking post-Revolutionaries to the past, now rift?[88] The memorandum to Decazes continued by insisting that the corporate world, with its traditional brakes on individualism, with its hierarchy and networks of influence, was gone, never to return. The break with that age is complete. " 'The nation is reduced to dust,' " Cuvier explained. " 'Each person is isolated and has only his own wealth and his own talent to aid him.' " "The government might seek the support of men, but 'it would only find isolated individuals.' "[89]

Reading the *Eloges historiques* on the same level of abstraction as we did the memoirs of Cuvier, we see that of the three major thinkers considered in this book, the one assumed to be least relevant today might have been the most profound. For what is being addressed by Cuvier in these life histories is the question raised by Stendhal not in *The Red and the Black* but in *The Charterhouse of Parma,* the master-piece that followed. What happens next to Fabrice, lost at the battle of Waterloo, "stranded in time," poised, in the words of Victor Hugo, on the "hinge of history"? It was as solution to that great problem of the post-Revolutionary self—mentally disconnected from its past, yet undeniably knit from it—that Cuvier drafted his *éloges* (at least in part). We could talk here, Cuvier said in 1810, by way of introducing his *éloge* of Horace-Bénédict de Saussure (1740–99), of Bailly, Condorcet, and Lavoisier (these three victims of the Revolution), but "it is they . . . whose tumultuous lives . . . whose unfortunate ends, would have more vividly brought to mind memories that remain much too painful to bear."[90] "To expiate the crimes of that disastrous time, one would have to narrate them and, we admit it, we do not yet have the courage to do so."[91] It would be better, claimed Cuvier in an apostrophe, "if we present for public recognition those of your peers who, more prudent or more fortunate, sheltered themselves from the tempests which claimed you as victims."[92] What kind of self appears without connection to the greatest historical event of modern times, and the aspirations, the ambitions, that drove it?

Outram, whose biography of Cuvier was one of the first to ease his story away from a narrow history of science and place it in the "social-political world" in which he lived, suggests (in part) that

Cuvier's challenge was to answer the charge of responsibility on the part of scientists (as philosophes) and science (as materialism) for the radical stage of the Revolution. "To both right and left, in fact, the *savant* represented a scapegoat figure. The contemporary debate over the responsibility of men of learning for the Revolution made it an uphill struggle to define the social role of science in neutral and acceptable terms."[93] Thus, the insistent theme in the *Eloges historiques* of disengagement in politics (however artificially placed) makes sense, we might agree, as a crucial step in the process of reorienting science toward safer rhetorical ground.

But do not the *éloges* need to be put into a larger context still? So many life histories, so deeply grounded in the details of their age—what do they tell us? The forty or so biographies we have to work with here—the *éloges* of Cuvier, his autobiography, and the three dozen *Eloges historiques* written *by* Cuvier for the first class of the Institut de France, then the Academy of Science (1800–1832)[94]—together form a history of self-making in an era that began in the reign of Louis XV. The first of his subjects were born in the 1720s through 1740s. Cuvier was born in 1769, in the same year and month, it was noted, as Napoleon.[95] How does one become a self in an era of Enlightenment, in its heightened mood of individualism? How does one not lose oneself in isolation? Or lose to competition? What are the risks incurred in a world in which, to paraphrase Pierre-Paul Royer-Collard's comment on France after the Revolution, "only individuals are left standing'" where "men, thrust outside their rank by events, deprived of all resources and all hope," speak for the potentiality and fears of revolutionary change?[96]

Cuvier's answers in the *Eloges historiques* are clear. Against the backdrop of exotic locales—Guiana, Brazil, Senegal, the Alps (still terra incognita until our period)—and tortuous theories—Lamarck's, to his mind, but also Michel Adanson's (1727–1806) and, to a degree, Claude-Louis Richard's—Cuvier posed the fate of two types of selves, the solipsistic self, forever lost in the imagination, and the social self, tied to the orbit of Parisian sociability, to the Republic of Letters, to the Academy of Science, to the judgment of one's peers, to organized life. The dangerous self is the solipsistic self, the self that wanders in itself, unmoored, cut off metaphorically or literally (or both). Safety lies in effacing the liberal self, the liberated self, to history—experienced as destiny, in a kind of secular quietism, I suggest—and to one's community, to the views of one's peers, which stands as a kind of apologia for the Empire and for opportunism overall, but also for collaboration in the positive sense of working together in the common cause and, finally, to facts, to a body of accumulating verifiable detail, valuable in itself, understood as a record, a recording of the world *dehors*. It is an uninspiring set of answers, to be sure, especially set next to those forwarded by Staël and Stendhal. But Cuvier's conformist arguments should retain our attention. The long-term importance of Doctrinaire liberalism for French culture is coming into view from a number of different historiographic angles.[97] By looking at the lives re-created for us by the friend of Royer-Collard and Guizot and other common associates, cannot we see more clearly how an "effaced" self views itself?[98]

Other Tales

Like the life of Cuvier as it was spun in his autobiography, the lives of many of the scientists honored in his *Eloges historiques* began with a set of problems rooted in family life.[99] Jacques René Tenon (1724–1816), for example, was born into a struggling family of surgeons in 1724. One of eleven children, he left for Paris at age seventeen, dependent on the charity of an uncle.[100] Jean-Charles Desessarts (1729–1811), whose recommendations on children's health must have influenced Rousseau, Cuvier suggests, was orphaned; his genial and wealthy uncle did nothing to help his career.[101] André Thouin's (1747–1824) father was head gardener at the Jardin du Roi. Thouin was cradled in the greenhouses, he played in the shadow of exotic plants, his life was charmed, and he was happy. But his father died when he was fourteen, and Thouin was left to support himself, his mother, and his several younger siblings.[102] René-Just Haüy's (1743–1822) father was a poor weaver who expected his son to follow in his career.[103] Fourcroy was from a noble family whose fortunes had declined. The problem of his father's poverty was compounded by the death of Fourcroy's mother when he was seven years old. So devastated was he that at the burial he tried to throw himself into the grave. At his *collège* a brutal prefect mistreated him.[104] Louis-Jean-Marie Daubenton (1716–1800) was not poor, but he was forced against his will to study for the priesthood, whereas Richard, as noted above, was expelled from the family home at age fourteen for refusing the religious life.[105] The *Eloges historiques* offer still more examples of this misery.

Like Cuvier's, these selves were driven by an inner need. Daubenton, for example, was sent by his parents from the Côte-d'Or to Paris to study theology. "Inspired, perhaps, by a presentiment of what he must be one day," he secretly followed lectures at the Faculty of Medicine and at the Jardin des Plantes. Following the death of his father, he became a doctor in Reims and returned to his hometown, where "he limited his ambition to the exercise of his art." "But," says Cuvier, "his destiny reserved a more brilliant theater for him."[106] The small town where he lived happened also to produce Buffon. He, too, was shaped by destiny, one that would lift up his childhood friend in its wake. In Cuvier's barbed word portrait, the young Buffon is drawn as an independently wealthy rake, whose "charms of body and mind, [whose] violent taste for pleasure, appeared to destine him toward a completely different career than science but who found himself drawn unremittingly back [towards science], however, by an irresistible inclination, that almost certain index of extraordinary talent."[107] Buffon's imagination was "ardent," his genius "exalted." He easily could have become "an elegant writer, a clever poet, but he would not have been a naturalist, he would not have been able to aspire to the role he sought for himself as the reformer of science"[108]—if not for Daubenton. Destiny linked them. In what will stand as Cuvier's basic distinction between good science and bad, Daubenton was drawn to facts and the work of observation, whereas Buffon was happy in "imaginary facts."[109] Daubenton was recruited as an inferior partner in Buffon's fabulously successful natural history, for Buffon understood that "his restless mind would not allow for this laborious type of work, that the weakness of his sight even forbade him to hope to indulge himself there with success."[110]

Other examples of the imperious draw of science fill the *éloges*. Claude Louis Berthollet (1748–1822), the chemist and great friend of Napoleon, succumbed in his youth. Born in the Savoy, he was educated in Turin. There, while his peers prepared for careers in the church or state administration, Berthollet studied medicine, drawn by "the irresistible attraction that led him already toward the sciences, in which he remains": "this same attraction" "made him run to Paris, the only city in which, he believed, he could at his ease satisfy the passion that controlled him."[111] Berthollet sought out the famous doctor Théodore Tronchin, who treated (as we saw in chapter 2) Louise-Germaine Necker for her depression and was influential in Paris and at Versailles. Though Berthollet's only claim on Tronchin was that they were from somewhat the same region, Tronchin became his patron. Berthollet's fortunes shifted in the fairy-tale fashion in which Cuvier's own life was turned: "Predisposed in his favor by his air of honesty and his reflective cast of mind, becoming more and more attached to him the more he got to know him, Tronchin made of him a sort of adopted child." Through Tronchin, Berthollet was hired by the duc d'Orléans and given access to the laboratory at the Palais Royal, and the important connection to Lavoisier followed.[112]

Lacépède was pulled to Paris, too, fatally, as Cuvier implied, torn between science and music, fact and fantasy, Buffon and Gluck. He knew the *Histoire naturelle* by heart[113] and at age twenty composed a *mémoire* on electricity, which he sent to Buffon. His "master's" "flattering reply" was all Lacépède needed to send him flying to Paris, "full of hope and fire," arriving in the middle of the night, scarcely waiting for the light of day to throw himself at Buffon's feet at the Jardin du Roi (a gesture repeated for Gluck in the afternoon).[114] An innocent, coddled by his widowed father, he was ignorant of the corroding effects of ambition: "Without a doubt he imagined that ambition and the desire for glory produced no other effects in men than those that emulation had engendered among his young comrades."[115] Adanson was sure of himself, too. He was introduced to natural history at his *collège*. The visiting British biologist John Turberville Needham gave him a microscope there and determined him on his career.[116]

"Burning from that moment on with the ambition to make a place for himself, at whatever the cost, among those who had pushed back the frontiers of natural history," he was driven not to Paris but to Senegal, the most remote place he could think of, in hopes of finding in the African jungle new species that might bring him acclaim. He chose what seemed to be the most forbidding of all places—" 'the most dangerous place' in the world, estimating that it would be the least known by naturalists."[117]

That the aspiring self, not science, is the subject of the *éloges* is Cuvier's own statement of his project, though of course we may suspect others. In one of his first *éloges*, that of the botanist Lemonnier (1717–99; read in 1800), Cuvier explains why associate members of the academy were not typically the subject of *éloges*. "If the Institute does not ordinarily publish a notice of the life of its associate members, it is not in order to establish a difference between them and the resident members. . . . It is rather because one does not know them. . . . We would not be able to render an account of the details of their private life, nor paint a picture of their moral character."[118] And, asks Cuvier, how could it be otherwise? We do not read the *éloges* to further our understanding of science. "It is not [for] the extracts of the works, always insufficient and, moreover, so well known, of these famous men; it is certainly not for the almost always incomplete indications of their discoveries, but it is the intimate knowledge of their person [*leur individu*], it is for the pleasure of being admitted, so to speak, to their society, to contemplate from nearby their qualities, their virtues, their faults even, in engaging tableaux."[119] It is here where we see Cuvier's break with the writers of the *éloges* who preceded him in the eighteenth century, in that the emphasis of the subsequent *éloges* shifts from accounts of the subjects' scientific accomplishments to accounts of their lives.[120]

What do we gain from our intimacy with "*leur individu*"? On the one hand, acquaintance with successful lives—models to emulate— are offered, but on the other, instructions on how *not* to behave are insisted on. "How many young minds have our literary solemnities inflamed and sent flying into careers, noble endeavors, without doubt,

but arduous and full of peril for, one must admit," he explained in
1819, "it is all too easy to lose one's way!"[121] It is precisely this other
function that Cuvier concentrates on from the *éloge* of Lemonnier in
1800 through his remarks in 1819 to his late *éloge* of Lamarck in 1832.
Is it not our principle responsibility, Cuvier asks, "to mark the false
routes that so many superior men have set off on, seduced by their
imagination or by the desire to earn too hastily the approbation of the
crowd?"[122] "The life of savants teaches us at each page that the great
truths have only been discovered and established by prolonged solitary
study, directed constantly toward a particular goal, guided unceasingly
by a skeptical and disciplined logic."[123] How does that self not get lost,
transplanted as so many savants are, from home, from habit, launched
by aspirations to parts unknown? "Everywhere," Cuvier warns, "we
see those who have failed to reach their goals."[124]

   The false path is marked out for us in the life of Adanson, as narrated
by Cuvier. "A burning desire" to place himself within "the first ranks"[125]
of natural historians had moved him since he first peered into the
spontaneous gift of Needham's microscope and heard his praises sung.
We saw above that his ambition drew him to Senegal. Like so many
enthusiasts, Cuvier explains, he saw only one way to make his mark—
"the simple way, that of multiplying" the description of species[126]—and
in 1748, at the age of twenty-one, he set sail on a ship of the Company
of Africa to that place almost unknown to natural history to make his
discoveries. There he worked as one obsessed. One sees him, Cuvier
imagines for us, at times "crossing the hot desert sands whose 60
degrees (C) shriveled the leather of his shoes" and "at times, drenched
by tropical storms, never allowing these conditions to get in the way
of his work."[127] For five years he labored, sometimes eighteen hours
a day, studying the plants and the animals of Senegal. He also drew
maps and took astronomical observations. He composed a dictionary
of the Nier people's language and observed their commerce, clothing,
arms, and household utensils. Nothing about the region was ignored.[128]

   But he was always alone. "Imagine," Cuvier begins, a young man of
twenty-one, practically just out of school, to a large degree still ignorant
of the methods of science—imagine that youth suddenly transported

to "a barbarian land [almost without books], with a handful of men
. . . who were ignorant of or disdainful of his researches; abandoned, as
it were, in the most profound isolation in a new world in which
everything—the plants, the animals, the sky, even, is different.
Necessarily, that man's thoughts would take a turn of their own."[129]
Such was Adanson and such was his problem. Isolated from the
scientific community, he did not know how to evaluate his ideas. His
thoughts turned inward. "Always alone with himself, taking every idea
as a new discovery, lacking objects of comparison, never exposed to
those little battles of society which so quickly allow one to take the
measure of one's forces," he would naturally be inclined to exaggerate
the worth of his ideas and not hesitate to express them.[130] Solipsistic,
he was also antisocial, ignorant of "that delicate art of convincing
others without upsetting their self-esteem, of imperceptibly shifting
their settled ways into new paths."[131]

So, explains Cuvier, when Adanson returned to Paris "with his rich
provision of facts and sweeping ideas, he sought immediately to take
the place among naturalists that he felt was his," and was rebuffed.[132]
Adanson had developed a system of plant classification with great
advantages especially for the organization of the study of collections
from abroad, but the state of natural history had changed during
the time he was gone.[133] Linnaeus and Buffon had "broken a path
toward the empire which they were to divide between themselves for
close to a half century."[134] Though Linnaeus's system had faults, and
Adanson's had strengths, Linnaeus's was adopted, since he understood the sociability of science and Adanson did not. The Swede was
"amiable, kindly, surrounded by enthusiastic disciples whom he made
into so many missionaries, and whose discoveries he assiduously used
to enrich his multiple editions. [He was] a favorite of the great of the
world, linked by an active correspondence to every influential savant,"
whereas Adanson, though French, "[kept] his desert manners, [was]
inaccessible in his cabinet, without students, almost without friends,
and communicat[ed] with the world only through his books."[135]

Twenty years later he approached the Academy with a massive
project of categorizing the entire world, an encyclopedia "he would

spend the rest of his life futilely attempting to publish."[136] "The boldest imagination," Cuvier insisted, "would recoil from the reading of the plan he submitted in 1774: the numbers alone were frightening"—"the history of 40,000 species . . . organized in alphabetical order in 150 volumes; 200,000 words . . . explicated in a universal glossary."[137] His project rejected, Adanson withdrew into retirement and even more into himself: "from then on, his ideas were neither nourished nor rectified by those of others; his genius worked only on his own store of ideas, and this was no longer restocked."[138] He became reclusive, avoiding the work of others, wasting his time duplicating research (on mosses, for example), and enfeebling science by refusing to publish his own.[139]

This litany of mistakes is repeated in the history of Richard, abandoned, as we saw, by his gardener father to pursue his dreams of botany. After saving up a small fortune through parsimonious living and ceaseless work in tutoring and drawing, he gained an audience with Necker and Louis XVI to propose a trip to South America. The king personally showed Richard a map of Guiana, pointing out promising regions to explore. It was decided that he would travel to its capital, Cayenne, and to Brazil and the Antilles, to evaluate the production of spices, gain information, and offer suggestions for improvement. This he did, but naively, with only his own funds, and with no written assurances of what might be his recompense. There he compiled a collection of plants and animals of immense importance to natural history. Other collectors, for instance, brought back dried plant specimens, which were useless. Richard produced drawings of living plants with such detail that they remain of value. So, too, were his observations of mollusks important, before which (and for a long time in Britain still) the focus of naturalists in the field had been on shells, and little was known about the animals themselves.

After eight years of work in the field, in the spring of 1789, Richard returned home, "with his store of treasures," to the most profound lack of interest in his project.[140] He had imagined "the most honorable welcome as recompense for his work: 'the savants and administrators would press equally around him, the first to inform themselves of his discoveries, the second to fulfill the public's debt.'" It was as if, Cuvier

explained, "he had remained buried in the depths of his woods."[141]
After "several tries to obtain justice," Richard withdrew, within himself
and from the scientific world; "he confined himself to his retreat,
living and studying for himself alone."[142] His refusal to publish, "his
obstinate silence," was "an immense misfortune for all branches of
natural history."[143] A foreign naturalist who saw Richard's work, Cuvier
lamented, claimed he was one of Europe's greatest botanists.[144]

The history of Guillaume-Antoine Olivier (1756–1814) reprises this
theme of Rip Van Winkle or Sleeping Beauty, but with a happy ending.
Olivier left Paris in 1792 on a mission to the east, to collect plants and
political information from the Ottoman Empire. When he returned in
1799, "he no longer found any of his friends in a position to be useful
to him," but, unlike Adanson and Richard, he slipped back into the
network of science. News of his discoveries had preceded him, and
"within three weeks he was made a member of the new Institute."[145]
The theme of dislocation in the *éloges* is countered elsewhere, too, by
a narrative of recovery. Read this most famous of all descriptions of
the reconstitution of the Academy of Science as the first class of the
Institute of France, which appears as the denouement in the story of
Adanson's life: "At a sign from the authorities and after four years of
being scattered to the winds, these illustrious men," Cuvier explains,
"quit as one the obscurity of their retreats to assemble together once
more": "Impossible to efface the impression of that first reunion, of
those tears of joy, of those questions pressed back and forth about
their misfortunes, their retreats, their occupations; of those painful
reminders of so many colleagues, victims of the executioner; finally, of
the sweet emotion on the part of those still young, called for the first
time to sit alongside men whose genius they had long been taught to
respect, learning now through this poignant spectacle to know their
hearts."[146] The passage prepares us for the redemption of Adanson,
who by 1789 had retreated far into himself and further away from the
world: "Fearing to lose even an instant, he sequestered himself even
more than ever from the world; he stole time from sleeping, from
eating. When, by chance, someone was able to penetrate his lair, he
was found couched in the midst of innumerable papers which covered

the floors, comparing and contrasting, connecting them in a thousand different ways; unmistakable signs of impatience advised one not to interrupt him again; he found ways even to avoid these tentative visits by withdrawing to a small isolated house in a distant neighborhood."[147]

After the first moments of joy, the eyes of the Academy turned to those who were missing, among whom was Adanson: "It was then only that one was apprised of the circumstances which caused his absence."[148] A delegation was sent: "It was so moving to see the poor old man bent before his fireplace, in the glimmer of a half-burned log, attempting with a feeble hand to trace out a few more words, neglecting all the cares of life, hoping that a new idea, like a sweet and good fairy, would alight upon his imagination."[149] Adanson was saved, folded at last within the community's embrace: "His retreat had finally to yield to the solicitations of his colleagues. He received them with tears of recognition. Stunned as much as touched by our interest, he regretted, no doubt, that in renouncing the pleasures of the world he had included in his sacrifice the joys of the heart."[150]

Richard's story, too, takes us to the succoring arms of friendship, though its ending appears not in his *éloge* but in Thouin's, where we see his success more sharply as Richard's failure is woven within. The parallels of their early lives are set out for us. Thouin, as we saw above, was born at the Jardin du Roi, and when his father died, he was left in charge of his family. Thouin was fourteen, the same age as Richard when his gardener father abandoned him. Emotional similarities ended there, however. Thouin, Cuvier emphasizes, "found hearts more humane" than did Richard.[151] Buffon became Thouin's patron and arranged for him to be granted his father's place as head gardener at the Jardin du Roi, despite his youth. He was seventeen when he took up the post.[152] Connections saved Thouin and his family. They also ensured a very successful career. Agronomists and others whom he taught at the Jardin du Roi traveled the world, sending him back collections from Guiana, Senegal, Pondicherry, and Corsica. "Exchanges of plants with foreign botanists" also "enriched" the greenhouses.[153] These connections made his name well known. By 1795 he was world-famous, and he easily became professor in charge of public education at the newly organized

Jardin des Plantes. Sociability saved Thouin, and its lack led Richard to his miserable end. Cuvier clearly makes this point. As children, their positions were similar, but Richard's fight against adversity was "precocious" and his struggles shaped "a personality which continued to multiply difficulties for himself throughout his entire life." "The other, seconded in his first efforts by a helpful hand, created for himself a pleasant and honorable position and exercised for more than half a century an influence as happy as it was extended and unimpeded."[154]

The Republic of Letters saved Pierre-Auguste-Marie Broussonet (1761–1807), too. Trained as a doctor in Montpellier, but only toward gaining training in science, in 1783 he was teaching at the Veterinary School at Alfort. He was a zoologist and botanist, with an interest in agronomy. He enthusiastically welcomed the Revolution as a movement of reform. He was with Bertier de Sauvigny, the intendant of Paris in charge of grain supplies, in 1789 when Sauvigny was murdered by the crowd. Cuvier refers to Broussonet's subsequent role in the Revolution with the explanation that "after those events that put an end to the Legislative Assembly [the attacks on the Tuileries Palace and the September Massacres in 1792] of which we conserve only too frightening a memory, [Broussonet] retired to his country estate outside Montpellier, hoping to find in the culture of the fields that repose which had eluded him from the moment he had begun to yield to the attractions of ambition."[155] But he was hounded as a federalist, and after being jailed for several days, Broussonet escaped to Spain through the Pyrenees. In Madrid he knew no one, and the royalist refugees refused him help.[156] From the point of view of both the left and the right, he was the enemy. "Happily," Cuvier exhales, "there exists in the midst of political associations an association of quite another order, which looks to be of service to all, which refuses to take part in their continual disagreements, the true friends of science, as devoted to their country as any other class of men, are united to each other by those same lines which attach them to the greater cause of humanity."[157] And so, "It was enough that the name of M. Broussonet be uttered and that his situation be made known, for him to receive from all those who cultivated the sciences—without distinctions based on country, religion, or political affiliation—welcome, protection, and help of all kinds."[158]

Broussonet's "arms were too weak to protect himself from the universal delirium," and he almost lost sight of himself.[159] Fourcroy, Cuvier suggests, lost himself in the "delirium" of politics that began for him with the sound of his own voice. In 1784 he gave a lecture at Alfort in place of his patron, Bucquet. Fourcroy had resisted—he had never spoken in public before. Prevailed upon, he spoke for two hours, "without hesitation, or confusion, as if he were already a professor at the height of his power. He has often related how during that stunning ordeal, he saw nothing, heard nothing, had abandoned himself entirely to the situation."[160] In 1784 he was made professor of chemistry at the Jardin du Roi, largely as a result of his popularity as a speaker. "The voice of the public spoke so strongly in favor of Fourcroy" that he was chosen over Berthollet, the much stronger scientist.[161] He was a master speaker: "Logic in its organization, a wealth of expression, nobility, exactness, elegance in his elocution, as if his words had been carefully chosen; a swiftness, a brilliancy, an originality in his turns of phrase as if they had come to him through inspiration; his voice mobile, resonant, silvery, lending itself to any pitch and range, able to penetrate into the further recesses of the auditorium; nature had given him all."[162] For twenty-five years, Cuvier explains, the amphitheater at the Jardin des Plantes was "the seat of his glory," "*le principal foyer de sa gloire.*"[163] It twice needed to be expanded to accommodate those crowding in to hear him speak on chemistry: "You might have seen hundreds of listeners of all classes, of all nations, spend entire hours crowded together, forgetting almost to breathe, their eyes fixed on his, hanging on his words . . . while his fiery eyes scanned the crowd. He knew how to pick out from the ranks of those even most far away that difficult mind which remained skeptical, and the slower thinker who did not yet understand. He redoubled for them his arguments and examples, he varied his expressions until he found those that would reach them. Language appeared to multiply its riches for him. He would quit a topic only when he saw that his many listeners were equally persuaded."[164]

The problem for Fourcroy was that he too was captivated by his ideas. "Some say," reports Cuvier, "that the habit of speaking with such warmth on behalf of each opinion that he took up weakened a bit the natural effect that his eloquence would otherwise necessarily have had."[165] This weakened him as a politician, though it partially explained for Cuvier his commitment to the Convention. Fourcroy was always too much interested in the approbation of the crowd, in persuasion itself, disconnected from reason—a delirium in itself. "In the end," explains Cuvier, the tensions within Fourcroy—"his works so multifarious," the "double existence" of scientist and politician, superficiality and fact—destroyed him. "Seized at last by a sudden attack, just as he was signing some dispatches, he cried out: *I am dead,* and he was, in effect."[166]

Two selves are offered by Cuvier as models for the scientific self. They appear in the brilliant word pictures of Haüy and Adanson. Haüy, son of a poor weaver with few prospects, was ordained a priest in Paris. In the 1770s he began to teach at the Collège du Cardinal Lemoine. At first his interests lay in botany, but he happened to hear Daubenton's lectures on mineralogy at the Jardin du Roi. In an example of paradigm change—Cuvier so much as suggests—Haüy solved the problem of how to categorize minerals that the field had run aground on.[167] It took an outsider, Cuvier explains, to see what to do. The Jardin du Roi had many qualified scientists who, says Cuvier, would leave the fields of botany and mineralogy just where they had found them. "It was on account of learning these sciences later in life," Cuvier explains encouragingly, "that M. Haüy envisaged them differently. The dissimilarities, the lacunae in the sequence of ideas keenly struck a good mind which, at the height of its power, was thrown all of a sudden into the study of something new."[168] Haüy "laid out the foundation of the mathematical theory of crystal structure,"[169] which we are led to appreciate, though the interest in the *éloge,* as usual, is in the life and not the science.

Haüy's story had much to offer for the development of Cuvier's themes of the self standing independent from history while resting dependent on its peers. The critical episodes began with the fall of the constitutional monarchy. In August 1792 Haüy was jailed along with other nonjuring priests. For Haüy, this was a matter of small importance; "cell for cell, for him there was little difference: reassured above all in finding himself in the midst of many of his friends, his only care was to have his cabinets brought to him and to endeavor to put his crystals in order."[170] Fortunately, Cuvier says, he had friends who were better informed. Geoffroy Saint-Hilaire, a former student at the Collège du Cardinal Lemoine, mobilized the scientific community in his behalf and secured an order for his release. Immediately, Geoffroy ran to where Haüy was held (Saint-Firmin), document in hand. But it was rather late in the evening and Haüy was so comfortably ensconced that Geoffroy could not prevail on him to leave that day. "The next morning he had to be almost dragged away. One trembles still," Cuvier claims, "to consider that the day after that was the 2nd of September!"[171]

Cuvier draws Haüy for us again during the Convention, when, despite his continued nonjuring status and the active performance of his clerical duties, he remained on the Commission for Weights and Measures well after Lavoisier was executed and others were purged.[172] This detachment from politics was not the same as an alienation from other people; "simplicity of manners . . . was everything to him."[173] Indeed, it seemed its parallel. Cuvier described Haüy walking the streets of his neighborhood, outside the Jardin des Plantes, seemingly transcendent of time and place. "His antique clothing, his air of simplicity, his excessively modest way of speaking, these were not such as to identify him" as the famous scientist he actually was, in touch with his age, and the materialist core of its beliefs.[174]

Cuvier also offers us the life of the alpinist Saussure. Born in 1740, Saussure, known for his work in geology, meteorology, botany, and most of all through his multivolume *Voyages dans les Alpes*, was a patrician of Geneva. Saussure was politically active in the revolutionary movements there, taking "a voluntary oath to liberty, equality, and fraternity in 1793" and working on "committees to draw up a new revolutionary constitution"[175]—though we do not learn of these activities from Cuvier's *éloge*. The *éloge* of Saussure begins with a preface, discussed above, on the subject of the impossibility of integrating the history of the Revolution into the history of science at the time. Thus, he would read an *éloge* of Saussure in 1810, but not of Lavoisier, to launch the Institute's work of catching up with the lives of scientists who had died in the interim between the abolition of the Royal Academy of Science and its re-corporation in the first class of the Institute of France.[176] Cuvier presents Saussure as one untouched by revolutionary politics, though we know that (like Cuvier) he was—but the major theme in his *éloge* is the power of physical reality to speak accurately to those who know how to listen, to represent itself, to destroy the chimera of constructs spun from reason, and reasoning alone.

Cuvier could not but be moved by the romanticism of the *Voyages dans les Alpes*. In this passage of the *éloge,* the tiny Alpine flower is contrasted with the sublimity of the peaks, echoing Saussure's language: "Occupied henceforth with objects much larger and which demanded much more arduous labor, Saussure always returned with pleasure to his first interests [in botany]. In the midst of his travels in the Alps, on the summits of the steepest slopes, during his profound meditations on the most imposing aspects that nature presents on the globe, he would carefully collect the smallest flower and contentedly record it in his notebook. He appeared to find something sweet in the discovery of these last living beings nestled against the immense ruins of nature."[177]

The Alps and the other mountain chains that Saussure began to explore in the 1760s were exotic and almost unknown to science. They were understood to hold the secret to the earth's foundation, and thus to the frisson of fear their physicality had begun to evoke was added the tension of hovering at the gap between theology and science. Moreover, their natives were picturesque, generous, and timelessly poor, offering yet another set of contrasts to enlightened thinkers. Here is Cuvier describing the exertions of Saussure:

> To make long treks in those high valleys to which vehicles never approach, to share with the poor inhabitants their hard

black bread, to have for shelter only their huts, smoky and open to all the winds, to have as a path only the rocky bed of a torrent, to cling with one's hands and feet to the sharp edge of crags, to leap from one of their points to another above a precipice, to be surprised, sometimes by winds which knock one over, sometimes by fogs which hide the path and freeze one's chest, to sound at each instant that snow which hides perhaps a crevice to engulf you, to remain for days and nights on the glaciers, those fields of ice where the outer limits of life are reached, and to which only a love of science could draw a living being: such was the existence to which the historian of the Alps was condemned.[178]

Cuvier embraces the enthusiasm the redoubtable peaks inspired in Saussure. In the "Discours préliminaire" to Saussure's *Voyages dans les Alpes,* the pure air of the mountains, the noble character of the natives, and the steadying corrective of their sublimity are evoked, and Cuvier seems to approve: "He describes himself, on the summit of Mount Etna, seeing men and their empires in all their insignificance."[179] But, says Cuvier, it is true that "a philosopher need not go so high to see that, and if Saussure had carried with him only these vague dispositions, we would not be writing his *éloge*."[180] Saussure's excursions—to the top of Mont Blanc for an unprecedented four and one-half windblown hours, on Monte Rosa, on the Col du Géant—involved very precise high-altitude observations for which he either invented or improved measuring instruments such as the thermometer, the hygrometer, the electrometer, the anemometer, the barometer, and others.[181] Out of his experiments with these instruments emerges, Cuvier explains, the science of meteorology.[182] More directly to Saussure's point, his almost twenty years of detailed observations in the mountains destroyed the Cartesian theory of the earth and established the groundwork for an accurate understanding of the formation of mountains and thus the topography of the globe. To Cuvier's point, these observations stand alone. They are not twisted, so to speak, into theory: "With such a volume of important material, it took courage to resist the temptation to put it together in a system."[183]

The *Eloges historiques* were self-serving, of course. No one listening was fooled when Cuvier argued that his *éloge* of Lamarck was well-meaning, and neither can we be misled. Two types of scientists exist in the world, Cuvier explained in his preface. The first remain in the world of fact: those who "bring only to the light of day unquestionable truths, verifiable by demonstration, which lead to provable results, and who never put forward anything based on guesswork or chance."[184] These are "geniuses without peers" who hold up "torches to light the route of science."[185] Others—Lamarck, as it happens, was one of these—were fully as capable but "were not able to resist combining their observations and deductions with fanciful conceptions; believing it possible to leap ahead of experiment and calculation, they laboriously constructed vast edifices on imaginary bases, comparable to those enchanted palaces in our old tales that vanish at the shattering of the talisman on which its existence depends."[186] The *éloges* rest as models, and not everyone can reach the highest ranks of science, but it is Cuvier's responsibility to "distinguish by notable examples those subjects amenable to our efforts, and the obstacles which would bar our efforts to pursue them."[187] Thus, the *éloge* of Lamarck, which, while noting with praise the useful contributions he had made to science, stressed instead those works "where indulgence of a too lively imagination had led to highly problematic results and to indicate, as much as possible, the underlying causes and occasions for these errors, or, if one may express it in this way, their genealogy,"[188] which this nephew of pastors then proceeded to do.

Clearly, Cuvier's ambition was deployed in the biographies he wrote by virtue of his position as perpetual secretary of the Academy of Science. They explicitly marked out the territory that Cuvier as "gatekeeper of natural history" would allow. We will see this Cuvier in action in the next chapter as we follow the clash with his erstwhile friend Geoffroy Saint-Hilaire. The lack of politics, the absence of history, is a mirror trick of the biographies. Cuvier and his peers were deeply involved in politicking and deeply implicated in the Revolution. But is that not Cuvier's point all along—to propose what a deracinated self might look like as we turn our selves and our desires into fables, as careerism trumps heroism in the post-Revolutionary state?

The following chapter rests as a pendant to this, as Etienne Geoffroy Saint-Hilaire in his youth was alter ego to Cuvier. Geoffroy's break with Cuvier became a public statement against careerism, his personal struggle against Cuvier's control a plunging back into history of the liberal post-Revolutionary self.

5

FRIENDSHIP MATTERS; ARGUMENTS FROM EGYPT; CODA ON NAPOLEON

Friendship Matters

The famous debate between Cuvier and Etienne Geoffroy Saint-Hilaire on the floor of the Academy of Science in July 1830 remains good copy. Almost all its historians relate the following exchange between Goethe and his friend Frédéric Soret, with its unforgettable punch line:

> The news of the Revolution of July, which had already commenced, reached Weimar today, and set everyone in a commotion. I went in the course of the afternoon to Goethe's. "Now," he exclaimed as I entered, "what do you think of this great event? The volcano has come to an eruption: everything is in flames, and we no longer have a transaction behind closed doors."
>
> "A frightful story," I replied. "But what else could be expected under such notorious circumstances and with such a ministry, than that matters would end with the expulsion of the royal family?"
>
> "We do not appear to understand each other, my good friend," replied Goethe. "I am not speaking of those people at all, but of something entirely different. I am speaking of the contest, of the highest importance for science, between

Cuvier and Geoffroy Saint-Hilaire, which has come to an open rupture in the Academy."

This expression of Goethe's was so unexpected that I did not know what to say.[1]

Goethe, of course, had more to say. In articles immediately translated in the *Revue encyclopédique* and the *Annales des sciences naturelles,* Goethe imagined the quarrel's startling effect on the formerly placid scientific community: "At a meeting of the French Academy, on February 22 this year, there occurred an important event that cannot fail to have significant consequences. In this shrine of science, where everything proceeds most respectably in the presence of a large audience, where we encounter the moderation, even the hypocrisy, of well-brought up people, where only moderate responses are made in the event of differences of opinion, where the doubtful is rather set aside than disputed—here there erupts a quarrel on a scientific point, a quarrel that threatens to become personal, but, looked at closely, comes to mean much more."[2] The debate centered on the organization of nature. Was there a unity to nature—a basic model for all organisms—or were there four disconnected sets or models, *embranchements,* as Cuvier always insisted? Geoffroy lost the argument in the Academy of Science and at the Collège de France, where it continued until Cuvier's collapse in 1832, but history decided in Geoffroy's favor, as Goethe had predicted. A new book on Geoffroy (subtitled "A Visionary Naturalist") explains how biogenetics has returned Geoffroy to the "first level of the international scientific scene" for his efforts to establish the "unity of organic composition."[3] Readers may be more familiar with Geoffroy as a French herald of Darwin. Unity of composition implied change and progress and was opposed to Cuvier's notion of fixity. The association with evolution was tightened by Geoffroy's devotion to Lamarck (though not transformism) in the face of Cuvier's disapproval, whose violence we felt in his *éloge* of Lamarck, which, by the way, was transparently an attack on Geoffroy as well—Lamarck's follies stood in for Geoffroy's in this last (1832) display of Cuvier's contempt.

For Geoffroy, the conflict was always personal. In Geoffroy's account of the debate, the quarrel was set in the context of friendship, an understanding that more than anything removes it from its place as a footnote in the history of science and repositions it in the center of our history. As Geoffroy framed the story, it is a tale of love and betrayal, a tragedy, at the heart of which ties of affection were found broken on the altar of ambition. "Three years younger than Baron Cuvier," Geoffroy explains in *The Principles of Zoological Philosophy* (discussed in March 1830 in the Royal Academy of Sciences), which stands as his apologia, "I nevertheless preceded him by eighteen months in my career of instruction. This circumstance, my position at the Royal Garden, brought us into contact, and led us to our relations." He continues: "These relations began for us at our entry into social life: they soon became intimate. Then what cordiality, what concern, what mutual devotion was there between us! At present should disagreements about the facts of science, however grave they may be, prevail over the sweetness of those memories? Our first studies in natural history, even some discoveries: we made them together; we behaved with the impetus of *the most perfect friendship,* to the point where we observed, we meditated, we wrote reciprocally, the one for the other. The anthologies of the time include writings jointly published by M. Cuvier and me."[4]

Geoffroy would repeat himself in his speech at Cuvier's funeral—why at Cuvier's last moments did he not remind Cuvier of their sweet moments of friendship, he moaned—and also in his *Etudes progressives d'un naturaliste:* "Throughout 1795 and 1796, we lived together—we ate at the same table, took walks together, worked alongside each other in the public collections which we studied together; our writings were signed by both of us."[5] Theirs was a marriage of minds, an intimacy, a "perfect friendship" that his friends, we recall, had warned him not to trust. Ensconce Cuvier at the Jardin des Plantes and you will find yourself edged out, as the "friend" who helped the needy "bitch" in the *Fables of La Fontaine.* Described in chapter 4, the passage continues:

The other wanted back
Her house, her room, her bed.
But now the Bitch bared every tooth in her head.

Help Cuvier he did, if recklessly, from this point of view.[6] Without him, Geoffroy claimed, Cuvier would have moldered in Normandy forever, ignorant of his potential, a mystery even to himself: "Still very young, M. Cuvier thought he had written only fragments of works; and already, without his knowing, unbeknownst to everyone, he had laid down the lasting foundation of zoology; I had the inexpressible happiness of having been the first to sense and to reveal to the world of science the significance of a genius about which he remained ignorant."[7]

We recall from the previous chapter that Henri Tessier wrote to the scientific world in Paris in 1793 to tell them about Cuvier. Geoffroy explains that although Tessier did write to A. A. Parmentier, it was only after Geoffroy urged him to that Tessier wrote to Jussieu and others, then making his *"anecdote prophétique"* about having found a pearl in the dung of the country. And even so, Geoffroy explains in this, his revised version of the fable, Cuvier's fortunes were not much advanced by these efforts. Geoffroy then suggested that Cuvier send him samples of his research. So impressed was Geoffroy by his reading of Cuvier's work that he was prompted to make the prophecy that has won its own resonant place in the story of Cuvier's career: "Come quickly to Paris, come play among us the role of another Linnaeus, of another founder of natural history."

"Cuvier put trust in my appeal," Geoffroy concludes, "the rest is well known."[8]

What happened? "Did I really open the hostilities? And to what extent?" These are the questions that Geoffroy poses on behalf of his readership: "This point of fact seems to me to have excited some curiosity; thus an explication is desired. I shall give it by presenting in published form the writing by which the susceptibility of Baron Cuvier was offended, and which was followed on his part, on February 15, by an improvisation as ardent as it was bitter."[9] Geoffroy's audience had spilled over from science into politics, if it ever was thoroughly distinct.

Though the point of contention was the humble mollusk, the *Journal des débats* that spring took Cuvier's side. *Le temps* and *Le national*, the liberal journals, supported Geoffroy.[10] In public opinion, Cuvier's attack on Geoffroy came to stand for how the powerful crush the voice of dissenters. Geoffroy himself described how Cuvier's circle had closed him out in the 1820s, silenced his voice by not responding to it, whispered criticisms so he could only half hear.[11] In a letter to a friend he complained about "the king of kings, this haughty Agamemnon": "he mumbled these words, directed towards my ears: *always looking for arguments and I have so many to endure*. Twice, I heard them. Twice I pretended not to have. I avoided all the inconveniences of that provocation by prudently retiring."[12]

Geoffroy's situation inspired François-Vincent Raspail, a republican critic of establishment science, to claim Geoffroy as an ally in his battle against authority. In "Scientific Coteries," published in 1830 (in the *Annales des sciences d'observation*, which he edited), Raspail describes what would happen to any aspiring young scientist working against (or outside) the "leading factions": " 'First, he will not be attacked to his face, but he will be ridiculed in secret. His discoveries will be bantered about in soirées, banquets, and concerts. . . . The scientific or literary journals that might be at his disposal will be prohibited from occupying themselves with the work of a recalcitrant, of this obscure innovator! Attacked from all sides, he will be cited by no one.' "[13] Should he not desist, "he will then be attacked head-on, his work destroyed through sarcasm, gross omissions, and mutilated quotations."[14] This was exactly Geoffroy's experience, as Balzac, too, described it. That author had the "ass" in his "Ass's Guide for the Use of Animals Who Wish to Achieve Honors" (1842) sell out to the Baron Cerceau (that band of iron that encircles a cask), while the "great philosopher" (Geoffroy) was mocked: " 'Dare say that I am an ass, I who have given you here the method to succeed and the epitome of all the sciences.' "[15] *Histoire naturelle drolatique et philosophique des professeurs du Jardin des Plantes* appeared several years later, comparing Cuvier's *Analyticus diplomaticus* with Geoffroy's *Transcendentalus honestus*. *Analyticus diplomaticus* was "more courtier than naturalist. . . . He elevated himself to the level of the great by his submission to the will of successive powers," whereas *Transcendentalus honestus* was "good, honest, an enthusiast of elevated and profound thoughts to whose research he devoted his life."[16]

The larger question is implied in the story of the debate. How did one person, one unit of being, as Geoffroy had cast his relationship with Cuvier during the Revolution, split into two in such a way that one became for his contemporaries the embodiment of ambition and the other the lodestar for complaints about competitive individualism?[17] How did Geoffroy become his own self so that his image as alter ego to Cuvier was made possible? How did the otherness, so to speak, of his ego evolve? That problem is the subject of this chapter—not the bitterness of the Restoration or the politics of the July Monarchy, but the decisions made during the collapse of the Directory that set Geoffroy apart from Cuvier, adrift from his emotional home.[18]

The first was Geoffroy's decision in 1798 to join Napoleon's expedition to Egypt as a member of its Commission of Sciences and Arts, an invitation that Cuvier declined. "Come," Berthollet had urged them both, in the iconic moment of their relationship, "Monge and I will be your companions and Bonaparte your general."[19] Doubt remains as to why Cuvier stayed home. Hervé Le Guyader follows research from the 1930s in urging us to believe that Cuvier was sick and thus unable to go.[20] Outram argues that he was unwilling to leave Paris, the center of his power. Cuvier tells us this himself, in the autobiographical fragment we have consulted already: "My calculation was soon made. I was at the center of the sciences, in the midst of the finest collections, and I was certain of being able to produce better, more systematic and coherent work and to make more important discoveries than on even the most fruitful of expeditions."[21] We know well from Cuvier's *Eloges historiques* (which began while Geoffroy was away) how disparaging he was of the "field naturalists," whose search for specimens had them wandering the globe, wandering away, out of touch, out of mind, which, as we will see, would be exactly Geoffroy's complaint.[22] Perhaps Cuvier suspected, as Talleyrand himself may have with respect to Napoleon, that Geoffroy might never return to Paris, and if he did—time enough then to repair the friendship. Certainly, Cuvier (like Talleyrand with

Napoleon) left Geoffroy for dead, cutting him off with scarcely a word, until he knew for certain Geoffroy would return.[23]

The crisis that ensued for Geoffroy unfolded in the letters he wrote from Egypt. Reading these, we feel his abandonment—by Cuvier, by the scientific establishment, by history itself after 1799 (when Napoleon returned to Paris for the coup d'état). As we peer into Geoffroy's confusion, we see once again how the "moral self" in this era was shaped against the rasping problem of ambition—Cuvier's, Napoleon's explicitly, too, and his own. Other themes too reemerge in this, the close to our story. The trauma of violence and the piecing together of connections with others as a means of connecting with oneself are found in Geoffroy's letters. Do we also find in Geoffroy's experience the matrix for our own everyday solutions to the problem of self-assertion, a bildungsroman of our own maturity as we chart his transition from complacency to the various moral accommodations to competitive individualism we all must make?

Arguments from Egypt

Separation was on Geoffroy's mind from the moment his journey began. On April 29 he wrote to Cuvier from Lyons, after a hurried journey from Paris, during which they had stopped only to eat. Lyons was the first pause, and just for a day. Geoffroy took the opportunity to write: "I have just written to my father, my dear friend, my second letter will be for friendship." "I have left everything behind. Friendship alone, the memory of which will never leave me, causes me any regret!"[24] From the *Alceste,* which he boarded at Toulon, he said good-bye: "Good-bye, dear friend, I am at the point of losing sight of land. I have only the time to give you my love and commend my interests to you."[25] And again, several days later, "Adieu, mon cher ami." For eighteen months more he would still be saying good-bye. On the eve of a perilous trip to Upper Egypt, where the Commission of Sciences and Arts would explore the tombs of Thebes and other attractions, and on which Geoffroy, already sick, dreaded to commence, he said "adieu" for what he thought might be the final time, in his twelfth extant letter to Cuvier: "I am not without hope of seeing you again. I am about to undertake a very difficult journey in order to be worthy of returning to your society in a manner deserving of you."[26] And in November, several months after Napoleon had slipped back to France, leaving the army and the Institut d'Egypte to face the implications of his defeat, Geoffroy again said good-bye: "I am resigned to sharing the fate of the army; either the savants and the artists will remain with the army buried in the sands of Arabia, according to the apt phrase of one of your orators, or, better yet, they will regain France with it, thanks to the kind indulgence of our enemies."[27]

Geoffroy had left Paris behind, but until late 1799 he insisted on the continuity of his experience. Life abroad was like life at home. "I am in good health and I have such an appearance of well-being that Defalgo would convince me that I am still at the Museum of Natural History and that I have by no means subjected myself to a journey of 200 leagues," he wrote from Toulon.[28] From the *Alceste,* under sail for the first time: "So there, my dear friend, such is the company I keep. Could I feel any boredom at all, with men such as these? They treat me with infinite kindness: also, I repeat, I am just as comfortable here as at the Jardin des Plantes."[29] In August 1798, in Cairo after the Institut d'Egypte was established in the former palace of Qassim Bey, he explained how different Egypt seemed, how challenging it was to describe: "What experience I have gained! Such people, these Egyptians! All their customs and habits contrary to ours!" he gushed,[30] but he went on to explain how similar it all was: "The menagerie is beginning to fill up with animals. If I had our friends here, I would believe myself in France, as I find myself occupied by the same cares."[31]

Fearing to be dismissed as Geoffroy the Egyptian, as he jokingly worried in a letter to Cuvier from Cairo in August 1799—fearing to *be* Geoffroy the Egyptian perhaps, he also took pains to insist that he was virtually the same person abroad as in Paris.[32] "As for me," he wrote to Cuvier from the fleet—as if Cuvier would care—"transported to a sphere so foreign to my habits, the only surprise is not being surprised by everything I see. I live with sailors with the same sang-froid, the same calm, in the same good health that you knew me in

Paris."[33] In October 1798 he wrote to his "adoptive family," Jussieu and his colleagues at the Muséum, again asserting the invariability of his self: "The dangers, the fatigues, the deserts to cross, the Arabs to fight, have never astonished me. I am fortunate to have a character which allows me to stay calm in the midst of danger, to maintain the same sang-froid which I bring to the most insignificant things. It is to my character that I owe my health. It is that which gave me the courage to save myself from the sea when I fell overboard, four days before Malta," speaking for the first time of this near-fatal accident.[34]

Geoffroy was unperturbed, seamlessly and seemingly the same person, despite the novelty of the Egyptian campaign. The insistence on the constancy of his self places Geoffroy squarely within the post-Jacobin generation concerned to counter notions of the malleability of self, understood by 1798 to have empowered the radical Republic.[35] Though Geoffroy's environment might change, he would remain himself, so he would claim. That we are encountering in Geoffroy a post-Jacobin self is signaled by Geoffroy in that first letter to Cuvier from Lyons. Geoffroy—supporter of the Revolutionary project at least until 1792,[36] and beneficiary of the Revolution since 1793, when, in the reorganization of the Jardin des Plantes by the Convention, Geoffroy—trained in mineralogy—became professor of zoology[37]—he describes how he cried when he viewed the damage to the city wrought by the Terror in Lyons and pondered what the ruins implied: "My heart was torn apart at the spectacle of the *architecture of Robespierre*. I could not stop myself from crying at the misfortunes of this important city so horribly ravaged. Spread before one's eyes lie the hideous remains of a war sustained in order to satisfy the ambition of a few fanatics. Entire streets demolished, fragments of the most beautiful buildings scattered here and there, all its monuments destroyed, even to that famous clock, which was not spared and which hatred attacked."[38] One notes the association of ambition with the pernicious goals of the leaders of the radical Republic. We will see below how Napoleon too was openly criticized for the same "vice" after the debacle of the Syrian campaign and his opportunistic return to France.

The violence that would shadow Geoffroy through Egypt is prefig-
ured in his trip down the Rhône. Geoffroy traveled with a doctor named
Masclet. As young and enthusiastic as himself,[39] Geoffroy's friend
would die in Alexandria, as surgeon in chief of the army's hospital.
From nearby Rosetta in August 1798 Geoffroy wrote to his brother
Marc-Antoine (in Egypt, too, with the army corps of engineers) to
describe the Battle of the Nile, including the explosion of the flag ship
Orient, which he had witnessed, and the death of Dupetit-Thouars,
captain of the *Tonnant,* which was much discussed. "He died a hero.
A cannonball ripped off his two legs. Refusing all help, he sat himself
down on the quarterdeck and commanded maneuvers until his life was
extinguished."[40] The *Courrier de l'Egypte* reported that while seated on
the quarterdeck as described, another shot tore off his arm; "he called
for a pipe, and after having smoked for some minutes, his soul exhaled
while crying, 'Crew of the *Tonnant,* never surrender.'"[41]

These macabre images were succeeded in 1799 by reports of
Napoleon's massacre of three thousand prisoners at Jaffa and the
poisoning of French soldiers, also at Jaffa, along with other depreda-
tions and attendant cruelties—war crimes, as David Bell has urged us
to judge them.[42] We know Geoffroy was aware of these, or whispers
of these. Three members of the commission had died at Acre. And
at the June session of the Institut d'Egypte that Napoleon attended
before abandoning the army in Egypt, he was attacked by René-Nicolas
Desgenettes, chief medical officer of the army, for attempting to cover
up his crimes.[43] Excluded from a committee to report on the plague,
"Desgenettes leapt to his feet and, 'with a vehemence that astounded
the numerous audience,' spoke his mind. His crime, he declared, was
to have refused to give poison to the plague victims at Jaffa. And there
were other things which the General, in his contempt of all principles
of morality, had omitted to mention."[44]

Was Geoffroy a witness to the impaling of Soliman of Aleppo,
the assassin of Kléber, Napoleon's reluctant successor in Egypt?
Christopher Herold places the Commission of Sciences and Arts at
the funeral of Kléber, attending his coffin to his burial, the procession

in a party to the execution: "The procession halted, and the coffin was put down, on the hill where Soliman and his accomplices were awaiting execution. An artillery salvo gave the signal for that part of the ceremony to begin." First the executioner beheaded the accomplices, then Soliman's hand was forced into red-hot coals. Finally, Soliman was impaled. Herold refused to describe the "surgical details" of the operation that would have been observed by the crowd: "When [the executioner] had completed the preliminary part of the operation, the pole with Soliman on it was set upright and planted in the ground. . . . The funeral procession resumed its march, leaving the impaled Soliman to pray to God."[45]

Geoffroy's first encounter with revolutionary violence had triggered a breakdown.[46] We saw above how Cuvier credited Geoffroy with saving Haüy's life by arranging his release from jail on the eve of the September Massacres. Théophile Cahn explains how Geoffroy returned to the prison of Saint-Firmin, where more of his former teachers from the Collège de Navarre and the Collège du Cardinal-Lemoine were detained as nonjuring priests. In the midst of the tumult of September 2—the tocsin had sounded, the crowds had formed—he entered the prison with the aim of shepherding his teachers to safety. Faced with their refusal to leave—the priests feared their escape would lead to reprisals on those remaining—he devised an even more dangerous plan. "Pointing out to them a wall which would be easy to climb over," "Geoffroy spent the night of September 2–3 on the other side helping a dozen or so priests to escape": "Two days after the September Massacres, he returned to Etampes and his family. The emotions of the previous days were too strong for his constitution. He fell sick and was not able to return to Paris until the end of 1792," in the rather old-fashioned words of Cahn.[47]

Less well known is the episode that capped his experience of Egypt. Sometimes explained as a celebration of his powers of concentration, how else to read it today but as a manic response to violence and the stress of war? This is the siege of Alexandria, which led to the final defeat of the French, as Geoffroy describes it retrospectively:

It was possible to distract myself from all the brouhaha of the siege, and to subordinate all the military events, the bombs, the local fires, the surprises of the besiegers and the plaintive cries of the victims succumbing in the fight, to the examination of my problems in natural philosophy. . . . I was taken with a fever of work which lasted for three weeks up until the day of my embarkation. . . . It was necessary, in the short interval of three weeks, to pass through in my mind 64 times all my knowledge of science because of the 64 hypothetical formulas that I had to examine and compare. The phenomenal manifestations of my two fish had led me to pass beyond the circle of their consideration, to conclude from them the nature of nervous action, and from these examples of animal nature I passed to all the phenomena of the material world. Knowledge is so sweet when one has arrived at a series of deductions which appear to the mind with perfect lucidity.[48]

Indeed.

Why write to Cuvier? Not really to impart information about places seen. "I have nothing at present very remarkable to tell you about," he explained in that first letter from Lyons. "I will enter into details perhaps that you know more about than do I. That indulgence I refuse to grant because I do not write to instruct you but to render an account of the feelings that I have experienced in proportion to the distance that I have traveled from you, my excellent friend, and from the establishment that assured my happiness, from well-loved colleagues, and from family and very dear friends."[49] Geoffroy would make the same point in letters to his colleagues. He would share his experience in the expectation that for them, as for him, the importance of the exchange lay in staying emotionally connected. Distance was physical only. His adventures would be theirs, too, or the image of his experiences would keep him alive in the minds of his former associates. On the shores of the Mediterranean, he explained his plan: "Arrived at Toulon and about to depart," he wrote to the Muséum d'Histoire naturelle. "I have the honor of giving you my news. I dare to hope from your friendship, citizens and dear colleagues, that you would not solely welcome information on natural history but that you will allow me to speak to you from time to time about myself and to inform you of that which happens to me which might be felicitous or not. I merit this complaisance if it is a claim on you to be tenderly attached to you and to assure you of an unbounded devotion."[50]

It seems a banal gesture of self-importance to those of us who live in a world of blogging, perhaps, and one example out of many of the impulses of the eighteenth-century expressive self, but the trouble that Geoffroy takes to explain his epistolary strategy suggests that he was shaping his self to another key theme of Thermidor. In 1798 Guillaume le Febure in *République fondée sur la nature physique et morale de l'homme* wrote about the "positive need to interact with others and to express oneself." "From the sociable, that is communicative, and active nature of humans, republican writers derived the notion of the self-creation of humans through their action in society," James Livesey has argued in commenting on this and related texts.[51]

Furthermore, Geoffroy's letters suggest that that self came alive through heroic adventure.[52] In 1798 Geoffroy imagined how friends at home might see him—"Citizen Geoffroy, naturalist, employed in the expedition to the Mediterranean and embarked on board the *Alceste*," as his letters were to be addressed—striking out with Napoleon on a famous journey east. "We left on 30 floréal: I do not doubt that the journals will have already carried this news to you," he wrote to Cuvier, in a type of self-presentation that would characterize his letters through the end of 1799.[53] Two years later he would be imagining himself in his life's leading role. To Marc-Antoine he suggested that his time in Egypt was but the prelude to the real story of his life, which—he was too hopeful here—would soon commence, with himself in the starring role: "I think that the two years I have spent in Egypt are only the preface to a beautiful novel in which I will play the leading part" (if he did not die first), a reorienting but also recentering of his experience after the disappointments of the expedition.[54]

Alas, Cuvier did not respond to Geoffroy's pleas to continue the relationship through letters. These appeals begin as early as the boarding of the *Alceste*. "You have not written to me; for this, I reproach you," he says for the first of many times, followed by the injunction, which also will be repeated, "Love me always, never stop thinking of me like a brother, keep me in the minds of our comrades, of my colleagues: make sure that I am not forgotten. I embrace you tenderly, I salute your father. Go and make new good-byes on my part to monsieurs Daubenton, to the Jussieu family, to cit[izen] Desfontaines, etc."[55] In August 1798, from the palace of the Institute in Cairo, Geoffroy wrote to "begin again the complaints that I have subjected you to in my last letters; I will not stop reproaching you for not yet having written to me." He understood, of course, that after the Battle of the Nile, getting letters through was difficult.[56] "Figure as I have," as he would say again and again, "that the English, now masters of the Mediterranean, will let pass perhaps only one-tenth of the avisos charged with carrying our letters, consequently, write to me much more often, and do not fear to repeat what you may have already written."[57] This Geoffroy did, as we know from duplicates in the archives. At least one early letter got through in good time to Cuvier. On October 20, 1798, a letter to Cuvier was given to "our comrade Norry," who, wounded and sent home, managed to escape the blockade and return to Paris.[58]

In March 1799 Geoffroy received a letter from his father with a few lines from Cuvier.[59] In January 1800, on the eve of his supposed departure (he would not be evacuated until September 1801) Geoffroy made bittersweet reference to those lines: "Fortunately, there were two lines from you: without these few words, I would not dare count on the continuation of your friendship. . . . Good-bye, my dear Cuvier, I have paid you often with long letters for the two lines I received from you."[60] Several months later, still in Egypt, Geoffroy ended another letter with the same reproach: "Good-bye, my dear friend, I embrace you with all my heart. Recall me to the memory of our colleagues, the *philomatiques* and the academicians; I still hold some resentment toward you, you have never written while my father has been able to get letters to me."[61] In early September 1801 a letter expressed "fresh sorrows for me, my dear Cuvier." A boat had escaped the blockade and arrived laden with news, except for Geoffroy: "Not one of my friends, not even you, have thought to send me your news. Is it because I have inundated you with my letters that I deserve never to hear from you?"[62] This same letter contained a pathetic injunction: "Remember that we are forgotten children. See to it that we are called home."[63]

The perfidy of Cuvier needs no special pleading,[64] though an older historiography dismissed its relevance. What strikes the reader today is Geoffroy's response to the wall of silence that his letters to Cuvier encountered. Geoffroy himself, in Cairo, early on recognized that his letters home were monologues, at least some of the time, and that "Cuvier" was merely a rubric for his own thoughts: "I would certainly give you, my good friend, other details of this type, if I knew they would reach you, but I am, to the contrary, convinced beforehand that you will not receive my letter, which explains the negligence of my style and the slight incentive I have to draw you into things."[65] As he explained in a letter to his father, writing home was a way of simulating a connection in the absence of certainty that a letter would be read, a "table-turning exercise" in which the ghost of home was raised and embraced: "How many times have I rushed to write to you, but have you received even one of the fifteen letters I have addressed to you? Will you receive this one? I doubt it, but the mere hope that you might do so makes me write to you with delight. To speak to you by letter is a way of communicating with you, it is a means of nourishing my mind with your memory, of fixing it on the dearest thing I have in the world."[66]

"Cuvier" and "father" were strong aide-mémoires, channels to a deeper Geoffroy. Cuvier was a "brother," a "friend": he was also already the most powerful of savant Paris. The Cuvier addressed in the letters spoke to Geoffroy's ambitions, his need for affirmation, which became more desperate as it was unmet by Cuvier. On board the *Alceste,* as an early example of unfulfilled demands on Cuvier, Geoffroy wrote asking Cuvier to make him a corresponding member of the Academy of Science. Geoffroy explained that he had been accorded officer status with the fleet—"he could eat at the captain's table and with the generals"—but his treatment was based on the assumption that he had just been elected to the Academy. A news report about a different Geoffroy, an older distant relation, had confused matters. Now Geoffroy wanted to have his cake and eat it too, so to speak, to maintain his officer status but have it backed up for real.[67] Need we explain that no response was forthcoming from Cuvier or Paris? It was not until 1807 that Geoffroy was made a full member of the Academy, twelve years after Cuvier.[68]

Also ignored were urgent requests to Cuvier and his colleagues at the Muséum d'Histoire naturelle for scientific literature to help Geoffroy with the studies of fish and other subjects, upon which he had begun to work. Here is an example addressed to the Muséum, which followed pleas to Cuvier made as early as his first letters from Toulon. "I asked you, my dear colleagues, . . . if you would be willing to make up for [my needs] at least by sending me some new books on the sciences: I especially indicated to you the last two volumes of Ichthyology by our colleague Lacépède and the comparative anatomy of citizen Cuvier."[69] Geoffroy would continue to beg for the latest journals and reference works up until his last moments in Alexandria, expressing frustration that without them, his work was stymied.

Cuvier's own success, by contrast, continued its upward arc. Its trajectory was much on Geoffroy's mind. In April 1800 Geoffroy received the news of Cuvier's entry into the Collège de France, and he offered his congratulations. He had already been addressing him as such. "I have already had the pleasure of congratulating you on your nomination to the Chair of Natural History at the Collège de France," he wrote, continuing, "apart from our own intimate connection, I have received this news with much satisfaction."[70] The balance of the letter contrasted Cuvier's dynamism with his own stasis, as he filled his time with boring and useless work.[71] It also contrasted Geoffroy's life at that point with what it once had been in partnership with Cuvier: "It is not often that the viscera of fish offer up any interesting facts to me and then, this [tedium] has replaced that beautiful time of my life when we were busy together amassing new facts, and lived without even noticing the petty worries of society and the piddling passions of men."⁷² Here he is echoing the despair he expressed to Cuvier in 1799 after the departure of Napoleon: "I no longer remember without pain all that I have exchanged for my position now. I left true and good friends to throw myself into a society which has all the elements of a convent or which resembles that of a small provincial town. We watch each other in order to seize on each other's absurdities and to make them the object of our mockery."⁷³ In 1801, in Cairo, waiting for orders to depart for the coast, and eventually home, he wrote explicitly: "While I vegetate and sleep here, you are advancing the sciences."⁷⁴

At first Geoffroy wrote confidently to Cuvier. He seemed to expect that his words would impress Cuvier with his importance. Here I am on the ship, at the captain's table, supplied with fresh bread and pastries, he wrote from the fleet.⁷⁵ At Cairo, as the Institut d'Egypte was becoming established, he wrote to say that their institute was as important as Cuvier's, that the Egyptian institution had decided to send them its proceedings, and perhaps the Institut de France could be so kind as to do the same, savant to savant? "L'Institut d'Egypte is up and running: I assure you that our meetings are at least as inter-esting as those of the Institut de France. We have voted, on a motion of our colleague Bonaparte, to send to your Institute minutes of our meetings. Might you take toward us a similar measure and place us by this means au courant with the sciences developing in Europe?"⁷⁶ Note the reference to his "colleague" Bonaparte. Later still, in August 1799, Geoffroy suggested that he, himself, was as good as Cuvier. The tone is jocular but also insistent: "Prepare yourself to make the greatest sacrifice for me. I demand nothing less than the throne of anatomy. Should you hesitate, I reply thus: have you found in a single fish both the organization of quadrupeds and that of the cuttlefish? Have you explained the workings of the so admirable organs of the *Tetraodons*? No, you say, I have made other discoveries which merit me the first place. If that is so, accord me at least the second place."⁷⁷

No response. There was no response either to Geoffroy's triumphant description of other finds. One "no longer can say that Geoffroy is not a naturalist," he wrote after the discovery of those odd fish in

Upper Egypt and in the Red Sea.[78] "Oh! What a blow if I am still to be reproached for not being a naturalist because I have not traveled. That would be a great mistake! I am fully a naturalist on this score."[79] Can we read reports of Geoffroy's works as successive tactics taken to impress Cuvier, to appear as important in the virtual comparison Geoffroy set up? Perhaps now I will be worthy of you, he says repeatedly to Cuvier. In January 1800, after traveling to Suez, a journey as arduous as the one several months earlier to Thebes, but less promising of discoveries, he said about their friendship: "I have worked hard, however, in order to render myself more worthy by the privations that I have patiently suffered and by the research, so costly and tiresome, that I have done."[80] On the eve of his return to France in late September 1801, he wrote, "I hope to reenter France worthy of you and my illustrious colleagues. I have already obtained from you your love of work; I will renew myself in your company so as to gain all the other qualities still lacking in me."[81]

Formulas of politeness, perhaps—are not these phrases expressions of need, as well? The blankness of "Cuvier" suggests that the letters became a screen on which Geoffroy projected himself, first as boon companion to comrades in arms, next as pasha or bey ensconced in a palace served by slaves and directing the Institut d' Egypte.[82] Geoffroy's stature seems to have risen with his clamors for attention. After claiming status as the ranking anatomist (recall that Geoffroy's training was in mineralogy, and Cuvier was welcomed to the Muséum by Geoffroy because he could actually do the work of a zoologist), Geoffroy then proposed a grand theory of unity, potentially an explanation for how all forms of life are related, a theory that would, as we saw above, bring him into dramatic and public conflict with Cuvier, eventually exonerate him in the court of science, and reassure contemporaries—such as Goethe and French republicans—that all individuals form part of a cohesive whole.

Could Geoffroy have believed that his "discovery" of the unity of life would be welcomed in Paris? Toby Appel notes, "He seemed largely oblivious at first to the fact that such grand schemes were wholly out of favor with French physicists,"[83] though the letters to Cuvier from quarantine in Marseilles suggest that once back in France, he realized the need for damage control.[84] Isolated in Egypt, Geoffroy had drifted away from Cuvier's orbit, had escaped that normative regime we addressed in our earlier discussion of Cuvier's career. Of course, the villain of Geoffroy's story is ostensibly Napoleon. The "man of the century," as he was described by Geoffroy in a letter to his father as the expedition began, was understood in November 1799 (though word of the coup d'état had not reached Egypt) to have used the members of the Commission of Sciences and Arts to further his aims, to have embellished his life while fouling their own. In a letter to Cuvier that month he complained, "The poor savants of Cairo have been brought to Egypt in order that the history of Bonaparte records one line of glory more, and they are kept here so as not to read in Kléber's a single line of reproach." "Thus the small are always the playthings of the great," he added.[85] But his reproaches were all for Cuvier. The comparison of his life with Cuvier's would shape Geoffroy's self-image to its end. In the "Discours préliminaire" to his *Etudes progressives d'un naturaliste* he sketched a history of the Jardin des Plantes in seven stages, beginning with its founding by Gui de la Brosse. Stage 3 was led by Buffon, stage 5 by Cuvier; each of these was credited with expanding its scope. Stage 6 was led by Thiers, responsible for "its magnificence in buildings." Stage 7 (so he hoped) was just beginning. Who would be given credit for this next stage, when philosophy or theory would predominate? The text leaves no doubt that the name left blank in the table drawn by Geoffroy would be, if justice was served, his own.[86]

On the one hand, then, Geoffroy's need for recognition led to an ever-inflated self, one that floated him high above the restrictions of Cuvier. On the other, abandonment in Egypt led to a paring down of the self to its essentials, which, in the denouement of Geoffroy's adventures in Egypt, is exposed as his work itself, his collections, without which Geoffroy himself would not have survived. Geoffroy had recognized as early as November 1799 that the achievements of the Commission of Sciences and Arts would redeem the expedition: "Yes, my friend, it will happen that the work of the commission of arts will excuse in the eyes of posterity the levity with which our nation precipitated itself, so to speak, in the Orient. In deploring the fate of so many brave warriors who, after so many glorious exploits, have succumbed in Egypt, one will console oneself by the existence of a work as precious. The time will come when this same army, busy now with rubbing our faces in the dirt, will find honor in having looked upon us, and having been known by us."[87]

But it was the collections themselves, "the seeds, minerals, birds, butterflies [and] reptiles," in the derisive words of the French general who signed the capitulation, that steadied the thoughts of Geoffroy.[88] From 1799 onward his letters reveal him to be desperate to maintain his collections intact. He worried about the lack of packing fluid, the specimens' fragility. They were drying out, breaking apart. In Marseilles he had to beg for funds from Paris to ship them safely home. When the agreement between France and Britain established that the collections of the French scientists would go to London, Geoffroy protested. "If the collections were to go to England, Saint-Hilaire insisted, then he would go with them," as Maya Jasanoff has explained in her account of the expedition. Or he would burn them, " 'throw [them] into the Libyan sands, or . . . into the sea,' "[89] scatter and destroy them, much as he had earlier feared the commission itself would be "buried along with the army in the sands of Egypt."[90]

An act of heroism that succeeded in saving the work of the Commission of Sciences and Arts for France, with the exception of the Rosetta Stone and a dozen or so other major archeological finds, Geoffroy's gesture should be seen, as well, as a declaration of the kind of self he had discovered in Egypt during his more than three years of separation from Cuvier. In 1801 his work—*industrie*—in the terms of the age, was now inseparable from himself, and that *industrie* had a collectivist bent. It was on behalf of the entire group of savants that he spoke, and for their collections overall. It was also on behalf of France, faced off against Britain, that he launched his threats.[91] Patriotic, yes, but his defiance was also a defense of a type of self—citizen, if you will—whose worth was gauged on a scale of effort expended—"We spent three years conquering these treasures one by one, three years collecting them in every corner of Egypt, from Philae to Rosetta; each of them is associated with a peril surmounted, a monument etched and engraved in our memories."[92] It is this notion of the self, understood and known by its experience of useful production, that would come to stand against the self posed by Cuvier's accomplishments in administration, his seat on the Council of State, his control of the Academy of Science, and his direction of education in France.

Of course, Geoffroy's gesture had a careerist bent. It was his collections that, having finally arrived in Paris, generated a favorable report to the Muséum in his behalf in 1802, signed by Cuvier, Lacépède, and Lamarck and helped reintegrate Geoffroy into the life of the scientific community. Geoffroy maintained his friendship with Cuvier, at least superficially, expressing gratitude to Cuvier for letters Cuvier sent to him in quarantine at Marseilles. He continued to ask Cuvier for help.[93] Yet Geoffroy's understanding of work as an extension of the self—man as *Homo faber*, in an anticipation of Marx—and its collectivist aims was at odds with Cuvier's careerist profile. In the larger political battles of the 1830s, this view would help shape the republican as well as the scientific self.

Coda

Geoffroy's heroism also rests in contrast to Napoleon's behavior, at least as Geoffroy understood it in November 1799, and we might agree. Geoffroy was a serial hero; the endangered had always a claim on him. During the September Massacres, as we know, he saved his former teachers from the crowd. During the Terror, he hid the poet Jean-Antoine Roucher for a time in his rooms at the Jardin des Plantes, though Roucher, always on the move, was arrested and executed after returning to his home.[94] In 1808, on his way through the Spanish uprising to Portugal to supervise an exchange of collections with the Cabinet d'Ajuda in Lisbon, Geoffroy came to the aid of a Spanish woman hurt when her carriage overturned. Geoffroy gave her his carriage and continued on foot. Captured by Spanish partisans, he and his party would have been murdered had not the governor of the province recognized in Geoffroy his niece's savior (some accounts say his mother's)![95] Finally, in the Revolution of 1830, it was Geoffroy who protected the archbishop of Paris.

Napoleon's willingness to sacrifice others toward his own ends, or the needs of France, and the convenient collapse of the two identities, state and leader, are well established in that historiography that shares Germaine de Staël's skepticism about the character of Napoleon and a wariness about authoritarian states. Less well developed is an understanding of how ordinary people were drawn into identifying their own selves with that of Napoleon. David Bell opens a promising line of thought when he suggests in his cultural history of the Napoleonic Wars how Napoleon saw himself as a hero in a novel.[96] Could nineteenth-century people have "read" the exploits of Napoleon, as eighteenth-century people had begun to read novels, by intensely identifying with the major characters? Julien Sorel was swept away by reading the *Mémorial de Sainte-Hélène*. This practice might explain how the cult of Napoleon gained its appeal. As stories, poems, plays, and songs about Napoleon proliferated in the course of the century, so did access to this means of self-abnegation, which is one way to explain the presence of so many "Napoleons" in the asylums for the insane.[97] Could we go further and suggest that the benefits of substituting another's successes for one's own might help explain the sway of charisma? Few people today lose themselves entirely in fantasies of Napoleon, but more than thirty years after the murder of John Lennon—killed because how could there be two of them?—we might ponder how distinctively modern a phenomenon this escape from ambition is.

Napoleon denied that he was ambitious. When charged with that crime, he demurred: "His only concern throughout his career had been to promote the 'empire of reason,'" he explained in the *Mémorial de Sainte Hélène*.[98] As Talleyrand pretended to believe when he introduced Napoleon to the Directory in late 1797, so would Napoleon continue to claim: "'No one can fail to see his profound disdain for splendour, for luxury, for display, those wretched ambitions of ordinary souls. . . . Far from fearing his ambition, I believe that one day we shall perhaps have to beg him to return from the comforts of a studious retirement. All France will be free; perhaps he can never be. Such is his destiny.' " [99] Furthermore, fantasy identifications with Napoleon, like Stendhal's, rue the fate that destroyed him. Napoleon's career ended in failure, he died in exile, his empire reduced to Longwood.[100] His was a tragedy, not a comedy; there is no happy ending on Sainte Hélène. As Napoleon himself had warned in 1791, "Ambition, like all disordered passions, is a violent and unthinking delirium. . . . Like a fire fed by a pitiless wind, it only burns out after consuming everything in its path."[101]

6

AMBITION IN POST-REVOLUTIONARY LIVES

The breakdown of corporatism in France that accelerated from the middle of the eighteenth century onward heralded the unprecedented possibilities for self-invention and achievement that have come to define the modern world. At the same time, it prompted a set of anxieties no less constitutive of the modern self. Jan Goldstein identifies the imagination as one of these flashpoints and "the problem for which psychology [in the nineteenth century, as she argues] furnished a solution."[1] This book, traveling the same revolutionary ground, has explored others. A self no longer contextualized through membership in the corporate order was liable to wander, to lose itself, to set itself loose from the institutions of the old regime—and to set society's moral compass spinning by flipping its orienting poles. This was the problem identified explicitly by the Parlement of Paris in its remonstrance against Turgot's "edict abolishing the guilds, [in] 1776." As its president famously complained, "Each artisan will regard himself as a solitary being, dependent on himself alone, and free to indulge all the flights of an often disordered imagination."[2] His final thought described the main concern: "All subordination will be destroyed."[3] Social control would be lost.

The Six Edicts, which destroyed the guild system, abolished the *corvée* (forced labor on roads in the countryside), and freed the trade in grain from government control, were soon revoked. Turgot was dismissed in the face of protests by artisans worried about their livelihood, peasants in the midst of dearth, and *parlementaires* speaking in behalf of the "liberties" of corporations threatened by monarchical despotism. In the event, as we know, in the summer of 1789 the Revolution itself demolished corporatism. Property was understood as one of the rights of man and of the citizen. Careers were opened to talents, religious vows were no longer binding, the family was contractual, and the self was something to make of itself, no longer legally inscribed within a group. In that new age were new men born, blissful in that dawn to be alive, especially those with cultural or economic capital.

The Revolutionary self was premised on a materialist philosophy of mind, even if only inchoately observed. As opposed to the dualism of Judeo-Christianity, reaffirmed by Descartes (albeit in a way that opened up the natural world to the investigative eye of reason), the self understood as a part of nature was formed by its senses and so was able to be transformed for good or for ill by its environment (for ill in the example of Frankenstein's monster, who was "born" good in Rousseau's terms—not burdened by original sin—but brutalized by the reaction of his creator and others to his ghoulish appearance).[4] Rousseau was the most influential of the Enlightenment sensationalists, the abbé Etienne Bonnot de Condillac the most theoretical. Second-generation sensationalists—the Idéologues, such as P.-J.-G. Cabanis and A.-L.-C. Destutt de Tracy—were folded into the power structure of the Directory and early Consulate.[5] The *écoles centrales*, where Stendhal was introduced to their ideas in the late 1790s,[6] taught sensationalist psychology through the course on general grammar at the same time that it was put into practice as pedagogy. The second class of the Institute of France, the Class of Moral and Political Sciences, was their domain, until abolished by Napoleon in 1803.[7]

The festivals of the Revolution as choreographed by David put sensationalist psychology in play toward cultivating Republican minds. The "sensory organs" of patriots were "deliberately bombarded to shape their intellects."[8] Notice how closely the proposed education reforms of Louis-Michel Le Peletier, the former noble and first Republican martyr, followed Rousseau's dictates for the education of Emile.[9] The

Republic would take the place of the tutor in guiding the child toward an education wrought by the senses after being removed from the influence of mother and home: " 'At five years of age, then, the fatherland receives the child from the hands of nature; at twelve it returns him to society. . . . In public institutions . . . the child belongs to us in the totality of its existence. The material, if I may so express myself, never leaves the mold. No external object intrudes to deform the shaping you give it. Prescribe a measure: its execution is certain. Imagine a good method: it is followed instantly. Create a useful conception: it is put into practice completely, continuously, and without effort.' " [10]

This "porosity," [11] this fluidity of self, was attacked by counterrevolutionary Catholics who reasserted the integrity and dominance of the soul. [12] In the aftermath of the Terror, others, too, were troubled by the incoherency of self that materialism implied. Subject to change with the prevailing political wind, self and society alike lacked a fixed end, were rudderless. Would the Revolution have no end? Goldstein places the ideas of Victor Cousin in this political frame. Cousin, like the Catholics, defended dualism against materialism by replacing the Catholic *âme* with the bourgeois *moi*. This bourgeois self was stable because it was a priori to and independent of its environment. It was self-directing and self-affirming. It was bourgeois and male because access to its voice took the work of reason and techniques—a " 'technology of the self' in Michel Foucault's sense"—that were taught in elite schools: the Ecole normale supérieure, the Paris Faculty of Letters, and, from 1832 on, the "entire lycée system of France." [13] It solved the problem of stability in another way, too. As Goldstein explains, though theoretically democratic and universal, in a "historical context" the Cousinian *moi* was "hierarchical" and "disciplinarian." [14] "In other words, Cousin and the Cousinian movement deployed the concept of the *moi* in a startlingly literal politics of selfhood. The *moi* became a marker, both objective and subjective, that distinguished the central players in early nineteenth-century French society from the peripheral ones, the rulers from the ruled." She concludes, "Even if the working class had a modest title to mental virility [in Cousin's view], the exclusion of both workers and women from the corridors of power was, in the Cousinian canon, a given. Or more accurately, it was a given for which Cousin had additionally supplied a psychological rationale."[15]

The problem of the wayward self is played out in the story lines, the plotlines of this book. Julien Sorel's prototype, Antoine Berthet, executed for attempted murder in 1828, was led astray by his imagination, as both the prosecution and defense spun his life. The son of a blacksmith who "created a brilliant future for himself in his imagination, much more glorious than would be due to his talents alone," exclaimed at his sentencing that it was "at the foot of the guillotine that it must end, this horrible dream which has so disrupted my youth!" As Julien sighs on the eve of his own execution, "In the old days . . . when I might have been so happy . . . a wild ambition would drag my soul off to imaginary countries."[16] Cuvier's *Eloges historiques* also speaks to this theme, as he denigrates those scientists who broke from the control of the Academy of Science and its empiricist bent by theorizing and imagining how the laws of nature were arranged. Recall the description of Michel Adanson. His massive classification of the world's flora and fauna (*L'ordre universel de la nature*) having been rejected by the Academy of Science, he withdrew to a "small isolated house in a distant neighborhood," where "the poor old man" was found "neglecting all the [necessities] of life," "bent before his fireplace, in the glimmer of a half-burned log, attempting with a feeble hand to trace out a few more words" of his magnum opus, hoping "that a new idea, like a sweet and good fairy, would alight upon his imagination."[17] What could be more ridiculous? is Cuvier's point, more self-destructive and useless? Imagination could lead scientists literally astray by drawing them off to actual far-off lands. There, isolated, separated from Paris, they would become even more susceptible to the dangers of imagination, as was the case of Adanson in Senegal, Richard in Brazil and French Guiana, and Geoffroy, as we have seen, in Egypt, bumped from Cuvier's orbit into an eccentric circuit of his own.

So, too, do associated worries about the coherence of the self in the face of novel possibilities for self-making run through the lives we have encountered in this book. Stendhal has Julien Sorel shipwrecked on an island of no return when his ambitious factitious personas evaporate.

Stendhal himself draws on remedies devised by British thinkers, especially, to counter the damage to the self that a certain understanding of materialism implied.[18] When he muses in the *Life of Henry Brulard* on his response to the execution of Louis XVI—"The reader will perhaps think me cruel, but such I was at the age of ten and such I am at fifty-two"—he makes reference to the role of memory in integrating the various selves that changing life experiences might be said to engender: "From this memory, so present to my gaze, I conclude that in 1793 . . . I was engaged in the pursuit of happiness exactly as I am today; in other, more common terms: my character was absolutely the same as today."[19] Does this not echo Mandeville's assertion in *The Fable of the Bees* that " 'The consciousness of a man of fifty, that he is the same man that did such a thing at twenty, and was once the boy that has such and such masters, depends wholly upon the memory, and can never be traced to the bottom.' "[20] We have also seen how vocation works to solve the problem of fragmentation for Stendhal by presuming a self independent of time and place, in this way like the Cousinian *moi* but especially akin to the romantic genius of Staël and the destiny of Cuvier. A priori to one's life experiences, one's vocation, genius, or destiny can be discovered, nurtured, favored, or expressed but never (in theory) adopted.

It is a second set of anxieties, however, that has claimed our attention in this book and for which romantic genius, secular vocation, and destiny provided the salve. The personalities and sensibilities of the thinkers we have encountered in this work were shaped by conflict, deep internal conflict, between their own powerful ambitions and the ethical concerns that materialism raised in the wash of traditional France. What are the limits of self-assertion in the absence or diminished strength of the corporate order, legitimated by God? By following Staël, Stendhal, Cuvier, and even Geoffroy as they construed answers to this question, we have seen how uneasily individualism sat with moral assumptions of the common good. Romantic genius, secular vocation, and post-mythic destiny spoke to the pursuit of happiness, to the entitlement offered to the self by the principles of the Enlightenment. But it is not to self-fulfillment alone that these constructions were addressed.

Gifts of God or of the gods, they leveraged individual achievement as contributions to a greater good. And how could it be otherwise, given the theologico-political context within which their aspirations arose?

As Daniel Roche argues in *France in the Enlightenment,* "The period [the old regime from the 1760s, when our period of inquiry begins] marked a shift [not so much from community to individualism but] from one concept of community to another: from a strong concept based on a society of customs and traditions, on the monarchy, and on religion, in which individual identities were entirely determined by the community, to a weak concept [of community] more fragmentary and utilitarian." "In the new conception the community may be external to the individual, but the individual still discovers himself in the community: This is what links the old way of looking at things to the new."[21] But what moral valence exists in a system bound together by the opportunities of capitalism, as Roche describes in a softly Marxist kind of way? And how does the individual "discover himself," become him- or herself, in this type of system based on competition and exchange between individuals, their commerce (in the multiple, generous meaning this term had in the eighteenth century), *le doux commerce* that underlay the Republic of Letters from its foundation in early modern humanism?

This is the major question of British moral philosophy. Its answer, that our associations are regulated by empathy—the quality of feeling what others are feeling to the extent that we check our harm to others and license our generosity—shapes an age of sensibility, a culture of tears, as well as movements to abolish the slave trade, and later cruelty to animals and the abuse of women and children. Staël would call this quality sympathy and offer it as a way out of the solipsism that to her mind Napoleon represented.[22] It marked her kind of genius from his. Voltaire cast the problem in a nakedly materialist frame by suggesting that humans have a kind of instinct for justice. Was there not a basic human sociability, akin to that of other social creatures like the bees? In his *Traité de métaphysique* he spoke of the natural laws by which all living things are governed: "He [God] did the same thing with man that he did with many other animals. He gave to bees a powerful instinct by virtue of which they work together and gain their sustenance, and he endowed man with certain inalienable feelings, and these are the bonds and first laws of society."[23] Here Voltaire is adapting Newton's assumptions to the social world. In Ernst Cassirer's transcription, "Should nature everywhere have aimed at unity, order, and complete regularity and have missed only in the case of its highest creation, man? Should nature rule the physical world according to general and inviolable laws, only to abandon the moral world to chance and whim?"[24]

But can we be so sure? This widely naturalist view of human morality, which is back in play today after its disastrous detour through racist social Darwinism, suggests what was at stake in understanding competition, in finding a place for the aspiring self as the traditional landscape eroded.[25] This is the basic subject of modern philosophy, of course, from Hobbes through Rousseau, and was broadcast in the Revolution on the broadest possible screen. Here the lens has been trained on individuals themselves. Genius, romantic genius especially, which was our first example, is the clearest view of the problem from this more intimate perspective. We can easily see how genius, "the genius," comes to play a significant role in enlightenment cultures. As individualism was the basic principle of the new regime, the super-individual—one able effortlessly to succeed where others might fail—would seem to represent that principle most completely, to be a luminous marker of cultural value. Transcending the limits of daily life, the romantic genius becomes not simply a super-individual but a supra-individual, not bound "by the ordinary rules," as Staël explains in *Corinne*. Torchbearer of the future, "precursor of future reason" (Holbach), the genius is touched by the supernatural, representing "divine inspiration in a secularized world," as Staël's understanding of enthusiasm as the breath of God makes clear.[26] So, too, is the genius generative, a Prometheus unbound. We might see the effects of "spilt religion" here, the spillage of a Catholic imaginary into an enlightened sensibility, the genius in the role of bourgeois saint, or martyr, or God himself, as in the case of Frankenstein.[27]

Is there not a more obviously social dimension of genius that this train of thought leaves behind, leaping as it does from bourgeois needs to heaven itself? Of course, pace Stendhal, who for a time believed that "education alone makes great men; consequently, one has only to want to do so to become a genius," Mozarts are more than the product of their environment.[28] Some talents are beyond the reach of history. Yet in the "Preliminary Discourse" to the *Encyclopédie,* d'Alembert invited readers to understand genius in its social context, as we have sought to do in this book. There (in Cassirer's gloss) "the essential advantage of the eighteenth century over the preceding era consists in the fact that it has brought forth more geniuses, more truly creative minds. Nature always remains the same; hence every age has great geniuses. But what can they achieve if they live in isolation and are left to their own thoughts?"[29] We hear Albertine Necker de Saussure here in her evaluation of Staël: a genius, of course, so a phenomenon of nature, but "at the same time, it is also true that a rare concourse of outside forces favored the early development of her mind."[30] Cuvier's critiques of Adanson and Claude-Louis Richard are more precise echoes of d'Alembert's point about the fate of those geniuses who are left in isolation. Can we follow Marx in the *Grundrisse*—substituting *genius* for *human* as a subset of the latter—and see the genius herself in radically social terms, as "not merely a gregarious animal, but one that can individuate itself only in the midst of society"?[31] This is the conundrum faced by Rousseau. "Having equated the virtuous, the natural, and the asocial," as Carol Blum shows, what to do about his need "to dazzle and to fascinate"? What to do about the need "to dazzle and to fascinate," if not, as did Diderot, as does the genius, as do those with vocations and the men of destiny, to construe those desires in "socially useful" terms?[32]

"For how really to reconcile the principle of community and the principle of individuality which are contradictory by definition?"[33] This study of attitudes toward ambition plucks at a related knot at the heart of the modern self. Romantic genius, secular vocation, and post-mythic destiny are all about the exertion of one's will on the world. The singular achievement, the unfolding of one's irrepressible self, speaks to an "exaltation of the will," as it were, but also to a profound passivity, as one is swept away by genius, as one discovers one's vocation in the face of other plans, as one's life turns toward one's destiny, often without one's knowing it (*à notre insu le destin nous conduit*)—in the words of Stendhal as well as Cuvier's biographers. One is willful but also will-less in the competition for post-Revolutionary rewards. This passivity allows for a nostalgic organicism, we have stressed, infusing if not cloaking ambition with communal purpose.

But it is also embedded in a deeper history of volition. Note that the problem of the will is central to Rousseau's *Social Contract,* that most influential statement of the goals of modern life. The general will, that part of each of us that tends toward the good, transcends particular wills, the passions of individuals, which, left to themselves, would lead the strong to dominate the weak. It is only within the social contract that both freedom and equality are assured, that one's humanity is assured. Pierre Rosanvallon places the will at the center of modern politics: "In the *Social Contract* democracy is the regime defined by the fact that it is uniquely founded on the human will." "This sacralization of the general will" defines the moral purpose of the Revolution. Post-Revolutionary liberalism, therefore, in reaction to the Terror, "called for a more modest politics that would take its distance from too ambitious an exercise of the will."[34] Thus, we find Doctrinaire elitism and the effaced self that Cuvier imagined in his memoirs and *éloges* following a destiny disconnected from history and its supposed histrionics.

The question of free will—in the face of an all powerful God, how could free will exist?—is a central problem of Christian ethics from Augustine through Calvin and into Kant (whose *Critique of Practical Reason* was published on the eve of the French Revolution, in 1788). Does the theological problem of the will spill over into the debate on the self and self-assertion that we have described? After all, the problem of Jansenism (Catholics whose reading of Augustine inclined them toward a belief in predestination)[35] could ignite the politics of the Regency and Louis XV's reign until midcentury. The fate of the Huguenots (French Calvinists), even after the Revocation of the Edict of Nantes in 1685, was in contention, as the Camisard revolt led to a regional civil war from 1702 until 1715, and the Calas Affair of 1761 became a cause célèbre, when Voltaire took up the defense of the condemned Protestant and his *Treatise on Toleration* (1763) helped define the terms of the Enlightenment.[36]

The problem of free will runs as an undercurrent through the debate on ambition: how free is the liberal will in the face of natural law, how free should it be with respect to moral laws, and, finally, how free does one want to be, with the responsibility for self-invention that freedom would entail? These questions seem to course through the life of Benjamin Constant, the champion of French liberalism and thus of the freedom of the individual (asserting " 'the peaceable enjoyment of private independence' "; " 'the triumph of individuality' ") who ironically yoked his life to Staël's.[37] While attempting to break with Staël and live openly with his wife, Charlotte (the relationship was kept secret from 1804 until 1808, as he continued to live with Staël, his wife kept waiting in one set of lodgings after another), Constant toyed with quietism. He considered joining the *Ames intérieures,* a sect his cousins in Lausanne belonged to; for a time he effaced his self even further in a set of beliefs that called for abdication of the will, renunciation of the world, passivity, and sweet release.[38] Did quietism appeal, if briefly, to Constant as another alternative to the heady freedom and responsibility that self-assertion would imply? Was Constant recoiling from the existential "nausea" later felt so fluently by Sartre and hinted at in *Adolphe* (1816; begun 1806), Constant's novel that exposed his complex feelings to Staël?

In any case, it is through their own ambitions that the subjects of this book are brought to consider the ethical questions posed by the postcorporate world. What does my ambition make of me in the changing moral universe brought to light by the Revolution and the First Empire? A sensibility that negotiates between the rights of the individual and the needs of the community is one response; a collapse of the second into the first is another. This sensibility, fluid but vigilant, is worked out in a dance between imagination and behavior, between imagining a way one can be and acting it out, in the temporizing realm of real life. When Staël had herself painted as Corinne, when Stendhal referred to us all as Juliens, the fourth wall of drama was breached.

Stories are a key to this imagining. Jerome Bruner and other psychologists have explained "self-making" as a "narrative art." "Selfhood itself seems a product of our own story making."[39] One plots a model for oneself, a meaning for the disparate details of life, connecting the dots between selective events to make a whole, to make one's self whole. We have seen this process at work in the lives in this book. Cuvier patterned the events of his early life to picture his destiny, and Stendhal discovered coherence, a coherent self, in the disparate episodes of his experiences in Grenoble and Paris. " 'Individuals who have lost the ability to construct narratives have lost their selves,' " as Geoffroy writing from Egypt might agree.[40]

Eighteenth-century thinkers thought along similar lines. The self was built from outside sensations, but how did this work of construction happen? Smith and others had argued that self-making—identity—went along with sociability. Jerrold Seigel explains that view in his own recent book on the self: "Through its identification with others [an individual] internalizes features of their character, and makes those features the elements of personal identity."[41] These models could be literary, or mythic, and multiple: "literary modes of self-formation that corresponded to Smith's theory assumed that an individual would form him or herself by drawing on and synthesizing a variety of experiences and exemplars," Seigel explains.[42] Condillac agreed with his British fellows, "maintain[ing] that what allowed human beings to have unique personalities was that each one copied a different assemblage of models, in the process putting together 'a different combination of traits and habits.' . . . Models were not merely to be imitated, but internalized."[43] Seigel's major argument about the self is brought to light in this analysis. Whereas Renaissance self-fashioning (as described by Stephen Greenblatt)[44] was based on a small number of exemplars, "and often only a single one," a "prince or courtier," and even earlier "a king, a saint," what "marks this complex as modern is the way that individuals who entered into it moved between differing real and imaginary situations, drawing on a range of exemplars and models."[45]

Thus, we have measured the importance of Corinne, Julien, and the fabled Cuvier. Constructs of the imagination, they have stood as models for generations of feminists, alienated intellectuals, and scientist-saints dedicated simply to the public good. Corinne shaped the understanding of "the exceptional woman" from her conception at least until the advent of new feminism in the late twentieth century. Julien's disdain for bourgeois hypocrisy appealed to both the left and the new right in Europe. Perhaps it still speaks to a salutary suspicion of self-satisfied virtue on the part of the rich. Cuvier's *Eloges historiques* was assigned in French schools until well into the twentieth century. Their argument about the disinterested role of the scientist has been shaken only somewhat by a historiography that has asserted—for Pasteur, for Watson and Crick, for other examples—worldly success as a primary goal.[46] "Master fictions" in Euro-American culture, to borrow again Paul Cohen's phrase, they were also animating fictions in the lives of their creators. When Staël is also Corinne, when Stendhal sees himself as Julien, when Cuvier imagines himself as a folktale hero, the identification is profound, deeply felt, and captive, a branding but also, as for us, experiments, essays in dialogue with other images of the self, some more pragmatic, whose congress speaks to our efforts to unite the disparate desires of postcorporate life.

NOTES

Chapter 1. The Aspiring Self in France from the Old Regime to the New

1. As Jay Smith explains, "The term assumed a favorable connotation only when context altered its usual meaning." Pierre Richelet, in his *Dictionnaire Français* (1679–80), explained that the word "is taken positively when accompanied by some favorable modifier. One says 'a noble ambition,' 'a glorious, ingenious ambition.'" Smith, *The Culture of Merit: Nobility, Royal Service, and the Making of Absolute Monarchy in France, 1600–1789* (Ann Arbor: University of Michigan Press, 1996), 44. See *Dictionnaire de l'Académie française,* 1st ed. (1694), s.v. "ambition"; *Dictionnaire de l'Académie française,* 4th ed. (1762), s.v. "ambition"; and *Dictionnaire de l'Académie française* (1798, 1835), s.v. "ambition." In 1798 and 1835, as in previous editions, we are told that *ambition* has a positive connotation only when modified or explained. In 1798 an example of a positive use of ambition reads: "My entire ambition is to be of service to you." In 1835 the example is: "My ambition is limited to the fulfillment of my duties." Unless otherwise indicated, translations from French-language sources are my own.

2. Saint-Simon is quoted by Norbert Elias in *The Court Society,* trans. E. Jephcott (New York: Pantheon, 1983), 128.

3. Quoted ibid., 129.

4. Ibid., 130.

5. Emmanuel Le Roy Ladurie, *Saint-Simon, ou Le systeme de la cour* (Paris: Fayard, 1997), 195.

6. Daniel Roche, *France in the Enlightenment,* trans. Arthur Goldhammer (Cambridge: Harvard University Press, 1998), 279.

7. Elias, *The Court Society,* 132.

8. Quoted by Daniel Gordon in *Citizens without Sovereignty: Equality and Sociability in French Thought, 1670–1789* (Princeton: Princeton University Press, 1994), 56.

9. Bossuet is quoted and Delamare summarized by Gordon in *Citizens without Sovereignty*, 57.

10. Albert Hirschman, *The Passions and the Interest: Political Arguments for Capitalism before Its Triumph* (Princeton: Princeton University Press, 1977), 14–15.

11. Ibid., 15.

12. Ibid., 9.

13. Ibid., 10.

14. Ibid.

15. Smith, *The Culture of Merit*, 44. Smith goes on to note that "Jonathan Dewald [in *Aristocratic Experience and the Origins of Modern Culture* (1993)] writes that nobles 'placed ambition at the center of their lives,' but by *ambition* he means simply the desire to do well, to make one's 'fortune' in life. This ambition nobles certainly had." *The Culture of Merit*, 44n113.

16. Ibid., 44.

17. Roche, *France in the Enlightenment*, 287.

18. John Shovlin, *The Political Economy of Virtue: Luxury, Patriotism, and the Origins of the French Revolution* (Ithaca: Cornell University Press, 2006), 8.

19. Montesquieu's *Esprit des lois* is quoted by Hirschman in *The Passions and the Interest*, 10. Hirschman makes reference here to the "idea of an 'Invisible Hand' . . . formulated in connection with the search for glory, rather than the desire for money, by Montesquieu."

20. Hirschman, *The Passions and the Interest*, 16.

21. Vico is quoted ibid., 17.

22. Keith Baker is quoted by Michael Kwass in "A Kingdom of Taxpayers: State Formation, Privilege, and Political Culture in Eighteenth-Century France," *Journal of Modern History* 70, no. 2 (June 1998): 335.

23. Shovlin, *The Political Economy of Virtue*, 11–12.

24. The "cult of great men" is the subject of Jean-Claude Bonnet's *Naissance du Panthéon: Essai sur le culte des grands hommes* (Paris: Fayard, 1998).

25. Marisa Linton, *The Politics of Virtue in Enlightenment France* (Houndmills, U.K.: Palgrave, 2001), 114. (Though she gives the year as 1759.)

26. David A. Bell, *The Cult of the Nation in France: Inventing Nationalism, 1680–1800* (Cambridge: Harvard University Press, 2001), 123.

27. Ibid., 126.

28. Keith Michael Baker, "Transformations of Classical Republicanism in Eighteenth-Century France," *Journal of Modern History* 73 (March 2001): 36. On the consumer revolution in France, see William H. Sewell Jr., "Fashion and the Rise of Capitalism in Eighteenth-Century France," *Past and Present* 206 (February 2010): 81–120 (esp. 114–20), and Michael Kwass, "Ordering the World of Goods:

Consumer Revolution and the Classification of Objects in Eighteenth-Century France," *Representations* 82 (Spring 2003): 87–116.

29. Shovlin, *The Political Economy of Virtue*, 5; Baker, "Transformations of Classical Republicanism," 36.

30. Baker, "Transformations of Classical Republicanism," 36.

31. Dena Goodman, *The Republic of Letters: A Cultural History of the French Enlightenment* (Ithaca: Cornell University Press, 1994), 97; Antoine Lilti, *Le monde des salons: Sociabilité et mondanité à Paris au XVIIIe siècle* (Paris: Fayard, 2005), 190.

32. Lilti, *Le monde des salons*, 175; Goodman, *The Republic of Letters*, 97.

33. Friendship is attracting interest as a historical subject. For instance, the Institut historique allemand de Paris, in collaboration with the Sorbonne and the Ecole des hautes études en sciences sociales (EHESS) held a graduate student conference, "Friendship: A Social and Political Relationship in France, 12th–19th Centuries," in the summer of 2011. Lilti offers a bibliography of gift giving and friendship in *Le monde des salons*, 453n76.

34. Ibid., 186, 175. Goodman suggests that salon society was organized along lines of friendship as a counter to court society. Goodman, *The Republic of Letters*, 3. Lilti's book is about how the salons were part of the power structure of the old regime and not apart or distinct from it, or in opposition to it.

35. Lilti, *Le monde des salons*, 182, 183, 175–76. Lilti (183) explains how Diderot was reproached by the Baron d'Holbach and Mme d'Epinay for not attending their salons frequently enough. He was reproached on the basis of friendship but also with respect to what they had done for him.

36. Lilti argues that the critique of the salons, or rather of the corruptions of *la mondanité*, on the part of Rousseau and others led to a convergence between personal and political experience: to assert independence from the salons, to become an independent writer, was of a piece with the developing discourse of patriotism. Ibid., 411.

37. Marie-Jean Hérault de Séchelles, *Théorie de l'ambition* (Paris: Bouquet, 1802), ii, iv–v. Marat, on the other hand, could never crack the code of civility, and, if not for the Revolution, he would have remained "un ambitieux ordinaire." See Bonnet, *Naissance du Panthéon*, 275. Robert Darnton's early essay "The High Enlightenment and the Low-Life of Literature in Pre-Revolutionary France," *Past and Present* 51 (May 1971): 81–115, explained how Marat and other frustrated ambitious writers and scientists carried their resentments into the Revolution.

38. Jean-Jacques Rousseau, *Discourse on the Origin of Inequality*, in *The First and Second Discourses*, ed. Roger D. Masters, trans. Roger D. Masters and Judith R. Masters (New York: St. Martin's Press, 1964), 174–75.

39. The liberalization of the economy proposed by Turgot included the conversion of the *corvée* (forced labor on the part of peasants to maintain the roads) to a tax on nobles as well as the abolition of guilds and the freeing of the domestic

grain trade from government control. One recognizes that Séguier was speaking in behalf of the nobility and their privileges against fiscal aggression on the part of the Crown. And the work of Michael Sonenscher has shown that the "corporations were relatively open institutions . . . in contradistinction to the claims made by the Physiocrats and Turgot in 1776." Séguier's argument is a self-serving, political statement but one with resonance in the culture. One believes he believed it. Sonenscher, *Work and Wages: Natural Law, Politics and the Eighteenth-Century French Trades* (Cambridge: Cambridge University Press, 1989), 107. Séguier is quoted by Emma Rothschild, *Economic Sentiments: Adam Smith, Condorcet, and the Enlightenment* (Cambridge: Harvard University Press, 2002), 23, and also by Jan Goldstein, *The Post-Revolutionary Self: Politics and Psyche in France, 1750–1850* (Cambridge: Harvard University Press, 2005), 39. The document is translated in full in Keith Baker, ed., *The Old Regime and the French Revolution,* vol. 7 of *University of Chicago Readings in Western Civilization* (Chicago: University of Chicago Press, 1987), 122–23.

40. Rousseau, *Discourse,* 173.

41. Denis Diderot and Jean le Rond d'Alembert, *Encyclopédie, ou, Dictionnaire raisonné des sciences, des arts et des métiers,* s.v. "ambition."

42. Ibid.

43. Ibid., s.v. "homme."

44. See Elisabeth Badinter's fine study of women and ambition in the old regime, *Emilie, Emilie: L'ambition féminine au XVIIIe siècle* (Paris: Flammarion, 1983), 9.

45. Francis Steegmuller, *A Woman, a Man, and the Two Kingdoms: The Story of Madame Epinay and the Abbé Galiani* (New York: Knopf, 1991), 37. Grimm is quoted ibid., 38.

46. Jerrold Seigel mentions the importance of secular vocation in *The Idea of the Self: Thought and Experience in Western Europe since the Seventeenth Century* (Cambridge: Cambridge University Press, 2005).

47. Also see Elisabeth Badinter on relationships among the philosophes in her *Les Passions intellectuelle,* vol. 2, *Exigence de dignité, 1751–1762* (Paris: Fayard, 2002).

48. Goodman, *The Republic of Letters,* 108. She describes the quarrel ibid., 182–232. Also see Steegmuller, *A Woman, a Man, and the Two Kingdoms.*

49. Galiani's belief in collaboration expressed itself in the form of his essay, shaped as a three-sided conversation meant to emulate conversation in an idealized Parisian salon. Goodman, *The Republic of Letters,* 190–92.

50. Ibid., 205.

51. Quoted ibid., 201.

52. Lilti, *Le monde des salons,* 413. Salons remained influential in the first part of the Revolution, during the constitutional monarchy, but the Revolution "accentuated the polarization of polite society" under way since 1788. Ibid., 401.

53. William M. Reddy, *The Invisible Code: Honor and Sentiment in Postrevolutionary France, 1814–1848* (Berkeley: University of California Press, 1997), xi.

54. Jean-Clément Martin, *Violence et révolution: Essai sur la naissance d'un mythe national* (Paris: Seuil, 2006), 227.

55. Robespierre is quoted by Baker in "Transformations of Classical Republicanism," 48.

56. Robespierre, "Report on the Principles of Political Morality (5 February 1794 [17 pluviôse, year II])" in Baker, *The Old Regime and the French Revolution*, 369, 374.

57. See Patrice Higonnet, *Goodness beyond Virtue: Jacobins during the French Revolution* (Cambridge: Harvard University Press, 1998).

58. This outcome would be encouraged by overhauls in education and inheritance law, and by frugal living. See ibid., 197, for frugal living. See also Jean-Pierre Gross, *Fair Shares for All: Jacobin Egalitarianism in Practice* (Cambridge: Cambridge University Press, 1997).

59. Robespierre, "Report on the Principles of Political Morality," 374, 370.

60. The importance of classical republicanism to Jacobinism is Baker's point in "Transformations of Classical Republicanism."

61. On the Festival of the Supreme Being, see Jacques-Louis David's instructions, "Ordre, marche et cérémonies de la fête de l'Etre Suprême, qui doit être célébrée le 20 prairial" (Paris: Lerouge & Berthelot, n.d. [1794]), and Jules Michelet, *Histoire de la Révolution française* (Paris: Gallimard, 1952), 2:868–71. Michelet explains that—to the satisfaction of Robespierre's enemies—the statue of wisdom was scorched and blackened from the flames. Marie-Hélène Huet describes the ceremony at the Tuileries basin that inaugurated the festival but does not mention "ambition" as one of the vices torched; she describes those vices as "idols of the past": Huet, *Mourning Glory: The Will of the French Revolution* (Philadelphia: University of Pennsylvania Press, 1997), 37. Other accounts of the festival focus more on its culminating ceremony at the constructed mountain on the Champs de Mars than on the events described here. These accounts include Mona Ozouf's *Festivals and the French Revolution*, trans. Alan Sheridan (Cambridge: Harvard University Press, 1988), and Dan Edelstein's *The Terror of Natural Right: Republicanism, the Cult of Nature, and the French Revolution* (Chicago: University of Chicago, 2009), 232–49.

62. Robespierre, "Discours sur les rapports des idées religieuses et morales avec les principes républicains," in Jean Poperen, ed., *Textes choisis* (Paris: Editions Sociales, 1958), 3:159 ("Le vice et la vertu font les destins de la terre: ce sont les deux génies opposes qui se la disputent"). Baker discusses a related section of the speech "mark[ing] the line between two kinds of egoism: 'one vile and cruel . . . the other generous and beneficent,'" in Baker, "Transformations of Classical Republicanism," 50.

63. Dan Edelstein argues that the Festival of the Supreme Being was meant to usher in "a republic in which laws were superfluous," though the "dream of a Republic of Nature [lay] in shambles" after Thermidor "and in any case may have remained on the level of fantasy," he qualifies. (Overall, Edelstein's book demonstrates the "privileged, authorizing function" of natural right during the course of the Revolution.) Edelstein, *The Terror of Natural Right*, 257, 263.

64. Theodore Zeldin, *France, 1848–1945: Ambition and Love* (Oxford: Oxford University Press, 1979). First published as the first of two sections of *France: 1848–1945* (Oxford: Oxford University Press, 1973).

65. These include David Landes, *The Unbound Prometheus* (Cambridge: Cambridge University Press, 1969), and François Crouzet, "French Economic Growth in the Nineteenth Century Reconsidered," *History* 59 (1974): 167–79.

66. See Bernard-Henri Lévy, "New-Look Bonaparte: Nicolas Sarkozy's Book Is Not Only a Political Platform but Also a Self-Portrait," review of Sarkozy's *Testimony: France in the Twenty-First Century*, in *New York Times Book Review*, July 22, 2007. He was described in these terms particularly during his office under Chirac, throughout the campaign, and in the first months of the presidency.

67. Jonas Frykman and Orvar Löfgren, *Culture-Builders: A Historical Anthropology of Middle-Class Life*, trans. Alan Croz (New Brunswick: Rutgers University Press, 1987). Also see Jane Nadel-Klein, *Fishing for Heritage: Modernity and Loss along the Scottish Coast* (New York: Berg, 2003). Reddy, however, describes how anthropologists have recently been writing about emotions in cultural life.

68. Thomas Dixon, "Why I Am Angry: The Return to Ancient Links between Reason and Emotion," review of Robert C. Solomon, *Not Passion's Slave: Emotions and Choice*, Solomon, ed., *Thinking about Feeling: Contemporary Philosophers on Emotions*, and Anthony Hatzimoysis, ed., *Philosophy and the Emotions*, in *Times Literary Supplement*, October 1, 2004. Also useful is Amélie Oksenberg Rorty, "Enough Already with 'Theories of the Emotions,'" in Solomon, *Thinking about Feeling*, 269–78.

69. In addition to works discussed in this chapter, see Gail Kern Paster, Katherine Rowe, and Mary Floyd-Wilson, eds., *Reading the Early Modern Passions: Essays in the Cultural History of Emotion* (Philadelphia: University of Pennsylvania Press, 2004). Also important are Daniel Wickberg's "What Is the History of Sensibilities? On Cultural Histories, Old and New," *American Historical Review* 112, no. 3 (June 2007): 661–85, and Sophia Rosenfeld's "Thinking about Feeling, 1789–1799," *French Historical Studies* 32, no. 4 (Fall 2009): 697–706.

70. Philip Fisher, *The Vehement Passions* (Princeton: Princeton University Press, 2002), 201.

71. Ibid., 7.

72. William M. Reddy, *The Navigation of Feeling: A Framework for the History of Emotions* (Cambridge: Cambridge University Press, 2001), 129.

73. D'Alembert is quoted ibid., 160, 146–210.

74. Ibid., 180, quoting Higonnet, *Goodness beyond Virtue;* emphasis added.

75. Ibid., 196–208.

76. How to maintain a sense of self in the shifting political winds of the Revolution and beyond is an implicit question of Pierre Serna's recent study of French political culture, *La République des girouettes: 1789–1815 . . . et au-delà: Une anomalie politique, la France de l'extrême centre* (Seyssel: Champ Vallon, 2005).

77. Reddy, *The Navigation of Feeling,* 203.

78. Michel Crouzet, *Stendhal, ou Monsieur Moi-Même* (Paris: Flammarion, 1990), 118: "Après Ulm, après Austerlitz . . . une immense gloire semble attendre tous ceux qui vont participer à la grande entreprise."

79. Isser Woloch, *Napoléon and His Collaborators: The Making of a Dictatorship* (New York: Norton, 2001), 103.

80. Reddy, *The Navigation of Feeling,* 202.

81. Charles Taylor, *Sources of the Self: The Making of Modern Identity* (Cambridge: Harvard University Press, 1989), 321.

82. As Patrice Higonnet has noted: "Guizot, a Protestant intellectual and Louis-Philippe's prime minister in the 1840s, had been attacked for urging his compatriots: 'Enrich yourselves by saving and work.' (*'Enrichissez vous par l'épargne et par le travail,'* which French anticapitalist critics had derided and reduced to a mere *'enrichissez-vous'*: 'Get rich!')." *Attendant Cruelties: Nation and Nationalism in American History* (New York: Other Press, 2007), 97.

83. Rothschild, *Economic Sentiments,* 218.

84. Adam Smith, Jules Simon, and Lucien-Anatole Prévost-Paradol are quoted by Pierre Larousse, *Le grand dictionnaire universel du XIXe siècle* (Paris: Larousse and Boyer, 1865–90), s.v. "ambition." Simon and Prévost-Paradol both used the term *un pays libre.* Prévost-Paradol was a journalist who wrote books on the separation of Church and State and parliamentary government. He entered politics during the liberal phase of the Second Empire. According to *La grande encyclopédie,* having been sent to Washington in 1870 as a diplomat, when he heard of the defeat of France by the Prussians, "he resolved to die. During the night of July 1870, he stood in front of a mirror and shot himself in the chest. He died soon afterwards." Société anonyme de la grande encyclopédie, *La grande encyclopédie,* 31 vols. (Paris: H. Lamirault, 1886–1902), s.v. "Prévost-Paradol."

85. Jean-Baptiste-Félix Descuret, *La médecine des passions; ou, Les passions considérées dans leurs rapports avec les maladies, les lois et la religion* (Paris: Bechet jeune and Labe, 1841), 579. The translation is Zeldin's, in *Ambition and Love,* 91.

86. Descuret, *La médecine des passions,* 579.

87. Jan Goldstein, *Console and Classify: The French Psychiatric Profession in the Nineteenth Century* (Cambridge: Cambridge University Press, 1987), 158–59. Goldstein is summarizing Esquirol. The phrase quoted is Goldstein's.

88. Descuret, *La médecine des passions,* 579.

89. Goldstein, *Console and Classify,* 159.

90. Ibid., 161–62. Descuret, *La medicine des passions,* 580.

91. Goldstein, *Console and Classify,* 161.

92. Honoré de Balzac, *Histoire de la grandeur et de la décadence de César Birotteau* (1823); Gustave Flaubert, *Madame Bovary* (1857); Emile Zola, *Le Docteur Pascal* (1893).

93. Higonnet, *Goodness beyond Virtue,* 294.

94. Alan Spitzer, *The French Generation of 1820* (Princeton: Princeton University Press, 1987).

95. James Chandler, *England in 1819: The Politics of Literary Culture and the Case of Romantic Historicism* (Chicago: University of Chicago Press, 1998).

96. Jo Burr Margadant, "Constructing Selves in Historical Perspective," in Margadant, ed., *The New Biography: Performing Femininity in Nineteenth-Century France* (Berkeley: University of California Press, 2000), 7.

97. Chandler, *England in 1819,* 176.

98. Marc Fumaroli, *Chateaubriand: Poésie et terreur* (Paris: Editions de Fallois, 2003), 38.

99. Ewa Lajer-Burcharth, *Necklines: The Art of Jacques-Louis David after the Terror* (New Haven: Yale University Press, 1999).

100. "Normative domain" is Chandler's term.

101. Tzvetan Todorov, *Benjamin Constant: La passion démocratique* (Paris: Hachette, 1997), 30. Note that Carla Hesse speaks of Staël, Sand, Colette, and Beauvoir as having "transformed their lives into works of art" in *The Other Enlightenment: How French Women Became Modern* (Princeton: Princeton University Press, 2001), 146.

102. Jonathan Shaw, "The Mysterious Mr. Shakespeare," *Harvard Magazine,* September–October 2004, 56. Stephen Greenblatt refers to the "mystery" he "set out to solve" through writing the biography *Will in the World: How Shakespeare Became Shakespeare* (New York: Norton, 2004). Shaw summarizes Greenblatt's project in the quoted sentence.

103. Stendhal is quoted by Dorinda Outram, *Georges Cuvier: Vocation, Science and Authority in Post-Revolutionary France* (Manchester, U.K.: Manchester University Press, 1984), 50. Outram cites Louis Royer, *Stendhal au Jardin du Roi: Lettres inédites à Sophie Duvaucel* (Grenoble: B. Arthaud, 1930), 62.

104. Woloch, *Napoléon and His Collaborators,* 148. Woloch describes *Ambition [Napoléon] and Gourmandise [Cambacérès] Contemplate Their Victims.* "It depicts Napoléon surveying smoldering buildings at his feet which are labeled Madrid, Moscow, and Vienna."

105. Ibid., 34.

Chapter 2. Genius, Madame de Staël, and the Soul of Prodigious Success

1. John Isbell, introduction to Madame de Staël, *Corinne, or Italy,* trans. and ed. Sylvia Raphael (New York: Oxford University Press, 1998), xv.

2. Ibid., xi.

3. Gretchen Rous Besser, *Germaine de Staël Revisited* (New York: Twayne, 1994), 77, 159n5.

4. Paul M. Cohen uses the phrase "master fiction" to describe Stendhal's *Le rouge et le noir* in *Freedom's Moment: An Essay on the French Idea of Liberty from Rousseau to Foucault* (Chicago: University of Chicago Press, 1997), 19. Madelyn Gutwirth speaks of Staël as heroic in the concluding pages of *Madame de Staël, Novelist: The Emergence of the Artist as Woman* (Urbana: University of Illinois Press, 1978), 308.

5. Karyna Szmurlo, introduction to Szmurlo, ed., *The Novel's Seductions: Staël's "Corinne" in Critical Inquiry* (Lewisburg, Pa.: Bucknell University Press, 1999), 21. Carla Hesse discusses the trajectory from Staël to Sand to Beauvoir in *The Other Enlightenment: How French Women Became Modern* (Princeton: Princeton University Press, 2001), esp. chap. 6.

6. Benjamin Constant's comments on Corinne and Staël are described by Simone Balayé, "Benjamin Constant, lecteur de *Corinne,*" in Balayé, *Madame de Staël: Ecrire, lutter, vivre* (Geneva: Droz, 1994), 268.

7. Gutwirth, *Madame de Staël, Novelist,* 259. "Strangers, friends, and Staël herself routinely called the author Corinne after 1807," according to Isbell, introduction to *Corinne, or Italy,* xv.

8. The other famous depiction is François Gérard's [*Madame de Staël as] Corinne on Cape Miseno* of 1822, commissioned and painted after Staël's death.

9. Albertine Necker de Saussure, "Notice sur le caractère et les écrits de Mme de Staël," in *Œuvres complètes de Mme la baronne de Staël publiées par son fils, précédées d'une notice sur le caractère et les écrits de Mme de Staël par Madame Necker de Saussure* (Paris: Treuttel et Würtz, 1820), viii.

10. Quoted by Ghislain de Diesbach, *Madame de Staël* (Paris: Perrin, 1983), 159.

11. Gutwirth, *Madame de Staël, Novelist,* 299.

12. This is Erich Bollman's comment about Staël's life in Juniper Hall. Staël was in England in early 1793. Quote is from ibid.

13. Staël, *Corinne ou l'Italie,* ed. Simone Balayé (Paris: Gallimard, 1985), 514.

14. They are preparing for his return to Britain. Ibid., 442.

15. Staël, *Ten Years of Exile,* trans. Avriel H. Goldberger (De Kalb: Northern Illinois University Press, 2000), 119.

16. Staël, *Corinne, or Italy,* 247.

17. Ibid., 255; emphasis in original.

18. Staël, *Ten Years of Exile*, 119.

19. Staël, *Corinne, or Italy*, 255. Chateaubriand spoke more poetically for the common point of view in a letter to Staël in 1810: "If, like you, I had a beautiful château on the shores of Lake Geneva, I would never leave it. Never would the public get from me a single line. I would direct as much energy toward getting myself forgotten as I have madly directed at getting myself known. And you, dear Madame, you are perhaps made unhappy from that which would bring me joy. Such is the human heart." Balayé is quoting Chateaubriand in Staël, *Dix années d'exil*, ed. Simone Balayé and Mariella Vianello Bonifacio (Paris: Fayard, 1996), 226n2.

20. Necker de Saussure, "Notice sur le caractère et les écrits de Mme de Staël," vii.

21. Ellen Moers, "Mme de Staël and the Woman of Genius," *American Scholar* 44 (Spring 1975): 225–41.

22. Isabelle Naginski, "Germaine de Staël among the Romantics," in Madelyn Gutwirth, Avriel Goldberger, and Karyna Szmurlo, eds., *Germaine de Staël: Crossing the Borders* (New Brunswick: Rutgers University Press, 1991), 180.

23. Madelyn Gutwirth, preface to *Germaine de Staël: Crossing the Borders*, xi.

24. Edouard Toulouse, *Enquête médico-psychologique sur la supériorité intellectuelle* (Paris: Flammarion, 1896), ix, x, 281. Lombroso linked genius to madness. He is better known, of course, for his studies of "born criminals."

25. Havelock Ellis, *A Study of British Genius* (Boston: Houghton Mifflin, 1926), 1, 9.

26. Sandra M. Gilbert, "The Lucky Few," review of Andrew Steptoe, ed., *Genius and the Mind: Studies of Creativity and Temperament*, in *Times Literary Supplement*, August 27, 1999.

27. Andrew Steptoe, "Mozart: Resilience under Stress," in Steptoe, ed., *Genius and the Mind: Studies of Creativity and Temperament* (Oxford: Oxford University Press, 1998), 143.

28. See Andrew Elfenbein on misogyny and genius. "Only men are significant enough for their deviance to be worth noticing. In the rare cases when female geniuses are acknowledged, they run the risk of being labeled as too masculine": Elfenbein, *Romantic Genius: The Prehistory of a Homosexual Role* (New York: Columbia University Press, 1999), 4.

29. Penelope Murray, *Genius: The History of an Idea* (Oxford: Basil Blackwell, 1989), 6.

30. Ibid., 5. David T. Lykken, "The Genetics of Genius," in Steptoe, *Genius and the Mind*, presents a different translation of the same passage, same sense, 35. Plutarch's Archimedes is also referred to by Steptoe in his essay on Vasari's *Lives* in *Genius and the Mind*, "Artistic Temperament in the Italian Renaissance: A Study of Giorgio Vasari's *Lives*," 255.

31. Elfenbein, *Romantic Genius,* 5. Darrin M. McMahon takes up exactly this question in his major new book, *Genius: A History,* forthcoming from Basic Books. The genius of the eighteenth century—divinely inspired, secular saint, born with the Enlightenment—was both "modern man" and "modern god."

32. Naginski describes *Corinne* as "one of the 'hinges' of French romanticism" (playing on Victor Hugo's definition of "the battle of Waterloo as . . . 'the hinge of the nineteenth century' "). Naginski, "Germaine de Staël among the Romantics," 181.

33. Charles Baudelaire, "The Albatross," in *The Flowers of Evil,* trans. James McGowan (New York: Oxford University Press, 1993), 17.

34. Staël, *Corinne, or Italy,* 72. "Fiction as philosophy" is discussed by Hesse in the chapter by that title in *The Other Enlightenment,* esp. 130–46.

35. Staël, *Corinne, or Italy,* 21.

36. Ibid., 22; emphasis in original.

37. Ibid., 23.

38. Ibid., 24.

39. Ibid., 247–48.

40. Ibid., 268.

41. Ibid., 246.

42. Ibid., 250.

43. Ibid., 246.

44. Ibid., 318.

45. Ibid., 311.

46. Ibid., 401.

47. Ibid., 396.

48. Ibid.

49. "Destiny has struck me," says Corinne. Ibid., 325.

50. On Beauvoir's view of Staël and on the importance of Corinne's "swan song," see Nancy K. Miller, "Politics, Feminism, and Patriarchy: Rereading *Corinne,*" in Gutworth et al., *Crossing the Borders,* 193.

51. Staël, *Considérations sur la Révolution française,* ed. Jacques Godechot (1983; repr., Paris: Tallandier, 2000), 28.

52. The conversion of livres to francs is given by Diesbach, *Madame de Staël,* 23.

53. Daniel Roche, *France in the Enlightenment,* trans. Arthur Goldhammer (Cambridge: Harvard University Press, 1998), 477; J. Christopher Herold, *Mistress to an Age: A Life of Madame de Staël* (1958; repr., New York: Harmony Books, 1979), 24.

54. Diesbach, *Madame de Staël,* 28–29.

55. Sainte-Beuve is quoted by Gutwirth, *Madame de Staël, Novelist,* 290.

56. Diesbach, *Madame de Staël,* 29.

57. Gutwirth, *Madame de Staël, Novelist,* 259.

58. Mme de Staël died July 14, 1817, and Jane Austen four days later, July 18.

59. Gutwirth, *Madame de Staël, Novelist,* 19. This remains a common strategy.

60. Gutwirth translates this as "Master Holy-Desk"; Gutwirth, *Madame de Staël, Novelist,* 39.

61. Bonnie G. Smith, "History and Genius: The Narcotic, Erotic, and Baroque Life of Germaine de Staël," *French Historical Studies* 19, no. 4 (1996): 1059–81. Diesbach, *Madame de Staël,* 11, quotes Talleyrand, Montesquiou, and Pozzo di Borgo to this effect. Talleyrand married Catherine Grand. Not a great conversationalist, she did have a style of sorts. David Lawday repeats the anecdote of the Comtesse Adèle de Boigne. Grand arrived at a dinner party in pre-Revolutionary Paris wearing only her "long and full" blond hair. David Lawday, *Napoleon's Master: A Life of Prince Talleyrand* (New York: St. Martin's Press, 2006), 101.

62. Quoted by Charles Taylor, *Sources of the Self: The Making of Modern Identity* (Cambridge: Harvard University Press, 1989), 349.

63. Gutwirth, introduction to Gutwirth et al., *Germaine de Staël: Crossing the Borders,* ix.

64. Diesbach, *Madame de Staël,* 31. Gutwirth, introduction to Gutwirth et al., *Germaine de Staël: Crossing the Borders,* ix–x.

65. Necker de Saussure, "Notice sur le caractère et les écrits de Mme de Staël," xxi. Albertine Necker de Saussure was the daughter of Horace-Bénédict de Saussure, the Genevan botanist and geologist who wrote *Voyages dans les Alpes.* Albertine married Jacques Necker, who was the son of Madame de Staël's uncle.

66. Diesbach, *Madame de Staël,* 31.

67. Necker de Saussure, "Notice sur le caractère et les écrits de Mme de Staël," xxii.

68. Ibid., xxi.

69. Ibid.

70. Ibid., xxvii. Necker de Saussure is quoted by Herold, though he does not credit her by name. Herold, *Mistress to an Age,* 29.

71. Necker de Saussure, "Notice sur le caractère et les écrits de Mme de Staël," xxi.

72. Diesbach, *Madame de Staël,* 40.

73. Ibid.

74. Suzanne Necker is quoted by Gutwirth, *Madame de Staël, Novelist,* 28–29.

75. Necker de Saussure, "Notice sur le caractère et les écrits de Mme de Staël," xxiii.

76. She was eleven years old at the time, according to Necker de Saussure. Quoted in Diesbach, *Madame de Staël,* 36.

77. Necker de Saussure, "Notice sur le caractère et les écrits de Mme de Staël," xxv–xxvii.

78. Ibid., xxii.

79. Quoted and remarked upon by Simone Balayé, *Madame de Staël: Lumières et liberté* (Paris: Klincksieck, 1979), 16.

80. Staël, *Corinne, or Italy*, 313.

81. Ibid., 307.

82. Others have also pointed this out.

83. Staël, *Corinne, or Italy*, 300.

84. *Encyclopédie, ou Dictionnaire raisonné des sciences, des arts et des métiers, par une société de gens de lettres*, s.v. "génie," quoted by Kineret S. Jaffe, "The Concept of Genius: Its Changing Role in Eighteenth-Century French Aesthetics," *Journal of the History of Ideas* 41, no. 4 (October–December 1980): 594.

85. Necker de Saussure, "Notice sur le caractère et les écrits de Mme de Staël," xxxiv.

86. Diesbach, *Madame de Staël*, 26.

87. Holbach is quoted by Taylor, *Sources of the Self*, 353.

88. *Encyclopédie*, s.v. "génie."

89. Condorcet is quoted by Gutwirth, *Madame de Staël, Novelist*, 22.

90. *Encyclopédie*, s.v. "génie."

91. Staël, *De l'influence des passions sur le bonheur des individus et des nations: Suivi de Réflexions sur le suicide* (Paris: Rivages, 2000), 74–75. Translation is from Staël, *A Treatise on the Influence of the Passions, upon the Happiness of Nations. Illustrated by Striking References to . . . the French Revolution* (London, 1798), 73.

92. Jean-Baptiste Du Bos is discussed by Jaffe in "Concept of Genius," 583–84.

93. See Jan Golinski's discussion of Du Bos and Montesquieu in Golinski, *British Weather and the Climate of the Enlightenment* (Chicago: University of Chicago Press, 2007), 173–84.

94. Staël, *Corinne, or Italy*, 294.

95. Ibid., 28.

96. Anon., "Of Genius" (1719), cited by Leo Braudy in *The Frenzy of Renown: Fame and Its History* (New York: Oxford University Press, 1986), 418.

97. Staël, *Corinne, or Italy*, 37.

98. Ibid., 387.

99. And Staël is Corinne, as we saw above. "Europe in its entirety" saw her this way, in the words of Jacques Godechot in his introduction to *Considérations sur la Révolution française*, 20.

100. Doris Y. Kadish argues in this fashion. Corinne "is presented . . . as an antithesis" to Napoleon: "She is a peace-loving ruler whose crown is gained for merit, not traditional privilege, whose glory is aesthetic, not military, whose freedom is gained through the powers of the mind and the pen rather than brute force and the sword. She stands as an alternative to Napoleon's absolutist aspirations to royalty and aristocracy as emperor." Kadish, "Narrating the French Revolution: The Example of *Corinne*," in Gutwirth et al., *Germaine de Staël: Crossing the Borders*, 119.

101. Staël, *Corinne, or Italy*, 11–12.

102. Oswald has seen her on two occasions at functions with his father, but "he had not paid much attention to her." Ibid., 306.

103. Ibid., 327.

104. Condorcet is quoted by Gutwirth, *Madame de Stael, Novelist*, 22.

105. Staël, *Corinne, or Italy*, 249.

106. Ibid.

107. Ibid., 248.

108. Ibid., 254.

109. Ibid., 247.

110. Balayé's argument is about liberty. "She joined in the battle men waged for the liberty that must become the goal of humanity's struggle today, the duty it must assume. There lies the greatness of Mme de Staël." See Simone Balayé, "Stael and Liberty: An Overview," in Gutwirth et al., *Germaine de Staël: Crossing the Borders*, 21.

111. This theme is also addressed by John Carson in *The Measure of Merit: Talents, Intelligence, and Inequality in the French and American Republics, 1750–1940* (Princeton: Princeton University Press, 2007).

112. Quoted in Jaffe, "Concept of Genius," 585; emphasis in original.

113. Ibid., 587, 588–89.

114. Jonathan Ree, "How High Am I?" review of Alain de Botton, *Status Anxiety*, in *Times Literary Supplement*, May 14, 2004.

115. Quoted in Jaffe, "Concept of Genius," 592.

116. Taylor, *Sources of the Self*, 375.

117. Ibid.

118. Staël, *Corinne, or Italy*, 247.

119. "Nature, which did not want to make two leaves alike, has made human souls even more diverse"; ibid., 111.

120. Isbell's words are: "Corinne must die . . . because the Revolution and liberty died, in a text haunted by the dead which actually says 'there is no France any longer' . . . just as Napoléon conquered Europe." Isbell, introduction to Staël, *Corinne, or Italy*, xiii.

121. Taylor, *Sources of the Self*, 335.

122. Barbara Taylor, "Too Much," review of Thomas Laqueur, *Solitary Sex: A Cultural History of Masturbation*, in *London Review of Books*, May 6, 2004, 23.

123. Isbell, introduction to Staël, *Corinne, or Italy*, xv.

124. This despite the efforts of her biographers to cast her so.

125. "I am . . . going to be the first of a new genus—I tremble at the attempt"; Mary Wollstonecraft to her sister Everina, 1787, quoted by Lyndall Gordon, *Vindication: A Life of Mary Wollstonecraft* (New York: HarperCollins, 1995), epigraph.

126. Godechot, introduction to *Considérations sur la Révolution française*, 20.

127. Diesbach, *Madame de Staël*, 87.

128. Staël is quoted by Maria Fairweather in *Madame de Staël* (New York: Carroll & Graf, 2005), 59.

129. "And he died a broken man in January 1806"; David G. Chandler, *Dictionary of Napoleonic Wars* (New York: Macmillan, 1979), s.v. "Pitt," 345.

130. "*Fallait-il accepter ma vie pour la tyranniser ainsi?*" Staël to Narbonne, October 14, 1793, quoted by Diesbach, *Madame de Staël*, 140.

131. Staël to Ribbing, January 8, 1795, quoted by Diesbach, *Madame de Staël*, 163.

132. Fairweather, *Madame de Staël*, 240.

133. On the gardening metaphor, see Diesbach, *Madame de Staël*, 445.

134. Gutwirth, *Madame de Staël, Novelist*, 78.

135. See Simone Balayé, "*Delphine*, roman des lumières: Pour une lecture politique," in Balayé, *Madame de Stael: Ecrire, lutter, vivre*, 194n32.

136. Balayé, "Chronologie de la vie de Madame de Staël," in Staël, *Dix années d'exil*, appendix, 538.

137. Quoted by Fairweather, *Madame de Staël*, 188.

138. Diesbach, *Madame de Staël*, 87.

139. Récamier is quoted by Fairweather in *Madame de Staël*, 261–62. Fairweather cites *Souvenirs et correspondance de Mme Récamier.*

140. Linda Colley, *Britons: Forging the Nation, 1707–1837* (New Haven: Yale University Press, 1992), 183.

141. Mary D. Sheriff uses the phrase *exceptional woman: The Exceptional Woman: Elisabeth Vigée-Lebrun and the Cultural Politics of Art* (Chicago: University of Chicago Press, 1996). Angelica Goodden discusses Vigée-Lebrun's "self-presentation" and the "myth of innateness" described in her memoirs in Goodden, *The Sweetness of Life: A Biography of Elisabeth Louise Vigée Le Brun* (London: André Deutsch, 1997), 322.

142. Quoted by Fairweather, *Madame de Staël*, 168. Diesbach describes the reunion of Bollman with Staël and Narbonne in *Madame de Staël*, 125.

143. Colley, *Britons*, 151.

144. Diesbach quotes from the *Mémoires* of Barras in *Madame de Staël*, 196.

145. Emmanuel de Las Cases, *Mémorial de Sainte Hélène* (1823; repr., Paris: Seuil, 1999), 1:353. Translation from Emmanuel de las Cases, *Mémorial de Sainte Hélène: Journal of the Private Life and Conversations of the Emperor Napoleon at Saint Helena* (Philadelphia: H. C. Carey and I. Lea and A. Small, 1823), 2:100–101.

146. Bourrienne's *Mémoires* are quoted by Fairweather, *Madame de Staël*, 238. See also Godochot, introduction to Staël, *Considérations sur la Révolution française*, 18n30.

147. Las Cases, *Mémorial de Sainte Hélène*, 1:353. Translation from *Mémorial de Sainte Hélène: Journal of the Private Life and Conversations of the Emperor Napoleon*, 2:101.

148. Fairweather, *Madame de Staël*, 238. The slur on Josephine is not Staël's, however. See Staël, *Dix années d'exil*, 47n1.

149. Godechot, introduction to *Considérations sur la Révolution française*, 18.

150. Ibid. Godechot is summarizing the specious conclusions of Paul Gautier in his 1902 *Mme de Staël et Napoléon*.

151. Las Cases, *Mémorial de Sainte Hélène*, 1:353.

152. Noted by the editors Balayé and Bonifacio in Staël, *Dix années d'exil*, 47n1.

153. Staël, *Ten Years of Exile*, 5; see Staël, *Dix années d'exil*, 49n4.

154. They were shaped as well as by the American Revolution and the example of English social life. Staël, *Dix années d'exil*, 45.

155. Staël, *Ten Years of Exile*, 3.

156. Ibid., 4.

157. Its English title is *Fingal*. It was faked by James Macpherson and published in the 1760s.

158. Staël, *Dix années d'exil*, 47n4.

159. On 18 Fructidor elected royalists were forced out of government to forestall the destruction of the Directory.

160. Staël, *Ten Years of Exile*, 14. As Philip G. Dwyer notes, the contrast between Napoleon and the Directory was driven by Napoleon's own representation of himself: "The image portrayed was that of a young, dynamic conqueror; a hero; a selfless benefactor who not only brought peace to Italy, but whose virtues were extolled and contrasted with the corruption associated with the Directory." Dwyer, "Napoleon and the Drive for Glory: Reflections on the Making of French Foreign Policy," in *Napoleon and Europe*, ed. Philip G. Dwyer (Harlow, U.K.: Longman, 2001), 128.

161. Staël, *Ten Years of Exile*, 107.

162. Staël, *Dix années d'exil*, 49n4.

163. That quiet street is in the 7th arrondissement, where Julien Sorel would fall from his horse while riding with Mathilde's brother.

164. Staël, *Dix années d'exil*, 49n5; *Ten Years of Exile*, 197n7.

165. Staël, *Ten Years of Exile*, 7.

166. Fairweather describes the meeting as having really happened, citing *Mémorial de Sainte Hélène* in *Madame de Staël*, 240. Other biographers are, correctly, more skeptical.

167. See Diesbach, *Madame de Staël*, 492, on La Harpe as an enemy of the Neckers.

168. Quoted by Godechot in his introduction to *Considérations sur la Révolution française*, 19.

169. Maurice Levaillant, *The Passionate Exiles: Madame de Staël and Madame Récamier*, trans. Malcolm Barnes (Freeport, N.Y.: Books for Libraries Press), 7. And we learn from Diesbach that Staël wrote to her Austrian lover, O'Donnell,

an angry note in 1809 saying that, thanks to him, she had become simply "une machine à conversation." Diesbach, *Madame de Staël,* 409.

170. Levaillant, *The Passionate Exiles,* 8.

171. Constant is quoted by Diesbach in *Madame de Staël,* 314.

172. Diesbach, *Madame de Staël,* 313.

173. This was Isabelle de Charrière's famous criticism of Staël; Levaillant, *The Passionate Exiles,* 7.

174. Margaret Higonnet, "Suicide as Self-Construction," in Gutwirth et al., *Germaine de Staël: Crossing the Borders,* 71.

175. Quoted by Naginski, "Germaine de Staël among the Romantics," 180.

176. Staël, *Ten Years of Exile,* 3.

177. Ibid.

178. Ibid., 5.

179. Ibid., 3.

180. Ibid.

181. Staël, *Germany* (New York: H. W. Derby, 1861), 1:178.

182. Ibid.

183. Staël, *Ten Years of Exile,* 27.

184. Ibid.

185. Ibid.

186. Ibid., 28.

187. Ibid., 5.

188. Quoted in Steven Englund, *Napoleon: A Political Life* (New York: Scribner, 2004), 227.

189. See ibid., 225.

190. See Isser Woloch, *Napoleon and His Collaborators: The Making of a Dictatorship* (New York: Norton, 2001), 99.

191. He was taken from Baden, a "theoretically independent German state . . . just across the Rhine from France." David Lawday, *Napoleon's Master: A Life of Prince Talleyrand* (New York: St. Martin's Press, 2006), 145.

192. His crime was publishing "Letter on the Blind."

193. This account of the event is taken from Englund, *Napoleon: A Political Life,* 225.

194. Staël, *Ten Years of Exile,* 83.

195. He would remain in that position until 1810.

196. Balayé in Staël, *Dix années d'exil,* 172n1. Antoine-Jacques-Claude-Joseph, comte Boulay de la Meurthe, was "one of the earliest, ablest, and most devoted collaborators of Bonaparte," according to Woloch, in *Napoleon and His Collaborators,* 40. Talleyrand's most recent biographer says Talleyrand said it. Others agree. Lawday, *Napoleon's Master,* 147.

197. Ronald Schechter makes this quip also in his review of Xavier Martin, *Human Nature and the French Revolution: From the Enlightenment to the Napoleonic Code,*

H-France Reviews, January 21, 2003, www.h-france.net/vol3reviews/vol3no2 schechter.pdf.

198. Staël, *Dix années d'exil,* 172n1. Balayé is quoting from *De l'Allemagne.*

199. Staël, *De l'Allemagne,* ed. Simone Balayé, 2 vols. (Paris: Garnier-Flammarion, 1968), 2:181.

200. Kurt Mueller-Vollmer, "An American National Literature," in Gutwirth et al., *Germaine de Staël: Crossing the Borders,* 155n52.

201. Staël is quoted ibid., 155. Mueller-Vollmer describes the influence of *On Germany* on transcendentalism.

202. Staël, *De l'Allemagne,* publiée d'après les manuscrits et les éditions originales avec des variantes, une intro., des notices et des notes par la comtesse Jean de Pange, avec le concours de Simone Balayé, 5 vols. (Paris: Hachette, 1958–60), 5:189, note for line 13; Staël's draft version "A" of *De l'Allemagne* is being discussed.

203. Quote is from Staël's draft version "A" of *De l'Allemagne,* ibid.

204. Quote is from ibid.

205. Quote is from ibid., note for line 1.

206. Quote is from ibid.

207. Ibid., 203. Note that *calculation* is a term from Hobbes.

208. Ibid., 204.

209. Ibid., 199.

210. Ibid., 187.

211. Ibid., 204.

212. Ibid., 199.

213. Ibid., 191.

214. John Isbell, introduction to Staël, *Corinne, or Italy,* xv.

215. Necker de Saussure, "Notice sur le caractère et les écrits de Mme de Staël," clxxxix.

216. Quoted by Balayé in "Madame de Staël et l'Europe Napoléonienne," in *Madame de Staël: Ecrire, lutter, vivre,* 159.

217. Staël, *Ten Years of Exile,* 19.

218. Ibid., 27. But note that the translators describe him incorrectly as the bishop of Flanders.

219. Paul Gautier, *Madame de Staël et Napoléon* (Paris: Plon-Nourrit, 1902); Henri Guillemin, *Madame de Staël et Napoléon; ou, Germaine et le Caïd ingrat* (Bienne: Editions du Panorama, 1966).

220. John Isbell is quoting Mme de Chastenay in Isbell, *Birth of European Romanticism: Truth and Propaganda in Staël's "De l'Allemagne," 1810–1813* (Cambridge: Cambridge University Press, 1994), 5.

221. Paul Bénichou, *The Consecration of the Writer, 1750–1830,* trans. Mark K. Jensen (Lincoln: University of Nebraska Press, 1999), 161n143.

222. Ibid., 161n144. On counterrevolutionary arguments against the Enlightenment, see Darrin M. McMahon, *Enemies of the Enlightenment: The French*

Counter-Enlightenment and the Making of Modernity (Oxford: Oxford University Press, 2001), 56–152.

223. If it is not irrelevant, it is at least bizarre. Smith writes: "My contention is that by today's standards de Staël was quite bizarre as a historian. Bluntly, drugs and the body were two of her chosen venues to historical truth." Bonnie G. Smith, "History and Genius: The Narcotic, Erotic, and Baroque Life of Germaine de Staël," *French Historical Studies* 19, no. 4 (1996): 1062.

224. Lady Caroline Lamb quipped that he was "mad, bad, and dangerous to know."

225. Irshad Manji, "Why Tolerate the Hate?" *New York Times,* August 9, 2005, op-ed.

226. Staël, *De l'Allemagne* (1968), 1:93.

227. Staël, *Ten Years of Exile,* 16.

228. Staël is quoted by Balayé in "Madame de Staël et l'Europe Napoléonienne," in her *Madame de Staël: Ecrire, lutter, vivre,* 168.

229. Staël, *De l'Allemagne* (1968), 1:100.

230. Ibid., 171.

231. Ibid., 96.

232. Balayé's comment and quote of Staël are in "Madame de Staël et l'Europe Napoléonienne," 160.

233. Staël, *De l'Allemagne* (1968), 1:141.

234. Ibid.

235. Ibid., 140.

236. Ibid., 55.

237. Reduced in number by Napoleon from more than three hundred to fewer than forty. See Alexander Grab, *Napoleon and the Transformation of Europe* (New York: Palgrave Macmillan, 2003), 90.

238. Staël, *De l'Allemagne* (1968), 1:55.

239. "Il a plus que personne l'esprit que tout le monde a." Ibid., 56.

240. Ibid., 170.

241. Isbell, *Birth of European Romanticism,* 21.

242. Staël, *De l'Allemagne* (1968), 1:86.

243. Isbell, *Birth of European Romanticism,* 21n17.

244. Staël, *De l'Allemagne,* ed. Pange and Balayé (1958–60), 211. On the Humboldts' close connections to the Groupe de Coppet, see ibid., 211n1.

245. Staël, *Corinne, or Italy,* 111, discussed above.

246. Heinrich von Kleist, "The Monk and the Condemned Man," in Philip B. Miller, ed., *An Abyss Deep Enough: Letters of Heinrich von Kleist, with a Selection of Essays and Anecdotes* (New York: Dutton, 1982), 260.

247. Balayé, introduction to *Dix années d'exil,* 13.

248. Balayé, *Madame de Staël: Lumières et liberté,* 243.

249. Balayé is quoting Staël, ibid., 169.

250. Naginski, "Germaine de Staël among the Romantics," 180: "Her fictions pinpoint precisely that lack of equilibrium in the heroines' lives, thereby laying bare their 'genius' and the absence of a social space where that talent can be expressed."

251. Simone Balayé, "Le Groupe de Coppet: Conscience d'une mission commune," in her *Madame de Staël: Ecrire, lutter, vivre*, 326, 326n11.

252. Staël is quoted by Balayé in her introduction to *Dix années d'exil*, 7n1.

253. Balayé, "Le Groupe de Coppet." in *Madame de Staël: Ecrire, lutter, vivre*, 323. The Groupe de Coppet began to attract the interest of scholars in the 1970s. See the "Colloques de Coppet," including Simone Balayé and Jean-Daniel Candaux, eds., *Le Groupe de Coppet: Actes et documents du deuxième Colloque de Coppet, 10–13 juillet 1974* (Geneva: Slatkine, 1977), and Kurt Kloocke, ed., *Le Groupe de Coppet et l'Europe, 1789–1830: Actes du cinquième Colloque de Coppet, 8–10 juillet 1993* (Lausanne: Institut Benjamin Constant, 1994).

254. Who joined and when is detailed in Balayé, "Le Groupe de Coppet," 324–25.

255. Jean Roussel, "L'ambiguïté des lumières à Coppet," in *Le Groupe de Coppet: Actes et documents*, 173.

256. Balayé, "Le Groupe de Coppet," 332.

257. Ibid., 333.

258. Sismondi is quoted by Roussel, "L'ambiguïté des lumières à Coppet," 173.

259. Quoted by Paul Delbouille in "Le Groupe de Coppet: Une appellation reconnue?" in *Le Groupe de Coppet: Actes et documents*, 27n3.

260. "Un refuge, surtout un carrefour"; "foyer européen d'opposition à Napoléon Ier": Roussel, "L'Ambiguïté des lumières à Coppet," in *Le Groupe de Coppet: Actes et documents*, 171; Balayé, introduction to *Dix années d'exil*, 8.

261. Diesbach, *Madame de Staël*, 541. Staël probably believed this, and it is the reason she did not leave him anything in her will.

262. On the meaning of *communautarisme*, see Craig S. Smith, "France Has an Underclass," *New York Times*, November 6, 2005, 3.

263. See Dena Goodman, "Difference: An Enlightenment Concept," in Keith Michael Baker and Peter Hanns Reill, eds., *What's Left of Enlightenment? A Postmodern Question* (Stanford: Stanford University Press, 2001), 130.

264. As we saw in Staël's own salons. See Steven Kale, *French Salons: High Society and Political Sociability from the Old Regime to the Revolution of 1848* (Baltimore: Johns Hopkins University Press, 2004). Antoine Lilti, *Le monde des salons: Sociabilité et mondanité à Paris au XVIIIe siècle* (Paris: Fayard, 2005), 401.

265. In a letter to Constant in October 1815, quoted by K. Steven Vincent in his review of Harold Mah, *Enlightenment Phantasies: Cultural Identity in France and Germany*, H-France Reviews, April 29, 2004, www.h-france.net/vol4reviews/vol4no46Vincent.pdf.

266. Diesbach, *Madame de Staël*, 469.

Chapter 3. Vocation, Stendhal, and the Art of Living Ethically

1. Michel Crouzet, "Notice sur *Le rouge et le noir*," in Stendahl, *Le rouge et le noir*, ed. Crouzet (Paris: Garnier-Flammarion, 1964), 27.

2. Crouzet is quoting from Gilbert Durand, *Le décor mythique de la Chartreuse de Parme* (Paris: J. Corti, 1961), in "Notice sur *Le rouge et le noir*," 27.

3. See Theodore Zeldin's discussion of Edouard Charton's *Guide pour le choix d'un état, ou, Dictionnaire des professions* (Paris: Librairie Vve Lenormant, 1842) and Paul Jacquemart's *Professions et métiers: Guide pratique pour le choix d'une carrière à l'usage des familles et de la jeunesse* (Paris: A. Colin, 1892) in Zeldin, *France, 1848–1945: Ambition and Love* (Oxford: Oxford University Press, 1979), 88–98. Jan Goldstein describes Charton's *Guide* as "a popular practical handbook on choosing a career." Goldstein, *Console and Classify: The French Psychiatric Profession in the Nineteenth Century* (Cambridge: Cambridge University Press, 1987), 13.

4. Stendhal, *The Red and the Black,* trans. Lloyd C. Parks (New York: New American Library, 1970), 450.

5. Ibid., 449.

6. Ibid., 33.

7. Ibid., 34.

8. Ibid.

9. Ibid., 75.

10. Ibid., 115.

11. Ibid., 88.

12. Ibid., 99.

13. Ibid., 33.

14. Ibid., 34.

15. Shoshana Felman, *La "folie" dans l'oeuvre romanesque de Stendhal* (Paris: J. Corti, 1971), 24, 26; emphasis in the original.

16. Stendhal, *The Red and the Black*, 449.

17. Etienne Esquirol, "Monomanie," in *Dictionaire des sciences médicales* (Paris: Panckoucke, 1819), 34:116.

18. Ibid.

19. Jules C. Alciatore, "Stendhal et Pinel," *Modern Philology* 45 (1947): 130–33. Alciatore also shows how Stendhal borrowed directly from Pinel both in *Histoire de la peinture en Italie* and in *Vie de Rossini* to describe the "*dangers du génie.*" He argues, however, that Stendhal suffered from melancholy. Alciatore does not mention monomania.

20. Esquirol, "Monomanie," 124.

21. Ibid., 125.

22. "Stifled ambition" and "little stories" are Goldstein's translation of Pinel's terms. Goldstein summarizes Pinel's case studies discussed here in *Console and Classify*, 80–84.

23. Discussed ibid., 90. See Philippe Pinel, *Traité médico-philosophique sur l'aliénation mentale, ou La manie* (1800; repr., Geneva: Editions Slatkine, 1980), 106–34.

24. Etienne Esquirol, *Des passions considérées comme causes, symptômes et moyens curatifs de l'aliénation mentale* (1805; repr., Paris: Librairie des Deux Mondes, 1980), 17.

25. Alciatore, "Stendhal et Pinel," 129.

26. Victor Del Litto, *La vie intellectuelle de Stendhal: Genèse et évolution de ses idées (1802–1821)* (Paris: Presses Universitaires de France, 1962), 287nn63, 65; 288.

27. Pinel, *Traité*, 237, 238.

28. Stendhal is quoted in Del Litto, *La vie intellectuelle de Stendhal*, 289.

29. Ibid., 288.

30. Quoted ibid., 279.

31. Stendhal is quoted ibid., 281.

32. Stendhal is quoted ibid., 289.

33. The phrase is Goldstein's, in *Console and Classify*, 88.

34. Pinel, *Traité*, 237–39.

35. Goldstein, *Console and Classify*, 84.

36. Ibid., 93.

37. Goldstein summarizes the case ibid., 83. My summary is from a reading of Pinel, *Traité*, 233–37; the quotation is on 236.

38. The three bells are "a well-known signal in French villages that, after the various morning chimes, announces that Mass is about to begin" (*The Red and the Black*, 451).

39. Henri Martineau, in his introduction to *Le rouge et le noir* (Paris: Garnier Frères, 1962), xxvii, notes that Julien wakes up from a "noctambulistic state" as soon as he shoots Mme de Rênal.

40. Donald M. Frame, "Afterword," in *The Red and the Black*, 532.

41. Stendhal, *The Red and the Black*, 452.

42. Stendhal, *Le Rouge et le noir*, ed. Crouzet, 448.

43. Stendhal, *The Red and the Black*, 452.

44. Ibid.; Stendhal, *Le Rouge et le noir*, ed. Crouzet, 448.

45. Stendhal, *The Red and the Black*, 454.

46. Ibid., 456.

47. Ibid., 457.

48. The phrase is James Chandler's in *England in 1819: The Politics of Literary Culture and the Case of Romantic Historicism* (Chicago: University of Chicago Press, 1998), 298.

49. Stendhal, *The Red and the Black*, 475–76.

50. Pierre-Georges Castex reproduces these reports in his edition of *Le rouge et le noir* (Paris: Garnier, 1973) in "Le dossier du roman," 650–726. The quotations are from pages 664 and 665. On Berthet, see also René Fonvieille, *Le véritable Julien Sorel* (Grenoble: Arthaud, 1971).

51. The trial was in December 1827 and the execution in early 1828. Castex, "Le dossier du roman," 650–74.

52. Castex quotes Mérimée's preface in his introduction to *Le rouge et le noir*, xliv.

53. Castex quotes *Le pirate* in "Le dossier du roman," 669. To speak of wounds is to take the metaphor literally, of course. It may better be translated as "a plague of our civilization" when speaking of Berthet's plight.

54. Berthet grew up in Brangues, a village in the Dauphiné. His trial was in Grenoble. Julien lived in the Franche-Comté; the fictional town of Verrières stands in for Dole, a small town on the river Doubs about halfway between Dijon and Besançon.

55. Castex quotes *Le pirate* in "Le dossier du roman," 670.

56. Castex quotes *La gazette des tribunaux* in "Le Dossier du roman," 650–51.

57. Castex quotes *La gazette des tribunaux*, ibid., 651.

58. The de Cordons were not on the level of the Parisian de la Moles, however. The marquis was a peer.

59. Castex quotes *La gazette des tribunaux* in "Le Dossier du roman," 652; emphasis in original.

60. Castex quotes *Le pirate* in "Le Dossier du roman," 669.

61. Quoted by Castex in his introduction to *Le rouge et le noir*, lxxiii. The translation is from *The Red and the Black*, 505.

62. Castex quotes *Le pirate* in "Le dossier du roman," 663.

63. Jan Goldstein, *The Post-Revolutionary Self: Politics and Psyche in France, 1750–1850* (Cambridge: Harvard University Press, 2005), 60.

64. Ibid., 60–61.

65. Ibid., 11.

66. Quoted ibid., 167. Castex explains that the idea for *The Red and the Black* came to Stendhal during the night of October 25–26, 1829, in Marseilles. He subtitled his work-in-progress (initially titled "Julien") "Chronicle of the Nineteenth Century" and added "Chronicle of 1830" as he completed the book in the summer of 1830 in Paris. Castex, introduction to *Le rouge et le noir*, vii, xviii–xix.

67. Stendhal, *The Red and the Black*, 450. Martineau notes with reference to comments in a review published in *La revue de Paris* in 1853 that if Julien had waited—"a few hours, a few days at most"—Mathilde's father would have come around to the situation and continued to support the marriage. Why not? He had already embraced Julien as a son-in-law, despite his background and behavior. Martineau, introduction to *Le rouge et le noir* (1962), xx.

68. Charton, *Guide pour le choix d'un état*, 517.

69. Michel Crouzet, *Stendhal, ou Monsieur Moi-Même* (Paris: Flammarion, 1990), 118.

70. Crouzet, "Notice sur *Le rouge et le noir*," 23.

71. Thomas de Quincey, "The Casuistry of Duelling," quoted in Chandler, *England in 1819*, 295, 298.

72. Mathilde bribes M. de Frilair, who controls the jury; *The Red and the Black*, 480.

73. Stendhal, *Le rouge et le noir*, ed. Crouzet, 476.

74. Quoted in Fernand Rude, *Stendhal et la pensée sociale de son temps*, *Histoire des mentalités*, ed. Robert Mandrou (Paris: Plon, 1967), 254.

75. Babou is quoted in Emile Talbot, *La critique stendhalienne de Balzac à Zola* (York, S.C.: French Literature Publications, 1979), 8.

76. Rude is summarizing the Soviet linguist Viktor Vinogradov in *Stendhal et la pensée sociale*, 256.

77. Stendhal began work on *Lamiel* in 1839 and continued working on it until his death. See T. W. Earp, introduction to *Lamiel*, trans. T. W. Earp (New York: New Directions, 1952), 10–11.

78. Naomi Schor, *Breaking the Chain: Women, Theory, and French Realist Fiction* (New York: Columbia University Press, 1985), 142.

79. Eugen Weber, *Action Française: Royalism and Reaction in Twentieth-Century France* (Stanford: Stanford University Press, 1962), 81, 80.

80. Rude quotes Vinogradov in *Stendhal et la pensée sociale*, 256.

81. Rude, *Stendhal et la pensée sociale*, 256.

82. Rude is quoting and describing Gorki ibid., 255, 254.

83. Rude is summarizing Vinogradov ibid., 257.

84. Ibid.

85. Castex quotes *Le pirate* in "Le dossier du roman," 674.

86. Sorel is "rich." He sells land to Rênal at an exorbitant price. He is a much better bargainer in all things. See *The Red and the Black*, 26, 15. Note that William H. Sewell in *Structure and Mobility: The Men and Women of Marseille, 1820–1870* (Cambridge: Cambridge University Press, 1985), 249, explains that in Marseille "the most remarkable example of upward mobility actually came from *outside* this urban occupational hierarchy. In all the periods for which information has been recorded, sons of peasants had considerably higher rates of mobility into the bourgeoisie than workers' sons." Emphasis in original.

87. Perry Anderson, "Union Sucrée," *London Review of Books*, September 23, 2004, 11.

88. "La prison heureuse" is Stendhal's celebrated phrase. See Crouzet, "Notice sur *Le rouge et le noir*," 28.

89. Goldstein, *Console and Classify*, 161–62.

90. The figure is from Stendhal, *The Life of Henry Brulard*, trans. John Sturrock (New York: New York Review of Books, 2002), 317. See also the illustration on page 155. I am translating Stendhal, *Vie de Henry Brulard*, in *Oeuvres intimes*, ed. V. Del Litto (Paris: Gallimard, 1982), 2:813.

91. Victor Del Litto, "Notes et variantes," in Stendhal, *Vie de Henry Brulard,* 1408, in note 1 referring to p. 671.

92. Stendhal, *Vie de Henry Brulard,* 699.

93. Victor Brombert, introduction to *Stendhal: A Collection of Critical Essays,* ed. Brombert (Englewood Cliffs, N.J.: Prentice-Hall, 1962), 1.

94. He was, however, concerned already in 1789 by the Revolutionary "energy" of those deputies beholden to him. Stendhal, *The Life of Henry Brulard,* 57, 59.

95. Ibid., 633, 634.

96. Stendhal, *Napoléon: Vie de Napoléon, Mémoires sur Napoléon,* ed. Catherine Mariette (Paris: Stock, 1998), 257, 258.

97. Brombert, introduction to *Stendhal,* 1. On the cohort coming of age in the Restoration's first decade, see Alan Spitzer, *The French Generation of 1820* (Princeton: Princeton University Press, 1987), 3, 3–34.

98. Jean Starobinski suggests Stendhal played with some one hundred aliases. Starobinski, "Truth in Masquerade," in Brombert, *Stendhal,* 114. Brombert in his introduction (7) makes reference to Starobinski's points: the "only method whereby Stendhal's heroes can discover themselves is by 'trying themselves out' in an almost histrionic sense."

99. These professions were very visible and prestigious at the time.

100. "*Par protection et piston*": Crouzet, *Stendhal, ou Monsieur Moi-Même,* 76.

101. This was in 1806; Victor Del Litto, *La vie de Stendhal* (Paris: Editions du Sud, 1965), 113.

102. This is the first sentence of chapter 2 of *Henry Brulard.* According to Jonathan Keates, a "*commissaire des guerres* [was] a type of military bureaucrat whose job was to obtain provisions and supplies for the army." An *auditeur de Conseil d'Etat* was "attached to each councillor in a secretarial capacity. Being an auditor opened the way to a variety of influential administrative posts, including prefectures of the departments and, eventually, membership of the council itself." An *inspecteur du Mobilier et des Bâtiments de la Couronne* would approve "the bills presented to the court by cabinet-makers and upholsterers" and the like. Keates, *Stendhal* (New York: Carroll & Graf, 1994), 96, 117–18, 124.

103. Del Litto, *La vie intellectuelle de Stendhal,* 97.

104. Ibid., 103.

105. Ibid.

106. Casimir Périer's role in the July Monarchy is well known. Stendhal referred to Crozet as an "engineer-in-chief in Grenoble" and Edouard Mounier as a "peer of France" in 1835. *The Life of Henry Brulard,* 442, 67.

107. Crouzet, *Stendhal, ou Monsieur Moi-Même,* 17; Del Litto, *La vie de Stendhal,* 11. Simon Schama and others have given positive descriptions of eighteenth-century Grenoble, however. Schama, *Citizens: A Chronicle of the French Revolution* (New York: Knopf, 1989), 272–74.

108. Stendhal, *The Life of Henry Brulard,* 22.

109. Crouzet, *Stendhal, ou Monsieur Moi-Même*, 19.

110. Ibid.

111. Ibid. David Bell describes a *procureur* as "the equivalent of a modern English solicitor." An *avocat* was a barrister. David Bell, *Lawyers and Citizens: The Making of a Political Elite in Old Regime France* (New York: Oxford University Press, 1994), 30.

112. Stendhal explains in *Henry Brulard* that after the death of his mother, his father had contemplated taking Holy Orders, but he was restrained in this desire. Stendhal, *Vie de Henry Brulard*, 596. Richard L. Kagan discusses mobility within the legal professions of eighteenth-century France and describes "a high degree of continuity of vocation and career among families involved in the practice of law" in "Law Students and Legal Careers in Eighteenth-Century France," *Past and Present* 68 (August 1975): 58.

113. Stendhal, *The Life of Henry Brulard*, 78.

114. Crouzet, *Stendhal, ou Monsieur Moi-Même*, 19. Del Litto explains that membership in the *consistoire*, or assembly of forty *avocats* in charge of the order of *avocats*, came with personal nobility. Del Litto, "Notes et variantes," 1375n1.

115. Stendhal, *The Life of Henry Brulard*, 81, 82.

116. Crouzet, *Stendhal, ou Monsieur Moi-Même*, 26.

117. Stendhal, *Life of Henry Brulard*, 195.

118. "Quelle passion des *marchés:* ce sera le trait capital": Crouzet, *Stendhal, ou Monsieur Moi-Même*, 19. See the opening pages of *The Red and the Black* on Rênal's mania for buying land.

119. Stendhal, *Vie de Henry Brulard*, 596. Stendhal repeats this complaint some pages later. He was loved as the one who would carry on the family name, "but not at all as a son" ("mais nullement comme fils"); ibid., 606.

120. Quoted in Crouzet, *Stendhal, ou Monsieur Moi-Même*, 41.

121. Pointed out by Jules Alciatore, *Stendhal et Helvétius: Les sources de la philosophie de Stendhal* (Geneva: Droz, 1952), 210.

122. Stendhal, *Le rouge et le noir*, ed. Crouzet, 490: "Julien était près du désespoir."

123. Stendhal, *The Red and the Black*, 26.

124. Stendhal, *The Life of Henry Brulard*, 99.

125. Crouzet, *Stendhal, ou Monsieur Moi-Même*, 26.

126. Stendhal, *The Life of Henry Brulard*, 457.

127. Ibid., 464.

128. Quoted by Erich Auerbach, "In the Hôtel de La Mole," in Brombert, *Stendhal*, 43.

129. Stendhal, *Vie de Henry Brulard*, 944.

130. Ibid., 900.

131. Ibid., 947.

132. Stendhal, *The Red and the Black*, 96.

133. Keates, *Stendhal*, 42.

134. Stendhal, *The Life of Henry Brulard*, 423, 430; emphasis in original.

135. Alciatore, *Stendhal et Helvétius*, 209.

136. Martin Turnell, "*Le Rouge et le Noir*," in Brombert, *Stendhal*, 21.

137. Ibid.

138. Starobinski, "Truth in Masquerade," 126.

139. Del Litto, *La vie intellectuelle de Stendhal*, 39.

140. Stendhal claimed that when he arrived in Paris in 1799, "I had only my common sense and *l'Esprit* of Helvétius to rely on." *Vie de Henry Brulard*, 875. Del Litto says, however, that Stendhal probably had not yet read Helvétius. Del Litto, "Notes et variantes," 1504n4.

141. Del Litto, *La vie intellectuelle de Stendhal*, 41–42.

142. Ibid., 42.

143. Ibid.

144. Ibid., 41.

145. Victor Brombert, *The Hidden Reader: Stendhal, Balzac, Hugo, Baudelaire, Flaubert* (Cambridge: Harvard University Press, 1988), 164.

146. Crouzet, *Stendhal, ou Monsieur Moi-Même*, 118: "Alas, Stendhal created Julien out of his own experience of ambition, his *passion* to make his fortune at all costs." Emphasis in original.

147. Dorinda Outram, *Georges Cuvier: Vocation, Science and Authority in Post-Revolutionary France* (Manchester, U.K.: Manchester University Press, 1984), 50. Outram cites Louis Royer, *Stendhal au Jardin du Roi: Lettres inédites à Sophie Duvaucel* (Grenoble: Arthaud, 1930), 62.

148. Crouzet, *Stendhal, ou Monsieur Moi-Même*, 119.

149. Ibid., 77. Note that Cuvier spoke at Daru's funeral in 1829.

150. Stendhal, *The Red and the Black*, 487.

151. Crouzet, *Stendhal, ou Monsieur Moi-Même*, 117.

152. Stendhal, *Souvenirs d'égotisme*, in *Oeuvres intimes*, 2:430; emphasis in original.

153. Stendhal, *Vie de Henry Brulard*, 536.

154. Brombert, introduction to *Stendhal*, 6.

155. Patrice Higonnet, *Goodness beyond Virtue: Jacobins during the French Revolution* (Cambridge: Harvard University Press, 1998), 82.

156. Stendhal, *Souvenirs d'égotisme*, 429. Stendhal's search for unity resembles those of his characters, all of whom "realize that they can only exploit their genius by becoming something, by discovering some principle of unity within themselves." They need to become "integrated personalities." Turnell, "*Le Rouge et le Noir*," 21.

157. Stendhal, *The Life of Henry Brulard*, 5.

158. Ibid., 8.

159. Georges Blin, *Stendhal et les problèmes de la personalité* (Paris: José Corti, 1958), 1:5. Blin is citing *Souvenirs d'égotisme*.

160. Stendhal, *The Life of Henry Brulard,* 141.

161. Ibid., 117.

162. Ibid., 119. He notes also "the Gardon initiative" as being of a piece with the rest of his life. In this escapade Stendhal forged a document that would have enlisted him in the Jacobin organization for boys in Grenoble. Stendhal, *The Life of Henry Brulard,* 129.

163. "In loving her at the age of six, perhaps, in 1789, I had absolutely the same character as in 1828, when I was furiously in love with Alberthe de Rubempré." Stendhal, *The Life of Henry Brulard,* 33.

164. Stendhal, *Vie de Henry Brulard,* 700.

165. Stendhal, *The Life of Henry Brulard,* 454.

166. The phrase is Del Litto's, in *La vie intellectuelle de Stendhal,* 279.

167. Stendhal, *Vie de Henry Brulard,* 949.

168. A summary of evidence about the importance of Helvétius and the Idéologues is in Brombert, *The Hidden Reader,* 164–65. Del Litto describes it in detail throughout *La vie intellectuelle de Stendhal,* esp. pt. 1 and chap. 1 of pt. 2, 9–294. See also Alciatore, *Stendhal et Helvétius.*

169. Stendhal, *The Life of Henry Brulard,* 278, 268, 427.

170. Ibid., 17, 185.

171. Rowan Williams, "What Shakes Us," review of Andrew Shanks, *"What Is Truth?" Towards a Theological Poetics,* and Stanley Hauerwas, *With the Grain of the Universe: The Church's Witness and Natural Theology,* in *Times Literary Supplement,* July 4, 2003, 10.

172. William M. Reddy, *The Navigation of Feeling: A Framework for the History of Emotions* (Cambridge: Cambridge University Press, 2001), 204. Reddy is summarizing an argument made by Germaine de Staël in *De la littérature.*

173. Crouzet mentions the importance of "la prison heureuse" in "Notice sur *Le rouge et le noir,*" 28.

174. Pierre Larousse, *Le grand dictionnaire universel du XIXe siècle* (Paris: Larousse and Boyer, 1865–90), 24:1141.

175. Quoted in Denis Bertholet, *Les Français par eux-mêmes, 1815–1885* (Paris: Olivier Orban, 1991), 81.

176. Quoted ibid., 85.

177. *Le petit Robert,* 1984 ed., quotes Sainte Beuve s.v. "vocation."

178. Crouzet, *Stendhal, ou Monsieur Moi-Même,* 67.

179. Stendhal, *Vie de Henry Brulard,* 958.

180. Stendhal, *The Life of Henry Brulard,* 451.

181. Ibid.; emphasis in original. Stendhal often engaged in reflections of this sort after crossing into Italy.

182. Ibid., 203.

183. Ibid.

184. Ibid., 391. Stendhal's emphasis.

185. I suggested as much in the previous chapter.

186. Andrew Elfenbein, *Romantic Genius: The Prehistory of a Homosexual Role* (New York: Columbia University Press, 1999), 5.

187. Crouzet, *Stendhal, ou Monsieur Moi-Même*, 118.

188. Stendhal, *The Life of Henry Brulard*, 442.

189. Ibid., 81.

190. Crouzet, *Stendhal, ou Monsieur Moi-Même*, 43. Crouzet is quoting Félix-Faure's response to *The Charterhouse of Parma*.

191. Stendhal, *The Life of Henry Brulard*, 67.

192. Del Litto, *La vie intellectuelle de Stendhal*, 33.

193. Brombert is quoting from Stendhal's journal, April 1805. "The name of this illness is an 'exaltation of Rousseau.'" Brombert, *The Hidden Reader*, 165.

194. Charles Taylor, *Sources of the Self: The Making of Modern Identity* (Cambridge: Harvard University Press, 1989), 368–90.

195. "[Rousseau] is the starting point of a transformation in modern culture towards a deeper inwardness and a radical autonomy." Ibid., 363.

196. Ibid., 362.

197. He tried to read *Emile* and was baffled. Stendhal, *Vie de Henry Brulard*, 777–78. He did, however, borrow *Emile* from Dubois-Fontanelle at the école-centrale in 1796; ibid., 815.

198. Stendhal, *The Life of Henry Brulard*, 256–57.

199. Stendhal is quoted in Brombert, *The Hidden Reader*, 173.

200. Taylor, *Sources of the Self*, 376.

201. *Dictionnaire de l'Académie française*, 1st ed. (1694), s.v. "vocation," http://artflx.uchicago.edu/cgi-bin/dicos/pubdico1look.pl?strippedhw=vocation.

202. Taylor, *Sources of the Self*, 369–70. Taylor is describing the modern conscience.

203. Reddy, *The Navigation of Feelings*, 205.

204. Stendhal, *The Life of Henry Brulard*, 93.

205. Whitney Walton's work on nineteenth-century women writers suggests a similar strategy at work. By imagining approving fathers, important female writers allowed themselves to work within the patriarchal republican movement. Walton, "Republican Women and Republican Families in the Personal Narratives of George Sand, Marie d'Agoult, and Hortense Allart," in *The New Biography*, ed. Jo Burr Margadant (Berkeley: University of California Press, 2000), 99–136.

206. Stendhal, *Vie de Henry Brulard*, 708.

207. An example is a Sergent Réguinot, who wrote about the invasion of Russia and for whom Napoleon stood as a kind of guardian angel "who runs through his text like a protective, almost magical presence." Bertholet, *Les Français par eux-mêmes*, 82. Bertholet places Stendhal in this group, ibid., 88–89.

208. Pierre Pachet, *Les baromètres de l'âme: Naissance du journal intime* (Paris: Hachette, 2001), 125.

209. Ibid., 36–37. Pachet points to both the Christian tradition of self-examination and the influence of the Idéologues on Stendhal's impulse to keep a journal. Ibid., 128, 129. It is Stendhal's journals that interest Pachet, not the autobiographies

210. Maine de Biran is quoted ibid., 57.

211. Moritz is quoted ibid., 37.

212. "Suite" is Moritz's metaphor; see ibid.

213. Paul M. Cohen uses the term *master fiction* in *Freedom's Moment: An Essay on the French Idea of Liberty from Rousseau to Foucault* (Chicago: University of Chicago Press, 1997).

214. Taylor, *Sources of the Self,* 498.

215. Honoré de Balzac, *La peau de chagrin,* quoted by Toby Appel, "The Cuvier-Geoffroy Debate and the Structure of Nineteenth-Century French Zoology" (Ph.D. diss., Princeton University, 1975), 363. As Cuvier expressed it himself in the "Preliminary Discourse" to *Recherches sur les ossemens fossiles de quadrupèdes* of 1812 (later published separately as *Discours sur les révolutions de la surface du globe*), " 'I shall expound the principles underlying the art of identifying these bones, or, in other words, of recognizing a genus and distinguishing a species from a single fragment of bones.' " Cuvier is quoted in Martin J. S. Rudwick, *Georges Cuvier, Fossil Bones, and Geological Catastrophes: New Translations and Interpretations of the Primary Texts* (Chicago: University of Chicago Press, 1997), 186.

216. Stendhal is quoted by J. Théodorides in "Les relations de Cuvier et de Stendhal," *Biologie médicale* 1 (1961): 21–50. The quote is from Stendhal's essay in *New Monthly Magazine,* June 1826.

Chapter 4. Destiny, Cuvier, and Post-Revolutionary Politics

1. John Viénot calls him the "Napoléon de l'intelligence" in his *Georges Cuvier: Le Napoléon de l'intelligence* (Paris: Fischbacher, 1932). For George Louis Duvernoy he was "le législateur de la science": Duvernoy, *Notice historique sur les ouvrages et la vie de M. le baron Cuvier* (Paris, 1833), 1. Cuvier, Alexander von Humboldt, and Napoleon were born within a few weeks of each other in 1769. Humboldt was called the Napoleon of Science in a poem by Oliver Wendell Holmes.

2. Charles Léopold Laurillard, *Eloge de M. le baron Cuvier . . . discours couronné par l'Académie des Sciences, Arts, et Belles-Lettres de Besançon, 24 aout, 1833* (Paris: F. G. Lévrault, 1833), 24.

3. Cuvier is both hard to like and hard to ignore. His assassination of Lamarck in the infamous *éloge* of 1832, which we address in the second half of this chapter, helped shape French natural history's *sonderweg* where it wandered away from the logic that led to Darwin's theory and left it scrambling to recover prestige in the last years of the century by promoting once-discarded French ideas of change. He is also notorious for his treatment of Saartjie Baartman, the so-called Hottentot

Venus. See Rachel Holmes, *African Queen: The Real Life of the Hottentot Venus* (New York: Random House, 2007). Martin J. S. Rudwick, in the preface to his *Georges Cuvier, Fossil Bones, and Geological Catastrophes: New Translations and Interpretations of the Primary Texts* (Chicago: University of Chicago Press, 1997), xii, explains that William Coleman (author of *George Cuvier, Zoologist*, 1964) "had grown to dislike Cuvier the man" though Coleman's "infectious enthusiasm for the history of science, and particularly for Cuvier studies, . . . helped make me decide to become a historian of science too." Dorinda Outram's 1984 biography of Cuvier launched a new generation of Cuvier studies to which the work in this chapter is indebted: Outram, *Georges Cuvier: Vocation, Science and Authority in Post-Revolutionary France* (Manchester, U.K.: Manchester University Press, 1984).

4. The quote is from André Marie Constant Duméril, *Discours . . . prononcé aux funérailles de M. le Professeur Cuvier* (Paris: Muséum d'histoire naturelle/Firmin Didot frères, 1832), 2. This is the question all historians of Cuvier's life must ask. Note Outram's project in *Georges Cuvier*, as stated in her chapter 3, "The Conquest of the City": "Cuvier arrived in Paris at the beginning of 1795. By the end of the year he had been elected to the newly-formed Institut de France and had achieved not only the beginnings of a scientific reputation, but also public recognition and social success. The purpose of this chapter is to suggest the precise ways in which Cuvier achieved what seems so surprising a feat." Outram, *Georges Cuvier*, 49.

5. Its modern form is the graphite pencil.

6. For Cuvier's schedule and work habits, see Duvernoy, *Notice historique*, 87–88.

7. His memoirs are silent about certain aspects of his life, as we will see. Cuvier, *Mémoires pour servir à qui fera mon éloge, écrits au crayon dans ma voiture pendant mes courses en 1822 et 1823: cependant les dates sont prises sur des pièces authentiques*, published as "Extrait des *Mémoires* de G. Cuvier sur sa propre vie," in Pierre Flourens, *Recueil des éloges historiques lus dans les séances publiques de l'Académie des sciences*, 3 vols. (Paris, 1856–57), 1:169–93.

8. Vladimir Propp, *Morphology of the Folktale*, 2nd ed. (Austin: University of Texas Press, 1968). The importance of folktales to soldiers' and sailors' accounts of their experiences of the revolutionary wars is emphasized by David Hopkin. See Hopkin, "Storytelling, Fairytales and Autobiography: Some Observations on Eighteenth- and Nineteenth-Century French Soldiers' and Sailors' Memoirs," *Social History* 29, no. 2 (May 2004): 186–98.

9. Duvernoy, *Notice historique*, 3.

10. Cuvier, *Mémoires*, 170.

11. Outram, *Georges Cuvier*, 16. According to Coleman, the grandfather was a town clerk, a *greffier*. Coleman, *George Cuvier, Zoologist: A Study in the History of Evolution Theory* (Cambridge: Harvard University Press, 1964), 6.

12. Howard E. Negrin, "Georges Cuvier: Administrator and Educator" (Ph.D. diss., New York University, 1977), 26, 23.

13. Outram, *Georges Cuvier,* 16. Cuvier, *Mémoires,* 176.

14. Georges Cuvier, "Eloge historique de Richard, lu le 7 juin 1824," in Cuvier, *Recueil des éloges historiques lus dans les séances publiques de l'Institut de France,* 3 vols. (Paris: Firmin Didot frères, 1861), 2:334–36.

15. Stith Thompson, *Motif-Index of Folk-Literature: A Classification of Narrative Elements in Folktales, Ballads, Myths, Fables, Medieval Romances, Exempla, Fabliaux, Jest-Books, and Local Legends,* rev. ed., 6 vols. (Bloomington: Indiana University Press, 1955–58), 5:6–26 for Type L, "reversal of fortune." Also see Propp, *Morphology of the Folktale,* chap. 3, "The Functions of Dramatis Personae," esp. functions I, VIIIa, XI, XII, XIV, XV, XIX, pp. 25–65.

16. Robert Darnton, "Peasants Tell Tales: The Meaning of Mother Goose," in Darnton, *The Great Cat Massacre and Other Episodes in French Cultural History* (New York: Vintage, 1984), 9–72.

17. Outram, *Georges Cuvier,* 16. Negrin and Outram both signal the importance of Cuvier's replacing his brother in the family dynamic. Negrin, "Georges Cuvier," 32–34; Outram, *Georges Cuvier,* 16–17.

18. Thomas Crow, *Emulation: Making Artists for Revolutionary France* (New Haven: Yale University Press, 1995), 16. Jean-Germain Drouais, whose father died when he was twelve, and Anne-Louis Girodet-Trioson, whose father died when he was seventeen, are the painters in David's early circle on whom Crow focuses. We also read about Philippe-Auguste Hennequin, whose mother died when he was twelve and whose "distraught and distracted father cast him out of the house," and who desperately and unsuccessfully sought a place within the inner circle of David's early studio. "What follows is a history of missing fathers, of sons left fatherless, and of the substitutes they sought," Crow declares as he begins his book.

19. "Imagination of life" is Crow's phrase, which I place in the context of Jacobinism. Crow, *Emulation,* 2: "At moments in their collective work as artists, this imagination of life through the lens of exclusively male sociability presents itself as a moral, intellectual, and erotic utopia."

20. Terri Apter, "The Bounce," review of Camila Batmanghelidjh, *Shattered Lives: Children Who Live with Courage and Dignity,* Jane Waldfogel, *What Children Need,* and Stuart T. Hauser, Joseph P. Allen, and Eve Golden, eds., *Out of the Woods: Tales of Resilient Teens,* in *Times Literary Supplement,* July 21, 2006, 3.

21. Cuvier in his "Preliminary Discourse" to *Recherches sur les ossemens fossiles de quadrupèdes,* in Martin J. S. Rudwick, *Georges Cuvier, Fossil Bones, and Geological Catastrophes: New Translations and Interpretations of the Primary Texts* (Chicago: University of Chicago Press, 1997), 186.

22. Outram cites Cuvier's autobiography, which "puts the family's annual income at 800 francs at this period." Outram, *Georges Cuvier,* 204.

23. Reported by Duvernoy in "Notes additionnelles" to his *Notice historique,* 110–11.

24. Laurillard, *Eloge de M. le baron Cuvier,* 23.

25. William Hickey, *The Memoirs of William Hickey,* ed. Alfred Spence, 4 vols. (London: Hurst and Blackett, 1911–25).

26. François Pairault, *Gaspard Monge: Le fondateur de Polytechnique* (Paris: Tallandier, 2000), 18. Monge's grandfather had been a poor immigrant from the Savoy.

27. Ibid., 510, 508. Monge had signed the Convention's report certifying the death of Louis XVI.

28. Laurillard, *Eloge de M. le baron Cuvier,* 22.

29. Cuvier was able to do what he did because he devoted most of the substance of his *éloges* to the life stories of his subjects and not to descriptions of their scientific achievements, which filled much of the *éloges* of the old regime. Why Cuvier stressed the life stories of his subjects is outlined below. Fontenelle, Fouchy, Jean-Jacques Dortous de Mairan, and Condorcet, Cuvier's predecessors as secretaries of the Academy of Science, produced eulogies of deceased members of the Academy of Science during their tenures from 1699 to 1791. Paul is following Outram's argument about the purpose of the *éloges:* "If natural science was ever to acquire the kind of esteem (if not power) so ardently desired by Fontenelle and his successors, their eulogies perforce had to present the best possible image of the character of the scientists. Such a presentation could achieve maximum rhetorical effect, however, only if these men's quest for lasting fame were glossed over and the contradictions within their characters resolved. To some extent, these eulogists accomplished these results, but nowhere near as successfully as was subsequently done by Georges Cuvier in his *éloges* (1797–1832)." Note that Paul and Outram take into account two early *éloges* that Cuvier wrote for the Société philomatique de Paris in 1797. I consider the set of official *éloges* Cuvier delivered to the Institut de France, later the Academy of Sciences, dating from 1800. Charles B. Paul, *Science and Immortality: The* Éloges *of the Paris Academy of Sciences, 1699–1791* (Berkeley: University of California Press, 1980), 86.

For "destiny" (in sense of "a man destined to become a great engineer not being able to have been better placed by the accident of birth than in Lyons") see Fontenelle's *éloge* of Sébastien Truchet in Fontenelle's *Oeuvres complètes,* ed. G.-B. Depping (1818; repr., Geneva: Slatkine Reprints, 1968), 1:409. For nature overturning best-laid plans, see Fouchy's "Eloge of Mr. Bradley," reprinted in Paul, *Science and Immortality,* 141. On Banks, see Richard Holmes, *The Age of Wonder: How the Romantic Generation Discovered the Beauty and Terror of Science* (2008; repr., New York: Vintage, 2010).

30. Duvernoy is quoting Abbé Henri-Alexandre Tessier in *Notice historique,* 3. See also Negrin, "Georges Cuvier," 101–3.

31. Laurillard, *Eloge de M. le baron Cuvier,* 8. Propp describes the folktale hero in this way: "The hero of a fairy tale is that character who either directly suffers from the action of the villain in the complication (the one who senses some kind

of lack), or who agrees to liquidate the misfortune or lack of another person. In the course of the action the hero is the person who is supplied with a magical agent (a magical helper), and who makes use of it or is served by it." Propp, *Morphology of the Folktale*, 50.

32. Joseph-François Michaud, *Rapport fait à l'Académie française au nom de la députation envoyée à Montbéliard (jour de l'inauguration de la statue de Cuvier à Montbéliard, le 23 août 1835)* (Paris: Firmin Didot frères, 1835), 9.

33. Duvernoy, "Notes additionnelles," 110–11. Cuvier's father taught him how to construct things from paper.

34. Ibid.

35. Outram, *Georges Cuvier*, 18.

36. For more on prodigies see Paul Metzner, *Crescendo of the Virtuoso: Spectacle, Skill, and Self-Promotion during the Age of the Revolution* (Berkeley: University of California Press, 1998).

37. Laurillard, *Eloge de M. le baron Cuvier*, 24.

38. "The academy had been awarded university status by the Emperor Joseph II in December 1781." Outram, *Georges Cuvier*, 21, 22.

39. Cuvier is quoted by Negrin, who suggests the possibility that Cuvier may have been bested by his cousins and that Cuvier and his admirers remained anxious about this setback. Negrin, "Georges Cuvier," 40.

40. Cuvier, *Mémoires*, 171. This account is repeated in the *éloges* of Cuvier—as he intended it to be. For example, Laurillard explained that just as soon as the duke was presented with an account of Cuvier's talents, he offered him a place in his Academy. Laurillard, *Eloge de M. le baron Cuvier*, 8.

41. "Probably because of an epidemic in Stuttgart, and contrary to the impression given in his autobiography, Cuvier did not actually take up this place until two years later, in 1784." Outram, *Georges Cuvier*, 21.

42. Ibid.

43. Cuvier, *Mémoires*, 170.

44. Ibid., 176–77.

45. Duvernoy, "Notes additionnelles," 111; a cousin reported that his father, Cuvier's uncle, subscribed to Buffon. Coleman says that the uncle had a complete set of Buffon's *Natural History;* Coleman, *George Cuvier, Zoologist*, 24.

46. Laurillard, *Eloge de M. le baron Cuvier*, 8.

47. Duvernoy, "Notes additionnelles," to *Notice historique*, 112.

48. Cuvier, *Mémoires*, 173.

49. Ibid., 179–80.

50. Ibid., 179. As a result, his most important contributions to natural history were germinated then. Negrin explains that these are "Cuvier's two fundamental laws: the correlation of parts and the subordination of characters." Negrin, "Georges Cuvier," 73.

51. Cuvier, *Mémoires*, 179–80n1.

52. Outram, *Georges Cuvier,* 44. Outram warns that "the story of Cuvier and Tessier must be treated with caution as a narrative of real events." Also Negrin, "Georges Cuvier," 103.

53. Toby Appel, "The Cuvier-Geoffroy Debate and the Structure of Nineteenth-Century French Zoology" (Ph.D. diss., Princeton University, 1975), 144.

54. Ibid.

55. Ibid., 198n18. Appel cites Isidore Geoffroy Saint-Hilaire's biography of his father, *Vie, travaux et doctrine scientifique d'Etienne Geoffroy Saint-Hilaire* (1847; repr., Brussels: Culture et Civilisation, 1968), 65n. For the translation of La Fontaine, see *The Complete Fables of Jean de la Fontaine,* trans. Norman B. Spector (Evanston, Ill.: Northwestern University Press, 1988), 64.

56. The phrase is Appel's, in "The Cuvier-Geoffroy Debate," 145.

57. Stith Thompson, *Motif-Index,* "Magic," 2:48, 259. On "Helpful Animals" see ibid., 1:422–60, types B300–590.

58. Outram, *Georges Cuvier,* 44.

59. Etienne-Denis, duc de Pasquier, *Eloge de M. le baron Cuvier,* prononcé par M. le baron Pasquier, Chambre des pairs, séance du 17 décembre 1832, Impressions no. 11 (Paris, 1832), 52.

60. Etienne Geoffroy Saint-Hilaire, *Funérailles de M. le baron Cuvier: Discours de M. Geoffroy Saint-Hilaire, prononcé aux funérailles de l'illustre baron Cuvier, le mercredi 16 mai 1832* (Paris: Institut de France, Académie royale des sciences, 1832), 6.

61. Ibid.

62. Pasquier, *Eloge de M. le baron Cuvier,* 53.

63. Outram, *Georges Cuvier,* 44.

64. Coleman, *Georges Cuvier,* 8.

65. For instance, "[Sarah Wallis] Lee [a "close friend"] suppresses [in her 1833 biography, *Memoirs of Baron Cuvier*] the involvement with the administration of Bec-aux-Cauchois completely, or was never told about it." Outram, *Georges Cuvier,* 44.

66. Quoted in Lucien Jaume, *L'individu effacé, ou, Le paradoxe du libéralisme français* (Paris: Fayard, 1997), 27. Jaume explains that the essay was written by Chateaubriand or one of his supporters.

67. Rudwick, *Georges Cuvier, Fossil Bones, and Geological Catastrophes,* 182.

68. This work was published in 1826.

69. Cuvier's "Preliminary Discourse" is translated by Rudwick, in *Georges Cuvier, Fossil Bones, and Geological Catastrophes,* 183.

70. Ibid., 182–83; emphasis in original.

71. Cuvier is quoted by Negrin, "Georges Cuvier," 17.

72. Ibid., 82. According to Negrin, Cuvier saw "a rotting, corrupt society" in 1788 and early 1789. He understood the nobility "to be eclipsed by the dynamic force of the bourgeoisie," as Cuvier's remarks below underline.

73. Cuvier is quoted ibid., 84.

74. Cuvier is quoted ibid., 81.

75. "Savage ambition" is Cuvier's phrase. Negrin references Cuvier's *Tableau élémentaire de l'histoire naturelle* (1798) and *Le règne animal* (1817). Negrin, "Georges Cuvier," 156, 158.

76. Cuvier is quoted by Negrin, "Georges Cuvier," 157–58.

77. Laurillard, *Eloge de M. le baron Cuvier,* 24.

78. See François Pairault, *Gaspard Monge: Le fondateur de Polytechnique* (Paris: Tallandier, 2000). See also *Dictionary of Scientific Biography,* s.v. "Lavoisier, Antoine-Laurent."

79. Isser Woloch, *Napoleon and His Collaborators: The Making of a Dictatorship* (New York: Norton, 2001), 91.

80. Cuvier is quoted by Negrin, "Georges Cuvier," 157.

81. Cuvier is quoted ibid.

82. Louis-Guillaume Lemonnier was the brother of the astronomer Pierre-Charles Lemonnier. "Eloge historique de Lemonnier, lu le 7 octobre 1800," in Cuvier, *Recueil des éloges historiques,* 1:43.

83. Cuvier to Pfaff, September 22, 1789, quoted by Negrin, "Georges Cuvier," 86.

84. See Patrice Higonnet, "Terror, Trauma and the 'Young Marx' Explanation of Jacobin Politics," *Past and Present* 191 (May 2006): 159. Violence is at the center of Jean-Clément Martin's interpretation of the French Revolution, *Violence et Révolution: Essai sur la naissance d'un mythe national* (Paris: Seuil, 2006).

85. Michel Foucault, *The Archaeology of Knowledge* and *The Discourse on Language,* trans. A. M. Sheridan Smith (New York: Pantheon, 1972), 4.

86. "Preliminary Discourse," trans. Rudwick, in *Georges Cuvier, Fossil Bones, and Geological Catastrophes,* 193.

87. On the open-ended meaning of the phrase, see Outram, *Georges Cuvier,* 158. On Foucault, see ibid., 91, 155–56.

88. This despite Cuvier's accurate statement of the developing practices of historians.

89. Cuvier is quoted by Negrin, "Georges Cuvier," 160.

90. "Eloges historiques de Bonnet et de Saussure, lu le 3 janvier 1810," in Cuvier, *Recueil des éloges historiques,* 1:262.

91. Ibid.

92. "Pardonnez donc, ombres illustres," ibid.

93. Outram, *Georges Cuvier,* 2, 52.

94. Volume 1 includes éloges delivered 1800–1813, volume 2, 1815–26, and volume 3, 1827–32.

95. As "his biographers [*ses historiens*] never fail to mention"; Duvernoy, *Notice historique,* 2. "He left us at the same age Napoleon would have been,"

Stendhal wrote to Cuvier's stepdaughter after Cuvier's death; Stendhal is quoted in Jean Théodorides, "Les relations de Cuvier et de Stendhal," *Biologie médicale* 1 (1960): 45.

96. Royer-Collard's statement that "the Revolution left only individuals standing" is dated 1822 and is quoted by François Furet in *Revolutionary France, 1770–1880*, trans. Antonia Nevill (Oxford: Blackwell, 1992), 314. The second quote by an otherwise unidentified Adrien de S——n is taken from "Essai sur les causes qui ont contribué à multiplier le nombre d'auteurs," published in 1807 and quoted by Outram, *Georges Cuvier*, 52. The translation is mine.

97. Two of these recent works are Jan Goldstein, *The Post-Revolutionary Self: Politics and Psyche in France, 1750–1850* (Cambridge: Harvard University Press, 2005), and Jaume, *L'individu effacé*.

98. Outram notes Cuvier's friendships with Royer-Collard and Guizot as well as with Maine de Biran and De Gérando in *Georges Cuvier*, 106.

99. The standard work on this period and these people for the history of science is Charles Coulston Gillispie's *Science and Polity in France: The Revolutionary and Napoleonic Years* (Princeton: Princeton University Press, 2004).

100. "Eloge historique de Tenon, lu le 17 mars 1817," in Cuvier, *Recueil des éloges historiques*, 2:85–110.

101. "Eloge historique de Desessarts, lu le 6 janvier 1812," ibid., 1:339–50.

102. "Eloge historique de Thouin, lu le 20 juin 1825," ibid., 2:355–67.

103. "Eloge historique de Haüy, lu le 2 juin 1823," ibid., 255–92.

104. "Eloge historique de Fourcroy, lu le 7 janvier 1811," ibid., 1:299–335.

105. "Eloge historique de Daubenton, lu le 5 avril 1800," ibid., 3–34, and "Eloge historique de Richard, lu le 7 juin 1824," ibid., 2:333–52.

106. "Eloge historique de Daubenton," 4.

107. Ibid.

108. Ibid., 6.

109. Ibid.

110. Ibid.

111. "Eloge historique de M. Berthollet, lu le 7 juin 1832," in Cuvier, *Recueil des éloges historiques*, 2:297.

112. Ibid.; *Dictionary of Scientific Biography*, s.v. "Berthollet, Claude Louis."

113. "Eloge historique de Lacépède, lu le 5 juin 1826," in Cuvier, *Recueil des éloges historiques*, 2:375.

114. Ibid., 377.

115. Ibid., 374.

116. "Eloge historique de Adanson, lu le 5 janvier 1807," in Cuvier, *Recueil des éloges historiques*, 1:177–78.

117. Ibid., 179.

118. "Eloge historique de Lemonnier," 37.

119. Ibid. These lives were to become examples of how to behave and how not to behave ("Et deviendra tour à tour noble exemple pour l'émulation, ou salutaire avertissement pour le conduite"): "Eloge historique de Adanson," 176.

120. See note 29 to this chapter.

121. "Avertissement," in Cuvier, *Recueil des éloges historiques,* 1:lviij.

122. Ibid.

123. Ibid.

124. Ibid.

125. "Eloge historique de Adanson," 177.

126. Ibid., 179.

127. Ibid., 180. Readers of Adanson's *Voyage au Sénégal* encounter a calm, curious, and humane Adanson not at all like the manic collector described by Cuvier. See Michel Adanson, *Voyage au Sénégal,* ed. Denis Reynaud and Jean Schmidt (Saint-Etienne: Publications de l'Université de Saint-Etienne, 1996).

128. "Eloge historique de Adanson," 180.

129. Ibid., 181.

130. Ibid.

131. Ibid.

132. Ibid., 182.

133. *Dictionary of Scientific Biography,* s.v. "Adanson, Michel."

134. "Eloge historique de Adanson," 182.

135. Ibid., 191.

136. *Dictionary of Scientific Biography,* s.v. "Adanson, Michel."

137. "Eloge historique de Adanson, 192, 193.

138. Ibid., 199.

139. Ibid., 199–200.

140. "Eloge historique de Richard," 345.

141. Ibid.

142. Ibid., 347.

143. Ibid.

144. Ibid., 347–48. The foreign naturalist was Carl Sigismund Kunth.

145. "Eloge historique de Olivier, lu le 8 janvier 1816," in Cuvier, "*Recueil des éloges historiques,* 2:79.

146. "Eloge historique de Adanson," ibid., 1:202–3.

147. Ibid., 199.

148. Ibid., 203.

149. Ibid., 201–2.

150. Ibid., 203.

151. "Eloge historique de Thouin," 356.

152. *Dictionary of Scientific Biography,* s.v. "Thouin, André"; "Eloge historique de Thouin," 357.

153. *Dictionary of Scientific Biography,* s.v. "Thouin, André."

154. "Eloge historique de Thouin," 356.

155. "Eloge historique de Broussonnet, lu le 4 janvier 1808," in Cuvier, *Recueil des éloges historiques,* 1:221. Cuvier spells the name Broussonnet.

156. *Dictionary of Scientific Biography,* s.v. "Broussonet, Pierre-Auguste-Marie"; "Eloge historique de Broussonnet," 222.

157. "Eloge historique de Broussonnet," 223.

158. Ibid., 223–24.

159. Ibid., 221.

160. "Eloge historique de Fourcroy," 307.

161. Ibid, 308.

162. Ibid, 309.

163. Ibid., 308.

164. Ibid., 309–10.

165. Ibid., 332.

166. Ibid., 333.

167. "Eloge historique de Haüy," 261–66.

168. Ibid., 261–62.

169. *Dictionary of Scientific Biography,* s.v. "Haüy, René-Just."

170. "Eloge historique de Haüy," 275.

171. Cuvier is referring to the beginning of the September Massacres. Ibid., 276.

172. Ibid.

173. Ibid.

174. Ibid., 291.

175. *Dictionary of Scientific Biography,* s.v. "Saussure, Horace Benedict de."

176. The Institute of France was established in 1795, but the *éloges* began in 1800.

177. "Eloges historiques de Bonnet et de Saussure," 281.

178. Ibid., 284–85.

179. Ibid., 285.

180. Ibid.

181. These included a "cyanomètre," a "diaphanomètre," and a "eudiomètre" used to measure the color of the sky and the purity and composition of the air. Ibid., 287–88.

182. Ibid., 289.

183. Ibid., 294. Albert Carozzi argues that Saussure would have developed a theory about the formation of the earth had he not died so young. Carozzi explains that one is implied in the *Voyages dans les Alpes.* See *Dictionary of Scientific Biography,* s.v. "Saussure, Horace Benedict de."

184. "Eloge historique de M. de Lamarck, lu le 26 novembre 1832," in Cuvier, *Recueil des éloges historiques,* 3:179. Cuvier died in May 1832, and his *éloge* of Lamarck was read posthumously.

185. Ibid.

186. Ibid., 180.
187. Ibid.
188. Ibid.

Chapter 5. Friendship Matters; Arguments from Egypt; Coda on Napoleon

1. Toby A. Appel, *The Cuvier-Geoffroy Debate: French Biology in the Decades before Darwin* (New York: Oxford University Press, 1987), 1. An alternative translation is in Hervé Le Guyader, *Etienne Geoffroy Saint-Hilaire, 1772–1844: A Visionary Naturalist,* trans. Marjorie Grene (Chicago: University of Chicago Press, 2004), 261n21.

2. Le Guyader, *Etienne Geoffroy Saint-Hilaire,* trans. Grene, 262. Le Guyader is quoting from Goethe's "Principes de philosophie zoologique." Geoffroy quotes from this passage in his *Etudes progressives d'un naturaliste pendant les années 1834 et 1835* (Paris: Roret, 1835), xiv, citing the journal article and noting that it comes from the last essay Goethe published. Le Guyader, 261n21, says the Goethe article was published in *Revue médicale française et étrangère.*

3. Le Guyader, *Etienne Geoffroy Saint-Hilaire,* trans. Grene, 253. Le Guyader offers in evidence Stephen Jay Gould's laudatory essay in the *American Naturalist* in 1988; an essay in *Current Biology* in 1995 that speaks of Geoffroy's "old idea" being "given new life by studies of the signaling genes controlling dorsal and ventral development in Drosophila and Xenopus" (referring exactly to the subject matter of the 1830 debate, which had as it crux whether vertebrates and invertebrates were really the same basic model, just turned around); an essay in *Nature* in 1996 that highlighted Geoffroy in the authors' extract of their findings: " 'Functional studies seem now to confirm, as first suggested by E. Geoffroy Saint-Hilaire in 1822, that there was an inversion of the dorsoventral axis during animal evolution.' " Ibid., 253, 283.

4. Geoffroy's *Principles of Zoological Philosophy* is quoted ibid., 117; emphasis added.

5. Geoffroy, "Discours préliminaire" to *Etudes progressives d'un naturaliste,* xiv.

6. Since Geoffroy was made professor of zoology but had been trained in mineralogy and botany, it was perhaps in his interest to draw Cuvier—expert already in zoology—into partnership with him at the new Muséum d'Histoire naturelle. Théophile Cahn suggests this in *La vie et l'oeuvre d'Etienne Geoffroy Saint-Hilaire* (Paris: Presses Universitaires de France, 1962), 21, 24.

7. Geoffroy is quoting his own speech at Cuvier's funeral in his "Discours préliminaire" to *Etudes progressives d'un naturaliste,* xiii.

8. Ibid., xiv.

9. Geoffroy's preface to his "Report Presented to the Royal Academy of Sciences on the Organization of Mollusks on February 15, 1830," excerpted in his

Principles of Zoological Philosophy (1835), quoted in Le Guyader, *Etienne Geoffroy Saint-Hilaire,* trans. Grene, 126.

10. Cahn, *La vie et l'oeuvre d'Etienne Geoffroy Saint-Hilaire,* 203. Geoffroy reprinted essays in support of his position from *Le temps* and *Le national* in his *Principles of Zoological Philosophy;* these can be read in Le Guyader, *Etienne Geoffroy Saint-Hilaire,* trans. Grene, 209–24.

11. Geoffroy was never himself a social rebel. In the *Principles of Zoological Philosophy* he described the tactics he believed Cuvier and his supporters used to attack him. Le Guyader, *Etienne Geoffroy Saint-Hilaire,* trans. Grene, 116.

12. Geoffroy is quoted by Le Guyader, *Etienne Geoffroy Saint-Hilaire, 1772–1844: Un naturaliste visionnaire* (Paris: Belin, 1998), 117; emphasis in original. (This section is not in Grene's English translation.)

13. Raspail is quoted in Appel, *The Cuvier-Geoffroy Debate,* 196.

14. Raspail is quoted ibid., 197.

15. Balzac is quoted ibid., 194.

16. Quoted ibid., 199.

17. On the part of Fourierists, Saint Simonians, George Sand, Balzac, and the eccentric Raspail.

18. Here is Dorinda Outram on the effect on Cuvier of the rift between them and its timing: "The breakdown of his relationship with his friend and colleague Geoffroy St Hilaire was one of the decisive themes of Cuvier's entire life. Its final and public stages in its last two years were to leave an enduring mark on his scientific reputation and his power as a patron. In this earlier period, its effects on the style of Cuvier's science were crucial. It has often been asserted that there was little overt conflict between Cuvier and Geoffroy until the end of the 1820s. In reality, the first stages in the disintegration of their relationship came much earlier . . . in 1799." Outram, *Georges Cuvier: Vocation, Science and Authority in Post-Revolutionary France* (Manchester, U.K.: Manchester University Press, 1984), 60–61.

19. Isidore Geoffroy Saint Hilaire, in his *Vie, travaux et doctrine scientifique d'Etienne Saint Hilaire,* is quoted by Appel, *The Cuvier-Geoffroy Debate,* 72 (as well as by many others). Cahn explains that the types of books being collected for the expedition allowed the participants to assume that its destination was Egypt or perhaps Syria. Cahn, *La vie et l'oeuvre d'Etienne Geoffroy Saint-Hilaire,* 34.

20. Le Guyader prefers "to follow Bultingaire [L. Bultingaire's "Iconographie de Georges Cuvier," *Archives du Muséum,* 6th ser., 9 (1932): 1–12] who demonstrates that Cuvier was ill at the time," though he also notes that "Cuvier would never be a travelling naturalist. Everything he wanted to observe he had brought to the Museum." Le Guyader, *Etienne Geoffroy Saint-Hilaire,* trans. Grene, 259n11.

21. Cuvier is quoted in Outram, *Georges Cuvier,* 61.

22. Outram, too, points to this conclusion: "In rejecting Egypt and rejecting Geoffroy," Cuvier was deliberately "rejecting a whole way of doing science. Geoffroy's tales of hardship and travel pointed up the choice between natural

history as fieldwork, and natural history as work on the dead specimen in the Muséum. . . . The second, Cuvier's choice, . . . was far more useful, as Cuvier himself points out, in the rapid establishment of a scientific reputation and a scientific system." Outram, *Georges Cuvier,* 62.

23. Cuvier wrote to Geoffroy at Marseilles, where Geoffroy was in quarantine after leaving Egypt. That is, Cuvier wrote only when he knew Geoffroy was safe and on his way home. Outram says about this: "It is now impossible to decide whether Cuvier in fact answered these pathetic appeals or whether he simply ignored them, but whether his letters were lost or never written, it is unlikely that their relationship recovered from this degree of tension. It is in fact, more than likely that Cuvier did not reply to Geoffroy for it is noticeable that there are no references in other letters to his intentions to write to Geoffroy." Ibid., 61–62.

24. Geoffroy, in Lyons, to Cuvier, April 29, 1798, in Etienne Geoffroy Saint-Hilaire, *Lettres écrites d'Egypte à Cuvier, Jussieu, Lacépède, Monge, Desgenettes, Redouté jeune, Norry, etc., aux professeurs du Muséum et à sa famille,* ed. E. T. Hamy (Paris: Hachette, 1901), 1.

25. Geoffroy, in Toulon, to Cuvier, May 18, 1798, ibid., 36.

26. Geoffroy, in Cairo, to Cuvier, August 16, 1799, ibid., 137. Comments about the challenges of this journey through the desert appear in other letters to the Muséum. See Cahn's comments on the significance of this August 1799 trip for the *Description de l'Egypte* that the Commission of Sciences and Arts produced: Cahn, *La vie et l'oeuvre d'Etienne Geoffroy Saint-Hilaire,* 40.

27. Geoffroy, in Cairo, to Cuvier, November 27, 1799, in Geoffroy, *Lettres écrites d'Egypte,* 145.

28. Geoffroy, in Toulon, to Cuvier, May 9, 1798, ibid., 26.

29. Geoffroy, on board the *Alceste,* to Cuvier, May 23, 1798, ibid., 46.

30. Geoffroy, in Cairo, to Cuvier, August 28, 1798, ibid., 80.

31. Ibid., 81.

32. "Comment se portent tous nos amis? Est-il quelquefois question du Geoffroy Egyptien dans vos conversations?" Geoffroy, in Cairo, to Cuvier, August 16, 1799, ibid., 137.

33. Geoffroy, on board the *Alceste,* to Cuvier, May 23, 1798, ibid., 42.

34. Geoffroy to Antoine-Laurent de Jussieu, October 20, 1798 (probably), ibid., 99. The letter was read to the Muséum in March 1799. See the editor's note that this was his first mention of the incident, 99n1.

35. Born in 1772, he had just turned twenty-six when the expedition began.

36. *Dictionary of Scientific Biography,* s.v. "Geoffroy Saint-Hilaire, Etienne": "While retaining a deep attachment to the priests who had supported his career, Geoffroy embraced revolutionary ideas. He frequented the clubs and committees and adopted a philosophical deism and a generous humanitarianism that he preserved for the rest of his life." Outram says these claims are suspect. Note that Cahn is silent on this issue.

37. The appointment was at the renamed Muséum d'Histoire naturelle.

38. Geoffroy, in Lyons, to Cuvier, April 29, 1798, in Geoffroy, *Lettres écrites d'Egypte,* 3–4; emphasis in original.

39. Masclet was twenty-seven.

40. Geoffroy, in Rosetta, to Marc-Antoine Geoffroy, August 1798, in Geoffrey, *Lettres écrites d'Egypte,* 60. Geoffroy spells the name as Dupetitoir.

41. The article is quoted by Hamy in Geoffroy, *Lettres écrites d'Egypte,* 60n2. Herold says this account "seems scarcely credible," and one can agree; J. Christopher Herold, *Bonaparte in Egypt* (New York: Harper and Row, 1962), 119.

42. David A. Bell, *The First Total War: Napoleon's Europe and the Birth of Warfare as We Know It* (Boston: Houghton Mifflin, 2007).

43. Herold, *Bonaparte in Egypt,* 317.

44. Quoted ibid., 317. The session took place June 29, 1799.

45. Ibid., 367–68.

46. Le Guyader says, however, that Geoffroy's troubles began in Egypt: "During his stay in Egypt, he began to exhibit the nervous disorders that would never leave him. He was subject to serious crises of cyclothymia, no doubt aggravated by the climate, with alternating bouts of intense excitement and great despondency. In the course of one of his euphoric moments he elaborated 'the universal law of the attraction of like for like [*soi pour soi*],' which he would take up again thirty years later, at the end of his life. He also erected a grandiose theory of the universe that would earn him sarcastic remarks from the mathematician and physicist Joseph Fourier." Le Guyader, *Etienne Geoffroy Saint-Hilaire,* trans. Grene, 6.

47. Cahn, *La vie et l'oeuvre d'Etienne Geoffroy Saint-Hilaire,* 20.

48. Geoffroy's passage from *Etudes progressives d'un naturaliste* is quoted in Toby Appel, "The Cuvier-Geoffroy Debate and the Structure of Nineteenth-Century French Zoology" (Ph.D. diss., Princeton University, 1975), 158–59. (The quote is not complete in the published version of 1987.)

49. Geoffroy, in Lyons, to Cuvier, April 29, 1798, in Geoffroy, *Lettres écrites d'Egypte,* 1.

50. Geoffroy, in Marseilles, to Cuvier, May 5, 1798, ibid., 15.

51. James Livesey, *Making Democracy in the French Revolution* (Cambridge: Harvard University Press, 2001), 55, 263n46.

52. See Bell, *The First Total War,* on Napoleon's "innermost self [being] defined by war," 206–7, 312–13. On Napoleon's seeing himself as "character in a novel," see ibid., 203.

53. Geoffroy, on board the *Alceste,* to Cuvier, May 23, 1798, in Geoffroy, *Lettres écrites d'Egypte,* 38.

54. Geoffroy, in Suez, to Cuvier, January 14, 1800, ibid., 163.

55. Geoffroy, in Toulon, to Cuvier, May 13, 1798, ibid., 31.

56. Owen Connelly notes that few letters slipped through the blockade: "The Directory had sent orders, which Napoleon had not received, to return with his

army, an impossibility. For most of his sojourn in Egypt, Napoleon and his army were, in effect, stranded. His communications with Paris were severed, and for a year he received almost no messages from the French government." Connelly, *Blundering to Glory: Napoléon's Military Campaigns* (Wilmington, Del.: Scholarly Resources, 1989), 56n3. Geoffroy, in Cairo, to Cuvier, August 23, 1798, in Geoffroy, *Lettres écrites d'Egypte*, 73.

57. Geoffroy, in Cairo, to Cuvier, August 23, 1798, in Geoffroy, *Lettres écrites d'Egypte*, 73.

58. Geoffroy, in Cairo, to Cuvier, October 20, 1798, ibid., 95.

59. He mentioned this in a letter to his brother. Geoffroy to Marc-Antoine Geoffroy, probably end of March 1799, ibid., 117.

60. Geoffroy, in Suez, to Cuvier, January 7, 1800, ibid., 157–58.

61. The *philomatiques* were members of the Société philomatique, a scientific society that Cuvier and Geoffroy belonged to. It was an alternative to the Academy of Science. Geoffroy, in Alexandria, to Cuvier, April 30, 1800, ibid., 184.

62. Geoffroy, in Cairo, to Cuvier, September 20, 1801, ibid., 202.

63. Ibid., 203.

64. Outram insists on it: Cuvier rejected Geoffroy. Outram, *Georges Cuvier*, 62–63.

65. Geoffroy, in Cairo, to Cuvier, August 23, 1798, in Geoffroy, *Lettres écrites d'Egypte*, 78.

66. Geoffroy, in Cairo, to Geoffroy Père [Jean-Gérard Geoffroy], September 10, 1798, ibid., 90.

67. Geoffroy, in Toulon, to Cuvier, May 18, 1798, ibid., 35.

68. Geoffroy closes his last letter to Cuvier from Toulon thus: "Adieu, dear friend. I am about to lose sight of land; I have only the time to embrace you and to commend my interests to you." Geoffroy, in Toulon, to Cuvier, May 18, 1798, ibid., 36. On Geoffroy's career, see Le Guyader, *Etienne Geoffroy Saint-Hilaire*, trans. Grene, 7. On Cuvier's lack of compliance, if not perfidy, see Outram, *Georges Cuvier*, 63.

69. Geoffroy to the Museum of Natural History, October 29, 1800, in Geoffroy, *Lettres écrites d'Egypte*, 189. This was read in August 1801 to the assembled professors of the Museum of Natural History.

70. Geoffroy, in Alexandria, to Cuvier, April 30, 1800, ibid., 178.

71. Ibid., 178–79.

72. Ibid., 179.

73. Geoffroy, in Cairo, to Cuvier, December 22, 1799, ibid., 152.

74. Geoffroy, in Cairo, to Cuvier, September 20, 1801, ibid., 202.

75. Geoffroy, on board the *Alceste*, to Cuvier, May 23, 1798, ibid., 44.

76. Geoffroy, in Cairo, to Cuvier, October 20, 1798, ibid., 97.

77. Geoffroy, in Cairo, to Cuvier, August 16, 1799, ibid., 129–30. The cuttlefish is a mollusk, the *Tetraodon* is a puffer, or blowfish.

78. These discoveries included electric fish.

79. Geoffroy, in Cairo, to Cuvier, August 16, 1799, in Geoffroy, *Lettres écrites d'Egypte,* 137–38.

80. Geoffroy, in Suez, to Cuvier, January 7, 1800, ibid., 158. These remarks echo comments he made to Cuvier on his way to Upper Egypt in August: "I am setting out on a very arduous journey in order that I may better merit a return to your company." Geoffroy, in Cairo, to Cuvier, August 16, 1799, ibid., 137.

81. Quoted in Appel, *The Cuvier-Geoffroy Debate,* 79–80.

82. Geoffroy insisted in a letter to his father that his slaves were not really slaves, but part of his "family." Geoffroy also commented on how slavery in Egypt was different from slavery in America. Presumably, by "America" he meant the Caribbean sugar islands. Geoffroy, in Cairo, to Geoffroy Père [Jean-Gérard Geoffroy], June 23, 1799, in Geoffroy, *Lettres écrites d'Egypte,* 121, 122.

83. Appel, "The Cuvier-Geoffroy Debate," 157. The book of 1987 has a different wording.

84. See note 93 below.

85. Geoffroy, in Cairo, to Cuvier, November 27, 1799, in Geoffroy, *Lettres ecrites d'Egypte,* 146.

86. Geoffroy Saint-Hilaire, "Discours préliminaire" to *Etudes progressives d'un naturaliste,* ix, xii.

87. Geoffroy, in Cairo, to Cuvier, November 27, 1799, in Geoffroy, *Lettres écrites d'Egypte,* 147.

88. Herold, *Bonaparte in Egypt,* 387.

89. Geoffroy is quoted by Maya Jasanoff in *Edge of Empire: Lives, Culture, and Conquest in the East, 1750–1850* (New York: Knopf, 2005), 217, 218.

90. Geoffroy, in Toulon, to Cuvier, May 13, 1798, in Geoffroy, *Lettres écrites d'Egypte,* 31.

91. This last is the conventional understanding of Geoffroy's behavior.

92. Geoffroy is quoted by Jasonoff, *Edge of Empire,* 218.

93. The help he requested related to strained relations with Fourier and criticisms of Geoffroy's theory that were circulating. He also asked Cuvier several times for help in straightening out housing problems at the Jardin des Plantes. Geoffroy, *Lettres écrites d'Egypte:* on Fourier, Geoffroy, in Marseilles, to Cuvier, December 19, 1801, 215–20; on housing, Geoffroy to Cuvier, November 18, 1801, 210; November 22, 1801, 212; December 19, 1801, 214–15. He also begged Cuvier to reassure him that his father was still alive: Geoffroy to Cuvier, November 18, 1801, 212.

94. Cahn, *La vie et l'oeuvre d'Etienne Geoffroy Saint-Hilaire,* 22.

95. Taken from Cahn's account, ibid., 56–57, and from Le Guyader, *Etienne Geoffroy Saint-Hilaire,* trans. Grene, 260n15.

96. Bell, *The First Total War,* 203.

97. Sudhir Hazareesingh, *The Legend of Napoléon* (London: Granta Books, 2004), 2.

98. Ibid., 169.

99. Talleyrand is quoted in David Lawday, *Napoleon's Master: A Life of Prince Talleyrand* (New York: St. Martin's Press, 2007), 106.

100. For a description of life at Longwood see Emmanuel de Las Cases, *Mémorial de Sainte-Hélène* (Paris: Seuil, 1968), 1:289–309.

101. Napoleon is quoted by Bell, *The First Total War,* 186.

Chapter 6. Ambition in Post-Revolutionary Lives

1. Jan Goldstein, *The Post-Revolutionary Self: Politics and Psyche in France, 1750–1850* (Cambridge: Harvard University Press, 2005), 19, 21.

2. Ibid., 21, 39.

3. Emma Rothschild, *Economic Sentiments: Adam Smith, Condorcet, and the Enlightenment* (Cambridge: Harvard University Press, 2001), 23.

4. This suggestion comes from Miranda Seymour in *Mary Shelley* (New York: Grove Press, 2000), 173: "His translation into a force of evil is directly influenced by his education. Instinctively benevolent, he learns from the history of mankind to murder and to be cunning in his crimes."

5. Goldstein discusses this in *The Post-Revolutionary Self,* 141.

6. Stendhal attended the one that had been established in Grenoble with his grandfather's support.

7. Goldstein, *The Post-Revolutionary Self,* 141–42.

8. Ibid., 87.

9. Le Peletier was murdered by a monarchist in January 1793 after voting for the death of Louis XVI.

10. Le Peletier is quoted in Charles Coulston Gillispie, *Science and Polity in France: The Revolutionary and Napoleonic Years* (Princeton: Princeton University Press, 2004), 161. Gillispie also describes the enthusiasm of the Convention for this proposal (which was not enacted). Note that girls as well as boys would be educated by the state, girls for six years, boys for seven. See also Carol Blum, *Rousseau and the Republic of Virtue: The Language of Politics in the French Revolution* (Ithaca: Cornell University Press, 1986), 186.

11. Goldstein, *The Post-Revolutionary Self,* 86.

12. Among them were Joseph de Maistre and Chateaubriand, for instance.

13. Goldstein, *The Post-Revolutionary Self,* 165, 183.

14. Ibid., 178.

15. Ibid., 179.

16. Stendhal, *The Red and the Black,* trans. Lloyd C. Parks (New York: New American Library, 1970), 505.

17. Georges Cuvier, "Eloge historique de Adanson," in Cuvier, *Recueil des éloges historiques,* 1:201–2.

18. Stendhal read Adam Smith in 1806 in Sophie de Grouchy's translation of *The Theory of Moral Sentiments.* He also encountered Smith in his reading of

Cabanis, Pinel, and Staël. Victor Del Litto, *La vie intellectuelle de Stendhal: Genèse et évolution de ses idées (1802–1821)* (Paris: Presses Universitaires de France, 1962), 289–93.

19. Stendhal, *The Life of Henry Brulard*, trans. John Sturrock (New York: New York Review of Books, 2002), 119.

20. Quoted in Jerrold Seigel, *The Idea of the Self: Thought and Experience in Western Europe since the Seventeenth Century* (Cambridge: Cambridge University Press, 2005), 122. Del Litto in *La vie intellectuelle de Stendhal* does not have Stendhal reading Mandeville in the period covered by his book. See Daniel Roche, *France in the Enlightenment*, trans. Arthur Goldhammer (Cambridge: Harvard University Press, 1998), 566–69, on the influence of Mandeville's ideas in France.

21. Roche, *France in the Enlightenment*, 251–52.

22. Adam Smith did likewise.

23. Voltaire is quoted in Ernst Cassirer, *The Philosophy of the Enlightenment*, trans. Fritz Koelln and James Pettegrove (1951; repr., Princeton: Princeton University Press, 1979), 245.

24. Ibid.

25. See Daniel Lord Smail, *On Deep History and the Brain* (Berkeley: University of California Press, 2008), 117: "Moods, emotions, and predispositions inherited from the ancestral past, where they evolved at the intersection of human biology and human culture, [are understood to] form a structural backdrop for many things we do and have done" and "cultural practices [in return, to have] profound neuro-physiological consequences."

26. See chap. 2.

27. Is this another case of " 'secularized theological concepts' " defining the modern world? Carl Schmitt is quoted in Pierre Rosanvallon, *Democracy Past and Future*, ed. Samuel Moyn (New York: Columbia University Press, 2006), 196. "Spilt religion" is the phrase of Theo Hobson in "In the Beginning," review of Michael Allen Gillespie, *The Theological Origins of Modernity* (Chicago: University of Chicago Press, 2008), *Times Literary Supplement*, February 6, 2009, 7. Darrin M. McMahon (author of *Enemies of the Enlightenment: The French Counter-Enlightenment and the Making of Modernity*) works along these lines in his forthcoming *Genius: A History*, presenting the eighteenth-century genius as a secular saint, a new god.

28. Stendhal is quoted in Del Litto, *La vie intellectuelle de Stendhal*, 42.

29. Cassirer, *The Philosophy of the Enlightenment*, 269.

30. Albertine Necker de Saussure, "Notice sur le caractère et les écrits de Mme de Staël," in *Œuvres complètes de Mme la baronne de Staël publiées par son fils, précédées d'une notice sur le caractère et les écrits de Mme de Staël par Madame Necker de Saussure* (Paris: Treuttel et Würtz, 1820), xvii.

31. Quoted in Rosanvallon, *Democracy Past and Future*, 173.

32. Blum, *Rousseau and the Republic of Virtue*, 57, 58.

33. Rosanvallon, *Democracy Past and Future,* 184.

34. Ibid., 190.

35. It inclined them as well toward a personal, emotional relationship with God and thus a distanced relationship to church hierarchy and alienation from papal authority—and support of the Gallican Church.

36. Jean Calas was convicted of murdering his son to prevent his conversion to Catholicism. On religion in the old regime, see Dale K. Van Kley, *The Religious Origins of the French Revolution: From Calvin to the Civil Constitution, 1560–1791* (New Haven: Yale University Press, 1996).

37. Constant quotes are in Seigel, *The Idea of the Self,* 268. On Constant see also Biancamaria Fontana, *Benjamin Constant and the Post-Revolutionary Mind* (New Haven: Yale University Press, 1991). In chapter 2 above we saw how Staël was the agent of Constant's "liberation" from Mme de Charrière and also the enabler of his own ambition: "The habit of work has come back to me; even the mirage of literary glory, which you were at such pains to destroy in me." Constant is quoted in Maurice Levaillant, *The Passionate Exiles: Madame de Staël and Madame Récamier,* trans. Malcolm Barnes (1958; repr., Freeport, N.Y.: Books for Libraries Press, 1971).

38. Dorette Berthoud, *Constance et Grandeur de Benjamin Constant* (Lausanne: Payot, 1944), 161–63. The group *Ames intérieures* was founded by a disciple of Mme Guyon, whose works Constant read. See also J. Christopher Herold, *Mistress to an Age: A Life of Madame de Staël* (New York: Harmony Books, 1958), 351. Constant and Staël were Protestants, members of the Reformed Religion, or Calvinists. Cuvier was a Lutheran.

39. Jerome Bruner, *Making Stories: Law, Literature, Life* (Cambridge: Harvard University Press, 2002), 65, 70.

40. Bruner is quoting an unpublished paper by Kay Young and Jeffrey Saver, "The Neurology of Narrative," ibid., 86.

41. Seigel, *The Idea of the Self,* 133.

42. Ibid., 166.

43. Ibid.

44. Stephen Greenblatt's *Renaissance Self-Fashioning: From More to Shakespeare* (Chicago: University of Chicago Press, 1980) helped introduce the subject of the self to cultural history.

45. Seigel, *The Idea of the Self,* 165.

46. Charle B. Paul has something to say about this with respect to Watson's *The Double Helix* in his *Science and Immortality: The Éloges of the Paris Academy of Sciences, 1699–1791* (Berkeley: University of California Press, 1980), 107–8.

INDEX

Absolutism: and court society, 6; and mathematics, 67; passions controlled by, 2–4; and state control of ambition, 2–4; theories of, 2, 65

Académie française: ambition defined by, 1; and eulogies of great men, 4–5; on genius, 45; on originality, 104

Academy of Science, Paris, 119; and Adanson, 135–36, 171; and Condorcet, 112, 213n29; Cuvier-Geoffroy debate in, 145–46; and *Eloges historiques*, 112, 121–28, 131, 143, 171, 213n29; and Geoffroy, 159–60; and Institute of France, 135, 141

Action française, 88

Adanson, Michel: and Academy acceptance, 136; Cuvier's *éloge* of, 127, 132–34, 139, 175; early years of, 130–31; isolation of, 131, 132–33, 135–36, 175; *L'ordre universel de la nature,* 133–34, 171

Alciatore, Jules, "Stendhal and Pinel," 77–78, 79, 96

Alembert, Jean Le Rand d', 33, 35, 45, 175

Ambition: as "bourgeois" desire, 3; and careerism, 144, 165, 169; as

competitive individualism, 16, 69, 173; conflict of ethics and, 172; conflict of friendship and, 8, 9; control of, 1–4; as cultural marker, 11–15; definitions of the word, 1, 3, 7–8, 10, 41; ethics of, 41, 177; and free will, 177; and French Revolution, 10, 123, 124; and gender, 9–10, 19; genius contrasted to, 41, 121; Hérault's theory of, 6; and independence, 7; and inequality, 7; and liberalism, 13, 22; and love of glory, 3, 4, 13, 41, 102, 121, 130, 163; lust for power, 3, 41; and madness, 16–17, 74, 77–81, 88, 166–67; and modernity, 22; and oppression, 7; and politics, 16, 151; in post-Revolutionary France, 7, 11, 22, 168–79; redeeming social value of, 3, 4; as self-fulfillment, 8, 11, 13, 175; social hazards of, 82, 89, 130; Stendhal's depiction of, *see* Sorel, Julien

Ames intérieures, 177
Anderson, Perry, 89
Appel, Toby A., 162
Arago, François, 111–12